AF622016

DYNAMICS OF A TRIBAL SOCIETY
A MICRO-STUDY

DYNAMICS OF A TRIBAL SOCIETY A MICRO-STUDY

Edited by

Dr. B. DATTA RAY

Secretary

North-East India Council for Social Research

Shillong-793003

DR. S.K. AGNIHOTRI *IAS*

Resident Commissioner

Government of Meghalaya

New Delhi-110001

UPPAL PUBLISHING HOUSE

NEW DELHI-110002 (INDIA)

UPPAL PUBLISHING HOUSE
3, Ansari Road, Daryaganj, New Delhi-110002

(c) Dr. B. DATTA RAY
Dr. S.K. AGNIHOTRI
First Published 1993
ISBN 81-85565-27-9

Printed in India
Published by B.S. Uppal for Uppal Publishing House
New Delhi-110002 and Printed at R.N. Printers
1/2208. Shanti Building, Shahdara, Delhi-110032

Preface

Dynamics of a Tribal Society: *A Micro Study* is an outcome of the Symposium organised by the North-East India Council for Social Science Research during August 22-23, 1991. It is very timely that the papers contributed by various scholars, researchers, administrators and opinion leaders to the Symposium have now been brought out in a book form. The main theme of the Symposium was Shillong 1981-91: A Multi Dimensional Study It was the second volume in the series of research studies conducted by the NEICSSR on the developmental aspects of Shillong, the capital city of Meghalaya. The first volume was published on behalf of the NEICSSR during 1984. The earlier works on Shillong include a *Profile of Shillong* which was published in 1979 by the Anthropological Survey of India. There was another attempt in 1977 by the defunct Shillong Political Science Association to initiate through a seminar the specific study on the Shillong Municipality. However, the study has not been published as yet.

Both the study of the Shillong Municipality and a *Profile of Shillong* while referring to the growth and development of Shillong in general, that of the *Shillong 1971-81* was an attempt to state and interpret the various changes and new development that had taken place in and around Shillong during the decade 1971-81. The present volume, *Dynamics of Tribal Society*:

A Micro Study, on the other hand, while stating and interpreting the various changes and the latest development that had taken place during the last decade 1981-91 has also stressed on the various issues of modern global and national problems having a direct bearing on the Shillong city like urban development, urban human ecology, status of education, science and technology, social problems of housing, sanitation, water supply, traffic congestion, crime and social tension, economic problems of planning strategy for development, variation in temperature and rainfall, and the system of mass communication.

Before 1864 Shillong was unknown to the outside world. Its present area was then covered by deep and evergreen forests with Laban as a small tribal Khasi village under the then United Khasi State of Shillong. It was in that year that the British created Shillong as the administrative village for Khasi and Jaintia Hills district. Two years later, in 1866, Col. Henry Hopkinson, Commissioner of Assem and Agent to the Governor General of India had strongly advocated in favour of Shillong as the future headquarters of Assam. Accordingly, in March 20, 1874 by the Government Notification No. 49, Shillong, the district headquarters of Khasi and Iaintia Hills, was also declared the capital of Assam with effect from that date. Therefore, Shillong is essentially the creation of British administration and its growth depends almost entirely on the growth of administration. Ever since then, Shillong has become not only the centre of administrative establishments-civil, military and para-military, but also the centre of learning, judicial organisations, church activities, commercial establishments. banking systems, and students, youth and general welfare movements.

Shillong, now the capital of Meghalaya, is still a city in a tribal setting. In some localities, this tribal setting has been overshadowed by non-tribal groups. It is also the seat of the North-Eastern Council which is the central agency for economic co-ordination of the seven States of North-East India as well as the only Central University in the region, the North-Eastern Hill University and other central agencies for the purpose of administration, development and security. Unlike other cities in the region. Shillong did not have an organic growth in its early years. But during the last decade (1981-91) a number of changes have taken place. In the field of land use pattern and in the structural and architectural designs certain developments can be discerned during the decade under study. The spread of urbanisation, ideas and changing life styles during the last decade have brought far-reaching effects on the urban population. The influx of population from the rural areas as well as from other parts of India has definitely raised the social, human, and civic problems. The development of the means of communications has also brought a sizeable number of daily floating population to Shillong which has become an additional problem for the civic authorities. Thus, Shillong city has become a real challenge to the developmental and governmental agencies. Inspite of the various problems, the managers of Shillong have been able to tide over the crisis and enter into the last decade of the twentieth century.

All the papers in the *Dynamics of a Tribal Society: A Micro Study* have shed more light on our knowledge of the general conditions of Shillong during 1981-91. There had been much progress in the fields of administration, education and other dcvelopmental activities. The volume has further added more insight into the understanding of the socio-economic problems of the city. It is hoped that it would be a source of help for future detailed studies of the various aspects of Shillong city in the coming decades. It is also hoped that it would be of great help to the city planners, administrators, scholars and the members of the general population who are interested in bringing back Shillong to its earlier status of the Scotland of the East.

DR. B. DATA RAY

Contents

1. Introduction 1

2. Shillong 1981-91: A Background Note 6
P.C. Barua

3. Shillong Urbanization: A Background Note 9
V.S. Mahajan

4. Shillong—1991: A Critical Analysis based on Geomorphology, Tectonic movement and Urban Human Ecology 15
A.K. Borah and N.N. Bhattacharyya

5. Variation in Temperature and Rainfall of Shillong during 1981-1990 28
Zahid Hussain

6. Status of Environmental Pollution in Shillong 1981-91: An overview 41
H. Nath and Abhik Gupta

7. Population Trend in Shillong, 1981-91 65
M.C. Pandey

8. Demographic Profile of Shillong 1981-91 72
R.P. Bhattacharjee

9. Change of Settlement Pattern in Shillong city through decade: A Micro Anaiysis 85
P.K. Guha

10. Populaton increase and Road Traffic Problems of Shillong 92
A. Saikia

11. Traffic Congestion in Shillong 102
Sazidual Alam

12. Changing Townscape of Shillong 112
H.K. Mazhari

13. Slums in Shillong: A Analysis of its Impact 117
W. Syiem

14. Umbra behind the beauty of Shillong: some observations 124
S.S. Datta Choudhuri

15. Water Supply of Shillong: Its Problem 132
Subrata Chakravorty

16. Planning Strategy for Development of New Town for Shillong 139
B.K. Panda

17. Meghalaya Urban Development Authority Shillong 150
H.K. Mazhar and B. Jones Dhar

18. Need for low Cost Sanitation in Shillong 156
Amesh Priya

19. Housing Strategy for Shillong 165
A.K.M. Karim

20. Hapazard Growth of IEWDUH (Barabazar) Shillong: A Case study 172
P.C. Biswas

21. The Muslims of Shillong: An Observation 178
Saifun Nessa

22. The Changing attitude towards working women: A Panoramic view through decade in Shillong 193
Geetanjali Baruah

23. The Growth of Science and Technology in Shillong 1981-91 202
Sarit Chaudhuri

24. Status of Education in Shillong during 1981-1991 226
Parijat Chakrabarty and Ms Sarbani Bhattacharya

25. Mass Media and Changing Shillong 236
M.P. Hazarika

26. Crime Profile in Shillong, 1981-1991 241
Mrinmayi Banerjee

27. Tension in Shillong in 1979 and 1990: An Over view 258
U.S. Bhattacharya

28. Social Instability in Shillong, 1980-1991 267
Rakhal K. Purkayastha

29. Electoral Politics of Shillong: A Case Study of Laitumkhrah by-election, 1990 285
S.K. Mukherjee

30. Urban Development in Shillong: An overview 293
S.K. Agnihotri

List of Contributors

1. Introduction

2. Shillong 1981-91: A Background Note
Prof. P.C. Barua
North Eastern Institute of Bank Management, Guwahati, Assam.

3. Shillong Urbanization: A Background Note
Prof. V.S. Mahajan
Centre for Indian Development Studies, Chandigarh.

4. Shillong—1991: A Critical Analysis based on Geomorphology, tectonic movement and Urban Human Economic
Mr. A.K, Borah
ICSSR Doctoral Fellow, Gauhati University, Guwahati.
Prof. N.N. Bhattacharyya:
Deptt. of Geography, Gauhati University, Guwahati.

5. Variation in Temperature and Rainfall of Shillong during 1981-1990
Dr. Zahid Hussain
Anthropological Survey of India, Shillong.

6. Status of Environmental Pollution in Shillong 1981-91: An Overview
Mr. H. Nath
Meghalaya Pollution Control Board, Shillong.
Dr. Abhik Gupta
Deptt. of Zoology, St. Edmund's College, Shillong.

7. Population Trend in Shillong, 1981-91
Prof. M.C. Pandey
Deptt. of Adult and Continuing Education, NEHU, Shillong.

8. Demographic Profile of Shillong 1981-91
Mr. R.P. Bhattacharjee
Statistical Officer, Deptt. of Economics and Statistics, Arunachal Pradesh, Shillong.

9. Change of Settlement Pattern in Shillong city through decade: A Micro Analysis
Mr. P.K. Guha:
Anthropological Survey of Shillong India, Shillong

10. Population increase and Road Traffic Problems of Shillong
Mr. A. Saikia
Govt. College, Itanagar, Arunachal Pradesh.

11. Traffic Congestion in Shillong
Mr. Sazidul Alam
Deptt. of Urban Affairs, Meghalaya, Shillong.

12. Changing Townscape of Shillong
Mr. H.K. Mazhari
Deptt. of Urban Affairs, Meghalaya, Shillong.

13. Slums in Shillong: A Analysis of its Impact
Ms. W. Syiem
Deptt. of Urban Affairs, Meghalaya, Shillong.

14. Umbra behind the beauty of Shillong: some observations
Dr. S.S. Dutta Choudhuri
Anthropological Survey of India, Shillong.
15. Water Supply of Shillong: Its prablem
Subrata Chakravorty
16. Planning Strategy for Development of New Town for Shillong
Mr. B.K. Panda
Deptt. of Urban Affairs, Meghalaya, Shillong.
17. Meghalaya Urban Development Authority Shillong
Mr. H,K. Mazhar
Mr. B. Jones Dhar
Deptt. of Urban Affairs, Meghalaya, Shillong.
18. Need for low Cost Sanitation in Shillong
Mr. Amresh Priya
Sulabh International—North Eastern Region, Guwahati.
19. Housing Strategy for Shillong
Mr. A.K.M. Karim:
Deptt. of Housing, Meghalaya, Shillong.
20. Hapazard Growth of IEWDUH (Barabazar) Shillong: A Case study
Mr. P.C. Biswas
Shillong Bar Association, Shillong.
21. The Muslims of Shillong: An Observation
Dr. Saifun Nessa
Deptt. of Sociology, St. Mary's College Shillong.
22. The Changing attitude towards working women: A Panoramic view through decade in Shillong
Ms. Geetanjali Baruah
Anthropological Survey of India, Shillong.
23. The Growth of Science and Technology in Shillong 1981-91
Mr. Sarit Chaudhuri
Anthropological Survey of India, Shillong.

24. Status of Education in Shillong during 1981-1991
Mr. Parijat Chakravorty
Deptt. of Education, Women's College, Shillong.
Mr. Sarbani Bhattacharjee:
Deptt. of Political Science, Women's College, Shillong.

25. Mass Media and Changing Shillong
Mr. M.P. Hazarika
Directorate of Information and Public Relations, NEC, Shillong.

26. Crime Profile in Shillong, 1981-1991
Dr. Mrinmayee Banerjee:
Anthropological Survey of India, Shillong.

27. Tension in Shillong in 1979 and 1990—An Over view
Dr. U.S. Battacharyya
Deptt. of Political Science, Lady Keane Girls College. Shillong.

28. Social Instability in Shillong, 1980-1991
Dr. Rakhal K. Purkayastha
Deptt. of Political Science, St. Anthony's College, Shillong.

29. Electoral Politics of Shillong: A Case Study of Laitumkhrah by-election, 1990
Mr. S.K. Mukherjee
Anthropological Survey of India, Shillong.

30. Urban Development in Shillong: An overview
Dr. S.K. Agnihotri
Deptt. of Urban Affairs, Meghalaya, Shillong.

1

Introduction

The first scientific attempt to study the cultural profile of Shillong was made in 1973 (B.B. Goswami ed.) We held also in 1981 a symposium on Shillong 1971-81 (B. Pakem ed.) recording the various changes and the new developments that took place in and around Shillong 1971-81 since formation of Meghalaya.

North East India Council for Social Science Research made a more detailed study of the multifaceted changes of Shillong including climatological and ecological condition social, cultural, economic, civil political life of Shillong witnessing a rapid transition from an expanded village to a city in a seminar held in August 1991. The papers included in this volume are paper read in the seminar dealing with increasing demographic pressure and resulting strain on the physical conditions of Shillong. Some of the papers deal with social and political issues of the present day tribal politics. There has been a spectacular growth of Shillong during the decade of 1981-91 following the pattern existing in the rest of the country—the inner city—the semi-urban zone and the outer transition zone. This growth has posed challenges in every field of social, cultural, economic and political life. In the absence of scientific urban planning, the problems of Shillong are likely to be unmanageable by the turn of the century.

Shillong as a centre of economic, political, social cultural and administrative activities, has always attracted people for providing opportunities. This is why a very large number of people migrate every year to it—resulting in an enormous stress and strain required for a livable urban environment. Some basic social, cultural, political, administrative and economic questions arise out of this situation. Can Shillong economy and support systems contain this rush of migration? What strategies and programme can be viable to strive support systems within the ambit of city economy? What are the strength and weakness of the organizations for city planning and development management and how can these be made responsive to the city decentralization? How to integrate the efforts of city decentralization through balanced dispersal of all kinds of settlements, urban and rural leading to rural-urban continuum in greater Shillong retion? People, politics, local government and city management are now interwoven. Greater Shillong environment management through citizen participation is a lively issue today.

Economic revitalization of Shillong, potentials, imperatives, role of political and administrative organizations and the cultural life need to be examined to understand the emerging image of Shillong. Shillong is rich in its heritage—cultural, economic and political. This heritage should be studied for understanding urban dynamics. It was necessary that we study the growth of Shillong as regional centre of north-east India in various fields, (b) the infrastructure and civil facilities in Shillong, (c) the problems of urban management including urban project implementation and management including urban project implementation and management and (d) formulation and enforcement of master plans for urban development.

The papers of P.C. Barua and V.S. Mahajan are background notes for appreciation of urbanization process, particularly of Shillong—a growing tribal city in north-east India. The papers by R.P. Bhattacharjee and M.C. Pandey presented the demographic profile of Shillong. While Pandey observed that the population in Shillong had grown at a very high rate during 1981-91. Bhattacharjee found that the population in the Shillong Municipal area was nearly stagnant during the period.

With the city having to accommodate larger population within the limited space the pattern of houses has undergone change. The tiny and beautiful Assam Type houses are being gradually replaced by multi-storied R.C.C. constructions. This changing house-pattern was the topic of discussion in the two papers by P.K. Guha and H.K. Mazhari. Focussing attention on the problem of urban housing with special represence to Shillong A.K.M. Karim has estimated that to meet the immediate shortage of housing in Shillong investment of the order of Rs. thirty crores would be necessary.

The increase in population and vehicular traffic in the city has strained the transportation system of the town. The papers by S. Alama and A. Saikia pointed out various push and pull factors leading to the present state of traffic conditions in the city. Steps to reduce the traffic congestion were also suggested.

W. Syiem in her paper highlighted the problems of slums in Shillong and narrated the measures taken by various development agencies for their improvement. She called for further steps and greater involvement of the public towards this end.

As a solution to the problems of over-crowding and congestion in Shillong, B.K. Panda in this paper suggested development of a new township close to the existing city. Mr. A.K. Borah also felt the need for development of stellite towns. In the same context B. Jones Dhar expressed the need of redefining the role of the State Development Authority, Shillong.

The recent development in the town has also disturbed the environment and the eco-system. An analytical paper by Zahid Husain pointed out the alarming changes in climatic conditions (mainly temperature and rainfall) and the resulting degradation of the eco-system in the Shillong city in the last few decades. The paper by H. Nath and Abhik Gupta showed that Shillong had long crossed the safety limits of air and water pollution. A.K. Bora and M. Bhattacharya's paper also had reference to these problems.

M.P. Hazarika narrated the increasing role played by mass-media in general and the local press in particular in the lives of the residents of Shillong.

U.S. Bhattacharya and R.K. Purkayastha gave an account of the ethnic and social disturbances in Shillong during 1979-91. They attempted to explore the root cause of these disturbances. A case study of a recent by-election in Shillong was presented by S.K. Mukherjee. Dr. Mrinmayi Banerjee narrated the rate of incidence of crimes in Shillong during the last decade. Her paper also had a presentation of the ethnic and age distribution of the convicts during the same period. Saifun Nessa described the emergence and growth of the Muslim organisations towards educational, religious and social upliftment of the Muslim society here. Geetanjali Baruah observed a favourable change in social attitude in Shillong towards working women, particularly towards educated women working outside the four walls of home.

There are a number of papers on the educational infrastructure of the city. Parijat Chakravarty and Sarbani Bhattacharjee gave an account of the educational facilities in the town. S.K. Choudhuri enlisted various scientific institutions operating in Shillong and described the activities and achievement of these institutions during the last decade.

The talk of glaring inadequacies of civic amenities in Shillong came up. S.S. Datta Choudhuri describes some of the measures adopted recently to solve these problems. S. Chakravarti pointed out that despite receiving high rainfall and being a place of streams and springs, Shillong on an average day has a shortage of water-supply of the order of 30 lakh gallons. A. Priya suggested adoption of low cost sanitary systems to deal with the problems of sanitation in the city. Regarding the haphazard growth of Iewduh (Barabazar), which is the prime commercial locality of the city, P.C. Eiswas argued that the absence of adequate regulations and timely steps were responsible for the present mess of the area.

S.K. Agnihotri's paper besides presenting a general background of the town, gave an account of the urban development schemes for Shillong that were implemented during the last decade.

We are grateful to Mr. B.S. Uppal and Uppal Publishing House, New Delhi for undertaking the publication of this volume. We are thankful to Government of Meghalaya for its support.

Shillong,
7 April 1992

B. Datta Ray,
S.K. Agnihotri

2

Shillong 1981–91 A Background Note

P.C. Barua

Shillong, the capital of Meghalaya, originally a non-tribal township in a picturesque tribal setting, is one of the largest and charming hill resort in the North-East region of India. Established in 1864 as a hill resort and later the most important army Cantonment of the region, it became the capital of undivided Assam. In 1972, the United Khasi and Jaintia Hills along with the Garo Hills district were carved out of Assam as a separate state, Meghalaya, with Shillong as the capital. Situated in the midst of Khasi Hills ranges at an elevation of 1500 meters, Shillong presents a beautiful picture of cliffs and not-too-deep ravines, brooks, a lake, water falls with the mild fragrance of wind-swept hissing pines.

The present Shillong urban agglomeration consisting of seven 'towns' viz. Shillong Municipality, Shillong Cantonment, Nongtaymmai, Mawlai, Pynthormukhrah and Mauaurting had a population of 1,74,703 as per 1981 census, where the population at the beginning of the century was only 9,621. During the last census decade (1971-81) the population of Shillong increased by 42.32 p.c., a very significant increase.

Shillong is mainly administrative and residential in its functional character and this character has been maintained basically. Administrative and residential land use component still covered more than 70 p.c. of the total developed area of the city. Its commercial and educational functions have developed more or less in proportion with the increase in the population, whereas the defence function has assumed much greater significance during the last three decades. The city which is traditionally an important seat of education for the whole of the North-East region, specially for the states other than Assam, had a considerable area of 3 p.c. of the built up area of the city under educational function at the close of the last decade.

The development of the suburbs have been towards east and west primarily, their development being directional rather than general. The total suburb area is estimated at 25 sq. miles with about 25,000 people.

The most significant point in respect of the influence of the city is its functional linkages with Brahmaputra Valley on the north and the Barak Valley and the adjoining States of Mizoram Manipur and Tripura on the south, south-west through Silchar, the largest town in that valley. Its interaction with the plains areas in terms of people, goods and ideas is as important as the city's interaction with its own hinterland on the surrounding areas.

Shillong is not an organic spontaneous growth like old cities such as Guwahati. It was established with specific purpose, the kernel being a health resort, an administrative-cum-military centre, a nodal point for spread of English education and Christianity. Being the node of the arterial road system, originally linking the two valleys and beyond to the sea coast port areas, it retains this function even after partition of the country through development of new road systems. Some of the earlier functions have diminished in importance while new dimensions may have been added to some others. The role of a particular function may have changed considerably.

Shillong is the centre for employment, a collecting and marketing point for products of the surrounding area, a distribution centre for incoming goods, a centre for providing higher education and specialised health services for the whole supporting area, providing entertainment and cultural contact facilities, a centre for dissemination of information through various communication media, and above all, a centralising point for the local as well as sub-regional thoughts and feelings. The duty has to offer all these and the allied community services to the neighbouring areas, nourish these areas with artifacts. It is a place of refuge to surrounding people and their ideas as well as a reservoir of new ideas.

Development of a city is subject to various simultaneous centripetal and centrifugal forces. Spatial forces, situational ones, forces of social and technological evolutions lead to basic changes. With fresh nuclei formation and consequent changes in the land use pattern, structural and architectural changes occur. Such developments during the last decade in Shillong call for an analytical study.

The dichotomy of the pre-modern society into rural and urban as the only two ends of a situation stands modified in so far as there is possibility of gratuated distribution from the least urban to the most urban and from the most rural to the least rural. And, the urban limits are not necessarily enduring even though there may be physical separation. Spread of ideas influencing human attitude, behaviour and life style as a whole transcend physical barriers and extend beyond the old kernels of the city. Spread of urbanisation during the past decade is an important part of the growth of Shillong.

3

Shillong's Urbanisation : A Background Note

V.S. Mahajan

Both population explosion as well as emergence of economic opportunities bring about a tremendous growth in the character of urban complexes, particularly when these also happen to be the seat of the government. The situation becomes all the more explosive if the rural population is being exposed to the urban values through media and at the same time there is slow emergence of job opportunities in the rural areas. Thus both these pull and push factors are behind the quick urbanisation of major towns and cities. Once the rural labour force has been attracted to the urban areas, there is no going back. That is, these people would no longer be interested to go back to their villages, even if they were not able to find opportunities to settle down in urban areas.

The life in urban complexes is far too alluring aad tempting that the youth having once drifted from his village, which lacks the urban glamour, is reluctant to settle down in his village.

For him these urban areas, despite all the sufferings he has to undergo in the new surroundings, are like new temples which attract him more and more to become a part and parcel of such life.

Besides, there are growing opportunities in these urban areas. Trade is growing so is industry and even still faster grow a host of services, from street vending to organised areas banking, transport, government, semi-government and private sectors. Thus there emerges one of the other opportunity for the villager who has made urban area as his home.

Further the rate of growth of urban areas picks up fast after their exposed to industrial culture, when there emerged a large demand for the Labour force to fill up several openings that are created in the wake of such development. And this is also desirable for unless there is mobility of labour force, initially of course from the surrounding areas, cost of production would not be that competitive as it would be when the labour is available plenty. Further, the experience shows that such vast conglomeration of labour also provides in the early stages of development, market for the products manufactured.

Thus such labour serves dual purposes. It helps to reduce the cost of production and at the same provides market for the commodities produced. Of course, later on, the picture becomes more complex. The products thus produced would find a wider market. Thus under such situation, the character of urban areas undergoes a fast change.

For instance, as the British industry started growing fast after the Industrial Revolution, it was able to attract the international market, with the result that apart from the local labour force there had as well occurred a considerable inflow of labour from other countries (including our own). If an analysis is made of the London population, between different time points, it would be observed that in the composition of its labour force the share of emigrants had been continuously rising. The inflow of such labour force is as well a great help to the manufacturers for otherwise they would have had to pay far higher wages to the local labour and this would have raised their cost of production as well as reduced their international competitions. Such immigrant labour has also been of help in keeping down the cost of services.

Thus at a higher stage of urbanisation, no city could exclusively rely on its own labour force (including those from the surrounding areas). If it has to expand and capture larger markets, it has to undergo structural changes in its mode of production as well as services. Such changes would be quicker and efficient if it has an open economy where labour from outside was as well welcome.

(2)

The above background on urbanisation is important to help us appreciate the character of our own urban growth in this country. It does help us to understand the complex forces that emerge with the fast growth of urbanisation. No city or town will remain static and when it does, it spells its disaster and would indicate the lack of spirit for growth and enterprise among its people. People would be lazy. Probably the laws are such that there do not encourage new investment as well labour from outside.

On the other hand, in a dynamic set up, each urban area must grow and faster it grows it shows its in-built capacity for development and to attract investments for industrial production and services.

We must, therefore, approach the urban growth in our country, where there has been all-time high growth after independence, in this context. It is a good sign of fast development.

In this process it is not only that big urban complexes alone have grown. In fact their growth has as well helped the growth of surrounding economies spread over a large area. Also, several one-time villages have now acquired the status of towns and thus become important focal point for trade and industry.

(3)

It is heartening to find that urbanisation in the north-east has been even faster than most of other areas in the country. If we study the history of development of capitals of the seven States in this region, we do notice a quick change in their urban character as well as rise in population, a considerable share of which has been due to the movement of population from the surrounding and even distant areas. Also there have occurred opportunities in services, industry, government and private sectors.

And in this process, not only the capitals of States, even district headquarters as well as other towns (particularly those commanding strategic location) have also made quick growth and the rate of growth of several lesser known district headquarters and towns has been even higher than state capitals. The story is the same whether we consider Assam, Meghalaya, Nagaland, Mizoram, Manipur, Tripura of even Arunachal Pradesh (which is no longer backward and cut off as used to be couple of decades ago). All these areas have made a good progress and thus the urban population in this area is fast growing.

(4)

Meghalaya, among all the states of north-east, occupies a unique position. And still more unique is the status of Shillong for its has behind it long history as the seat of the government for this area. When the British captured this region, they found Shillong much to their liking. Its topography as well as climate made them feel at home and thus they developed it into a beautiful hill resort as well as administrative capital of this region. Thus Shillong under-went a unique transformation in terms of education, health and housing facilities and above all economic development.

The town has further grown at a record level over the last couple of decades and has emerged the most important state capital in the region, next to Guwahati. It has maintained its cosmopolitan character and, the quick growth of an urban area is very much linked with the dynamic character of its enter-preneours, that is those who risk investment in industry, trade, transport and other areas.

This is exactly what has happened in Shillong. With its open approach, this area has not only attracted people from the surrounding area mainly coming in for employment, it has attracted skilled labourer from the distrant areas who have contributed significantly in areas like construction (as it is well known urbanisation leads to fast growth of construction activity), as well helped in diverse trades, services and industrial activities.

In the key areas of trade and distribution, which constitute the core activities in any economy, the outsiders have again played an important role. A study made of the trading com-munity of Shillong would demonstrate the key role played by this class in making available several new goods in accordance with the needs of the local population and at competitive prices.

As the city grow its character too grow complex. It make a heavy demand on the new areas of finance, banking, modern transport, educational skills and administration. If these services do not grow to the required level, the city's, development is going to be affected.

While one would appreciate the positive side of Shillong's growth, at the same time we could not overlook the negative side. While there has been rapid growth of population as well as a host of educational, administrative, social, trading and industrial activities and also Shillong services as a major cantonment for armed forces, the growth of basic services and housing has lagged far behind. This is particularly so in these three keay areas-housing, water supply and sanitation.

4

Shillong—1991, A Critical Analysis Based on Geomorphology, Tectonic Movement and Urban Human Economic

A.K. Borah
and
N.N. Bhattacharyya

Introduction

Shillong as a capital town was first built up with modern, semi-modern housing structures by the Britishers well back in 1874 to facilitate themselves to govern the then whole north-east India which now includes seven states, viz., Arunachal Pradesh, Assam, Meghalaya, Mizoram, Nagaland with exception of Manipur and Tripura. The geomorphological setting of Shillong has attracted the early British settlers to shift their capital from Cherrapunji due to the variation of rainfall and humidity between Cherrapunji and Shillong. The dampness as well as heavy rainfall of Cherrapunji perhaps did not suit the Britishers to govern region better. On the other hand comparatively dry and with slight variation (having difference of only +/−14 inches) in rainfall between Shillong and Gauhati had given a very suitable climate for the Britishers to shift their capital and to establish the same at Shillong which they considered as the Seotland of the East. There were other political considerations also in shifting the capital from Cherrapunji to Shillong. It is noted that besides the annexation of Jaintia hills and Cachar as well as gruesome war started with Angami Nagas necessitiated such shifting. Further such urgency was also caused by widespread rebellion steered by Khasi leader U. Bormanik Syiem as well as the rebellion under stewardship of Moniram Dewan in the Brahmaputra valley. Furthermore the annexation of Upper Assam from the Ahom King Purandar Singha in 1837-38 also necessitated such shifting. In this paper the authors are attempting to analyse the geomorphology (urban sites), tectonic movement and urban human ecology of the present Shillong and more specifically giving thrust on proper land used in the greater Shillong area in future through the application of the theories of urban growth/land use which fall well under purview of Urban Sociology.

Geomorphology of Shillong City

Located at 25 34° N latitude and 91 53° E longitude, Shillong is one of the most important cities of North-East India. The city lies on the mountain basin (1500 m) which is bounded on the south by the Shillong range, on the north-east by the Mawpet hills and on the east by the river-divide of the Umkhrah—Umshing water divide. The area of the basin is about 45 sq. km. and is asymmetrical in shape. The site of the city is made up hard sedimentary rocks like shales and sandstones (Shillong series), granites and metamorphic rocks with of course a little alluvium. Such advantages of the sites perhaps provided attraction for settlement by the Britishers in the area well back in 1874 and these continued to exert their influence on the growth of the city during the various annals of the history of urban morphological development of Shillong.

The present site of Shillong is divided into five physiographic units, such as the northern slope of Shillong range (1900 m), the Umshirpi valley, the Laitumkhrah-nowkhar upland, the Umkhrah village and the the Umkhrah-Umshing river divide. The northern slope of Shillong range is now occupied by Nongthymmai, Motinagar. Malki, Lumparing and Laban. The Umshirpi is a narrow valley commongly known as Happy Valley and is occupied by the cantonment area.

The Laitumkhrah-Mawkhar upland is located between the Umkhrah and Umshirpi valleys. The Umkhrah valley is the lowest in height (1404-1455 mtrs). This valley is wide near the Race Course presenting an unique natural panorama which is deemed as rarity. The land rises towards the north-east Shillong.

Thus the Umkhrah—Umshing divide is about 1410 metres above the mean sea level. The major parts of the Shillong Municipality lie between the Umkhrah and Umshirpi rivers.

The city of Shillong spreads northward to the Umshing river and then extends eastward from the divide of Umkhrah and Umshirpi rivers. The recent ribbon development with respect to the land use, demographic and socio-economic structure has given the city a star like shape [with extension to the north on the Gauhati-Shillong road, to the south-west on Cherra road and to the north-east on the new NEHU campus at Mawlai area. The Municipal area of Shillong 'occupies 49 percent of the total area of Shillong. The other areas such as the cantonment shares 9 per cent, Nonghtymmai 14 per cent and Mawlai 28 per cent of the total and area of Shillong. However with the influx of good number of people from in and outside of the state/region the population pressure on the land use of greater Shillong area is alarmingly increasing. Further with the population pressure concomitant problems like dysfunction in the multi-ethnic set up is coming up which cannot be neglected. Further, more satlelite settlement of various ethnic groups in the various ethnic groups in the various places of Shillong—the process of which has started right from the early settlement when Shillong became the capital town of the northeast India and segregation of one ethnic group who is trying to maintain its own identity in a particular setelite setting and having simply a relation based on organic solidarity in field of interaction with other different ethnic groups posing a serious threat to the total social fabric of this beautiful hill resort cit) of north-east. This aspect comes under human ecology a branch of urban sociology and it would be dealth in thc later part of the present work.

Tectonic Movement of the Shillong City Through Different Phases of Geological History and the Probable Seismic Risk

The Assam range, the Shillong plateau as it were is the northeasterly prolongation of the Indian peninsula. Since pre-Cambrian to the end of Miocene it had experienced earth movements leaving imprints of differant geological events. We find major folding and fracturing; development of a trough to accommodate the Shillong group of sediment—later to be uplifted with the culmination of low grade methamorphism because of the intrusion of Mylliem granite and Khasi Green stone. The pst pre-Cambrian saw the eruption of plateau basalt—the Sylhet trap along the southern fringe of the Shillong plateau by the end of Jurasic period. The Sylhet trap intraplate volcanism could be the herbinger of different tectonic movements leading to depositional sites through large scale subsidence resulting into marine invasion and deposition of Upper Cretaceous sediments over a rapidly sinking basin. Towards Palaeocene-Eocene shelf, conditions were established as evidenced by the deposition of the limestones and sandstones. During Mid-Eocene due to another spell of subsidence led to the deposition of coal bearing sandstones and limestones and in some parts of eastern Jaintia and Garo Hills. Till Oligocene we find sedimentation over the submerged parts of K&J Hills and Garo Hills.

A major upheavel of the plateau occured at the closing phase of Miocene—which shaped the present configuration. The impact of this upliftment is still evident from the frequent occurrence of earthquakes. A major earthquake struck the state in 1877 with 8.7 magnitude in Richter's scaleand in seismological his it is known as the Great Assam Earthquake. It stands as one most devastating earthquakes in the annuals of historical records because it was felt over a considerable area and caused damage at far greater distances than any other earthquakes in north-eastern region's history. A vidid description of this earthquake by R.D. Oldham bears the fact. It raged the entire town of Shillong to the ground. While government buildings including government press were dashed to the ground. The fate of Shillong jail was worst of all where during the duration of earthquake one Inspector General along with ten Constables died and the jail was also raged to the ground. Infact, what we see today is the newly built dwellings after that earthquake with a combination of modern and old practices of the construction of houses.

The death toll of mere 1500 or odd people does not signify its true nature. It is perhaps due to primitive style of dwellings made of wood/thatch/bamboo. However, the scenario has considerably changed with rapid urbanization and population growth. Concrete jungles have since developed at Shillong. Human memory is short and people built urban centres in or near active fault system capable of generation earthquakes, on the steep slopes etc. The large population currently living within the damage area of the 1897 earthquake means that widespread destruction and loss of life limb and property is likely if the sequence is repeated,

Now keeping the geomorphology of the Shillong city, its tectonic movement with possible seismic risk due to the presence of active faults as the cornerstones of the physical ecology of the city we now look into the human ecology of the city on the basis of certain well established theories of urban growth. A modest attempt is also made by the authors to see the applicability of these theories in the growth of Shillong city and its further expansion through the pocess of decentralization, ethnic group interaction etc.

Human Ecology of Shillong City

(Theories of Urban Growth of Burges, Homer Hoyts, Harris-Ullman are re-examined in the context of present Shillong City):

In reality human ecology generally deals with a specific concrete population of human beings. The ratio of increase or decrease of the population affects the land use pattern of a city and concomitant problem of adjustment also comes into being.

As stated earlier the present city of Shillong bears the legacy of the administration centre of the Britishers and this process could be explained through theories of urban growth with slight modification which are put forwarded by Burgess-Homer, Hoyt and Harris-Ullman. It started with the functioning of the government offices and this process itself helped to the growth of various zones which are the cornerstones of the theories of urban growth put forwarded by the different above mentioned writers.

In Burges theory it is shown that a city generally consists of vie concentric zones keeping at the core the central business district. This is followed by the zone of transition in a second ring where business district is placed by residential district/areas. The second zone blends into the third zone as Burgess contends that 'working homes of the factory workers and labourers etc. The next consists of large residential area of the city, where white collar workers and middle class families are found The last, i.e. the fifth one is the commuter's zone where suburban communities are found along the main roads of communication. When growth begins invasion of one zone to other zone occurs and it is followed by another new pattern of concentric zone.

Homer Hoyt put forwarded the sector concept after studying the residential areas of united States. He gave a theoretical explanation of land use in terms of wedge-shaped sectors radical to the city's centre along the main lines of transportation. In his analysis he took different income group classes of a city and showed that they are generally found in distinct areas.

After Homer Hoyt's Sector Theory there is Multiple Nuclei Theory of urban growth which was first suggested by Mckenzie, then expanded by Harris and Ullman and it is stated that there are a series of nuclei in the patterning of the urban land uses rather than the single central core used in other theories of urban growth. There are four factors which are creating different nuclei which are as under:

Interdependency of certain types of activities and their need for close physical proximity to one another.

Natural clustering tendency among certain types of activities which find in mutually profitable to congregate together.

Converse to No. 2 activities which have no particular affinity for one another and general heavy traffic, creating parking problems but ultimately it faces the same congragation. Finally related factor of high rents or high land costs, which have the effect of attracting or repelling used in the process of nucleition.

The concent entails clearer differentiation between factors which explains the structures and dynamics of change.

In the field of application of the above mentioned theories to the present Shillong taking into account past based on historical progression analysis with slight variation viz. renaming the business zone of Burges theory, more particularly to a pure administratlve zone and then by tailing off the industrial blue collar environment with due stress on the past records, the theory put forwarded by Burgess could provide an explanation of the early phase of expansion of Shillong city. If we presume Police Bazar —where agglomeration of Assembly Hall, Secretariate and other government offices are found—as Zone No. 1, it than gave rise to the business zone i.e. Police Bazar and Bara Bazar. The second and third zone covered the residential areas like Jail road, Keatinge Road, eastern side of Ward Lake, Oak land, Quinton Road, etc. at the initial stage. The fourth zone definitely refer to the residential places like Malki, Lumpering, Upland, Rinbong, Laban, etc. Ofcourse putting all these places under centain zones to explain the application of classical ecological concentric zone theory may raise doubts in various quarters, yet to create a base the present authors tries here with that first ecological theory. Commuters zone in Burgess theory falls under zone No. 5 is however to be seriously looked into and the commuters zone of Shillong in the early stage of urbanization as authors contends might be between Garikhana to erstwhile Mawlai Gate.

Homer Hoyt developed his sector theory of urban development by studying the data which were available regarding real property inventories of 142 American cities. In his theory his mostly talked about central business district and of low medium and high class residential. The theory contends that with the growing of city population high rent areas move outward along one sector and these areas are generally located along the transportation lines.

Now in the field of application this theory in case of Shillong city if we take Bara Bazar and Police Bazar as central business district than low class residential area could be Mawprem area, medium class residential area could be Jail road and high class residential area could be Lachaumiere (Upper and Lower), Fruit Garden, Laitumkhrah, Nongrim Hills, Motinagar etc. Keeping Hoyt's observation as a cornerstone of analysis for dividing residential areas of Shillong the present author's also feel, like Hoyt's that high class residential areas tend to be located usually on well drained high ground and have established transportation network. In that context the above mentioned places of Shillong could naturally be fall under high class residential.

Coming to the application of Harris and Ullamans' Multiple-Nuclei theory in the case of Shillong city the present authors contend that this theory of urban growth fits well in case of Shillong city as this theory postulates not one centre for the city but several nuclei. Each of the centres tends to specialize in a particular kind of activity—retailing, wholesale, finance, government offices, recreation centres, educational centres and the like. Several centres may have existed from the beginning of the city or many have developed later in the form of a division from one centre. In that context we find that Bara Bazar, Police Bazar and Garikhana come under one nuclei, though originally these were different nucleous of certain specific activities. With the passage of time these neclei formed one nucleous because of the extension of trade centre from Bara Bazar to Police Bazar and due to generation of heavy traffic this included Garikhana also and formed one nucleous.

Again due to high rent non-availability of space in central business nucleous the business and other activities started in different nucleous of Shillong city—like Laban Bazar, Laitumkhrah, Nongthymmai. Laban Bazar developed with the help of high class residential area influence. Laitumkhrah developed with the support of middle class residential and of educational institutions and finally Nongthymmai developed taking the bass of educational centre like Auxlium Convent, Police Station, NEHU's Mayurbhanj campus. Further middle class residential influence helped the growth of nucleous like lower Jail Road and more specially near Polo Ground.

A Critical Review of the Application of the Theories of Urban Growth in the case of Shillong City

The exercise that has been made in the preceeding paragraphs showed that no theories of urban growth could be applicable in totality in explaining starlike extension of the Shillong city. However, partially by changing certain indices of the above mentioned three theories the applicability of the same in the case of Shillong city so far as its land use as well as urban growth can be explained. But the moot point which the present authors are trying to focus that during the decade of 80-90's the growth of Shillong city was somewhat abrupt and the ribbon development occupied a prominent place in the expansion and over-urbanization of Shillong city. Intra-city population numbers are alarmingly increasing—though the purchasing right of non-tribals on land is not there—dovetailed with daily commuters who came from different places of Meghalaya for job, business etc. which creates serious problems like traffic congestion, absence of adequate measures for handling garbages and sewage of the city. Moreover emission of a huge quantity of carbon monoxide by hydrocarbon powered vehicles—the number of which are increasing rapidly—are changing the ecological setup of Shillong. Shillong is becoming more warmer during the decade of 90's. Unless the over-urbanization process in the existing nuclei is not stopped and repell the population pressures to new satellite towns which are to be built immediately with all modern facilities the problem of over-urbanization of Shillong city would pose a serious threat to its present city population and its environment.

Shillong is a city of the composition of multi-ethnic population and on the basis of recent Ecological theory put forwarded by Shevky-Bell-William method of Social Areas Analysis we can study the segregation of different communities of Shillong living in different places of Shillong. This theory is commonly known as Social Area Analysis and it is based on three indexes (1) 'Social Rank' (also called 'Economic Status', representing measures of occuption and education). (2) 'Urbanization', representing measuring measures of fertility, gainfully employed women and single-dwelling or multiple dwelling residence and

(3) **'Segregation'** (Ethic Status representing measures of ecological segregation of ethnic or racial groups).

After a careful analysis the present authors find that the third index fits well in case of Shillong city. Various ethnic groups are some how segregated in different ecological settings of Shillong and this process is already creating avalanche in the total social fabric of the city. Unless this problem is not carefully looked into, it may after some time raise its ugly head.

Conclusion and Suggestion

From the above discussion it appears that the growth of Shillong city followed various patterns right from 1874 and more particularly after 1897 Great Assam Earthquake. It followed for decades a moderate growth and with the formation of the sates i.e. Meghalaya, Shillong city has grown haphazardly and concomitant problems like, traffic congestions, inadequate sewage, garbage disposable pattern, more commuters and finally unplanned concrete jungles in the active faults without giving stress on seismic risk. These problems become acute during the decade of 1980's.

The need of the hour is to build satellite towns in up town areas of Shillong with all urban amenities to reduce population and traffic pressure on the main Shillong city.

However, the present authors suggest that the satellite towns should be built with the implementation of an integral programme of loss reduction strategies with special reference to seismic risk of the areas to be selected for satellite townships. This entails the following measures to be taken seriously:

1. Building codes for structures that can withstand the earthquake impact. In this connection the city development authority may contact Roorkee University.

2. Identifying and avoiding sites where impact of an event is expected to be servere. In this connection Geological Survey of India may be contacted to identify active faults.

3. Emergency preparedness and making comprehensive plans to deal with the entire spectrum of expected results of an event—including awareness programmes for public in general. In this connection Civil Defence Department of Meghalaya may be contacted.

Lastly from multi-ethnic societal point of view and on the basis of Social Area Analysis inter-cultural exchange, holistic approach for the development of a composite cultural pattern is a must to strengthen the social fabric of Shillong city.

Acknowledgement

The authors are thankful to Dr. M. M. Saikia, Sr. Assistant Director and Head, Geoscience Division for giving active guidance in writing the tectonic movement part of this paper. Further many thanks goes to Dr. Mohini Saikia, Director, College Development Council, Dibrugarh University for providing valuable information regarding Shillong city.

REFERENCES

1. Abramson, Mark (1976) *Urban Sociology* New Jersey, Prentice-Hall Inc.

2. Gist, Noel P. and Fava, Sylvia Fleis (1974), *Urban Society* New York, Thomas Y. Crowell Co.

3. Gupta, R. C. (1983), *Planning and Development of Towns* New Delhi, Bombay, Calcutta, Oxford and IBH Publishing Company.

4. Gutman, R. and Popenoe, D. ed. (1970), *Neighbourhood, City ond Metropolis—An Integrated Reader in Urban* Sociology, New York, Random House.

5. Marphy, Raymond E., (1966) *The American City, An Urban Geography*, (New York, McGraw-Hill Inc.
6. Singh, J.P., (1979) *Urban Land Use Planning in Hill Areas* A Case Study of Shillong, Delhi, Inter-India Publications.

5

Variation In Temperature and Rainfall of Shillong During 1981–90

Zahid Husian

Introduction

Temperature and rainfall are two basic elements of climate. These are main influencing factors, and impact of any variation in them can be seen on the life forms, environment and natural processes. Therefore, man has nowadays become more concerned about the climate. It is because the climatic elements have been affected by various developmental works, wanton destruction of forests, environmental pollution and different global phenomena, and the resultant variations have invariably been detrimental to the global ecosystem as a whole. Hence, sequential studies of the climatic factors are necessary to find out spatiotemporal variations, interrelations between them and its ecological implications.

* Researh Associate (Ecology), Anthropological Survey of India NER Centre, Upper Lachumiere, Shillong —793 001.

Such points about temperature and rainfall of Shillong town from the year 1981 to 1990 have been discussed and analysed in this paper. Moreover, to ascertain any variation or fluctuation in these climatic factors, the present data and results have been compared with that of the periods from 1970 to 1981, and from 1931 to 1960, presented and analysed a decade ago by the author (Husain, 1984). Basic data on temperature and rainfall of Shillong have been collected from the climatic records maintained by the authrities of the St. Edmund's College, Shillong. Tabulation, calculation and cartographic representation of the data have been done to facilitate discussion and analysis on the above mentioned lines.

Discussion and Analysis

Temperature

Average annual temperature of the years from 1981 to 1990 comes to 17.06° Celsius (Table 1). It is 0.18 °C or 1.07 per cent more than the average annual temperature of the years from 1970 to 1981 (Husain, 1984). But alarmingly, it is 0.36 °C or 2.16 per cent higher than the average of the 30 years from 1931 to 1960 (IMD).

The yearly variation shows that average annual temperature of the years 1985, 87, 88 and 89 was above the average of the decade (1981-90). While in rest of the six years it remained below the average (Table 1). Interestingly, during the whole decade the average annual temperature was above the average of 1970-81, except in the years 1981 and 1983. This certainly points towards gradual warming of the climate of Shillong. The year 1988 was comparatively more warm than rest of the years. It is worth noting that between 1951 and 1990 the highest recorded temperature was 34 °C on the 10th August, 1978. But during the last ten years maximum 31 °C temperature was registered on the 11th August 1984. However, the mercury touched 30 °C mark on a number of days (i.e., 28.8.82, 5.9.82, 20.8.83, 28.8.85, 18.7.87 and 20.8.90). These dates and the highest average monthly temperature (21.74 °C) of the ten years indicate that unusually month of August happens to be the hottest month in Shillong. The same was the case in the seventies also (Husain, 1984).

The lowest temperature of minus 3 °C was recorded on the 12th January 1989, though many a times the mercury dropped to zero and even below it during the decade. However, the lowest temperature between 1951 and 1990 was minus 4 °C on the 27th January, 1980. January with average temperature of 10 °C is the coldest month in Shillong. During the period under study, average monthly temperature remained above the annual average from April to October. Specifically it was around 20 °C during June, July August and September, which marks the warm summer season also (Table 1 and Fig. 1).

During the winter months the averagd range between the average monthly maximum and minimum temperature is higher or above the average range of the decade (Table 2). It means higher diurnal range of temperature is experienced in winters when clear nights are very cold. Maximum average range is 13.41°C in January, closely followed by 13.33 °C in December. The highest diurnal range of 18 °C was on the 23rd February 1981, when daily maximum temperature was 21.5 °C. It was due to sharp sun shine in clear sky allowing higher solar radiation during day time, whereas the faster outgoing radiation from the earth in the clear night caused sharp drop of mercurry. The narrowest diurnal range of half degree Celsius was on the 3rd August 1982, closely followed by 1 °C on the very next day when maximum temperature was 18.5 °C and 20 °C respectively on these days, which noticeably brought down the maximum temperature. In general the diurnal range is low during the summers, the lowest average being 5.73 °C in July.

It is quite interesting to ncte that in the seventies the average maximum diurnal range of 10.4 °C was recorded in March, while it was generally around 10°C in the summer months (Husain, 1984). Surprisingly, the trend has shifted to winter months in the eighties. Not only that, the average annual range has also broadened considerably from 8.0 °C to 10.43 °C. This is because of increase of maximum temperature and decrease of minimum temperature as a whole. The average annual maximum temperature has gone up from 20.92°C to 22.26 °C and the average annual minimum temperature has gone down from 12.92 °C to 11.84°C (Table 2). This clearly proves that the climate of Shillong is slowly getting more and more warm during summers; and more and more cool during the winters, the latter have become prolonged too. In the recent years, the cold has been experienced even upto April-May, which possibly retards flow of the characteristic strong winds in Shillong during March-April-May.

Rainfall

The average annual rainfall of Shillong is 2118.05 mm (Table 3). Though this average is 80.95 mm or 3.97 per cent higher than the average of 1970-81, but it is markedly lower by 12.31 per cent from the average 2415.30 mm of the 30 years (1931-60). If shows an undesirable decline in the total annual precipitation in Shillong. Though the immediate reason can be attributed to deforestation in and around Shillong, but the role played by the global factors in formation of the monsoon and spatial distribution pattern of rainfall in the Northeastern India have also to be taken into account for it.

The uneven distribution of rainfall over the months and years is quite evident from Figure 1 and Table 3. From November to March, the average monthly rainfall is below 50 mm, the lowest being 9.38 mm in January. Winters are usually dry. Maximum rainfall occurs in July, the average being 513.44 mm, and the highest monthly being 858.00 mm in 1984. Average monthly rainfall of July has increased during the eighties. Every third or fourth year experiences low rainfall.

Table 1. Average monthly temperature of Shillong, 1981-1990 (in degree Celcius)

Year	*Jan.*	*Feb.*	*March*	*April*	*May*	*June*	*July*	*Aug.*
1	2	3	4	5	6	7	8	9
1981	8.87	10.86	14.84	15.74	18.91	21.54	21.91	21.65
1982	10.95	11.54	14.84	18.55	20.32	21.14	21.82	22.53
1983	9.22	10.79	15.03	18.53	19.13	21.35	21.55	21.17
1984	8.73	12.26	17.74	19.97	20.04	21.21	20.64	21.74
1985	10.38	10.71	17.78	19.81	19.15	21.57	21.04	21.89
1986	11.62	11.47	16.93	18.50	18.58	21.62	21.47	21.70
1987	11.85	13.10	15.55	18.66	20.38	21.56	21.52	20.87
1988	10.61	13.32	15.85	20.09	19.77	21.28	21.67	21.49
1989	8.13	10.63	15.53	20.02	20.96	21.48	21.19	21.78
1990	9.60	12.26	13.94	17.46	19.48	21.52	21.85	21.59
Average of the decade	10.00	11.69	15.80	18.73	19.67	21.43	21.47	21.74

September	October	November	December	Average Annual	% Variation from the average
10	11	12	13	14	15
20.92	17.99	14.93	11.09	16.60	−2.70
20.63	17.26	13.32	10.26	16.93	−0.76
19.58	18.75	14.78	10.32	16.68	−2.23
19.23	18.13	13.97	10.68	17.03	−0.18
20.56	18.45	13.34	12.37	17.25	+1.11
19.48	16.13	13.80	11.95	16.94	−0.70
20.84	17.69	15.24	12.42	17.47	+2.40
20.89	18.41	15.01	11.86	17.52	+2.70
21.30	19.22	13.94	11.32	17.13	+0.41
20.61	17.39	16.20	11.78	16.97	−0.53
20.40	17.94	14.45	11.41	17.06	

TABLE II

Range between the decadal average monthly maximum and minimum temperature of Shillong, 1981-90 (in degree Celsius)

Temperature	*Jan*	*Feb.*	*March*	*April*	*May*	*June*	*July*
1	*2*	*3*	*4*	*5*	*6*	*7*	*8*
Maximum	16.70	18.14	21.73	24.28	24.36	25.27	24.84
Minimum	3.29	5.25	9.87	13.30	14.98	17.58	18.09
Range	13.41	12.89	11.86	10.88	9.38	7.69	6.75

Temperature	*Aug.*	*Sept.*	*Oct.*	*Nov.*	*Dec.*	*Annual Average*	*Annual Av. of 1970-81*
9	*10*	*11*	*12*	*13*	*14*	*15*	*16*
Maximum	25.55	24.24	23.29	20.87	18.07	22.26	20.92
Minimum	17.73	16.57	12.60	7.97	4.74	11.84	12.92
Range	7.82	7.67	10.69	12.90	13.33	10.42	8.00

TABLE III

Monthly rainfall in Shillong, 1981-1990 (in mm)

Year	*Jan.*	*Feb.*	*March*	*April*	*May*	*June*	*July*	*Aug.*
1	2	3	4	5	6	7	8	9
1981	35.50	20.00	68.80	127.00	369.50	242.50	489.00	269.00
1982	5.50	1.00	62.00	142.00	170.50	622.00	328.75	369.25
1983	4.00	36.00	41.50	118.00	223.50	195.50	827.00	396.50
1984	16.50	2.50	18.00	97.60	142.50	316.00	858.00	309.75
1985	7.00	23.60	8.00	64.50	386.00	347.00	363.50	321.00
1986	0.00	16.00	20.00	82.00	189.50	184.00	154.80	182.00
1987	2.50	41.25	79.50	105.00	115.00	540.00	619.00	292.50
1988	7.00	18.00	46.50	68.10	575.20	561.00	512.00	572.25
1989	13.50	41.75	74.75	32.20	170.00	315.25	839.50	160.75
1990	2.25	21.75	50.00	193.50	280.75	278.75	142.85	148.50
Average of the decade	9.38	22.19	46.83	103.07	262.25	360.20	513.44	302.13

Spt.	Oct.	Nov.	Dec.	Total Annual	% Variation from the average
10	11	12	13	14	15
176.00	16.50	0.00	87.50	1900.50	−10.27
320.25	52.75	70.50	2.00	2147.25	+ 1.38
439.50	241.50	7.00	12.50	2542.50	+20.04
305.00	114.50	2.50	35.50	2218.35	+ 4.74
203.50	33.50	11.50	0.00	1769.10	−16.48
288.00	342.50	45.00	5.00	1508.80	−28.77
390.50	77.50	40.00	14.00	2316.75	+ 9.38
196.00	211.50	220.50	0.00	2988.05	+41.08
273.75	282.70	12.00	4.85	2221.00	+ 4.86
207.50	235.20	5.50	1.50	1568.05	−25,97
280.00	160.82	41.45	16.29	2118.05	

Total annual rainfall has also been uneven during the decade. The driest year was 1986 with 1508.80 mm annual rainfall, which was 28.77 per cent less than the average. The wettest year was 1988 with 2988.05 mm rainfall, being 41.08 per cent higher than the average. Significantly 1986 and 1988 are the driest and wettest years respectively between 1951 and 1990. Table 3 also depicts that the annual rainfall in seven years was above the average. Though it may appear against the general view that the rainfall in Shillong is decreasing, but it is not so because the average annual rainfall is, in fact, lower than the average of the 30 years (1931-60). Hence, a declining trend is easily discernible. During the decade, the heaviest daily rainfall of 193 mm was recorded on the 3rd July 1983. However, between 1959 and 1990 the heaviest daily rainfall of 252.50 mm was received between 7.30 a.m. of the 24th June and 7.30 a.m. of the 25th June 1988.

It is significant to note that in the recent years Shillong has experienced heavy hailstorms during February and march. Once it was so heavy that the landscape looked like a snow covered area for time being, a scene never seen before.

Conclusions

From the foregoing text the following conclusions can be derived.

(1) There has been mild and gradual increase in the average annual temperature of Shillong. (2) The summers have become more warm, while the winters have become more cold particularly the nights. (3) cold season is prolonged now, which seems to affect flow of the strong winds during March-April-May and effectiveness of the southwest monsoon too. The latter thus causing decline in total rainfall. (4) the diurnal range of temperature has widened and the greater range regime has shifted from March to December-January, indicating relatively more cold nights and warm days during the winters. (5) Opressive conditions prevail during summer days due to warm and moist

weather. By the beginning of the 21st Century, fan will become an inevitable need of the Shillongites to get relief from such uncomfortable weather conditions. (6) Though the average annual rainfall is slightly higher than the average of 1970 to 1981, but it is definitely less than the average of 1931 to 1960. The overall decreasing rainfall is one of the reasons behind little warming of the climate of Shillong. Moreover, it has also affected the already depleting sources of water (due to deforestation), causing great inconvenience to the citizens of this capital town.

Passing reference can be made here about some ecological changes resulting due to some variations in the climatic factors. The meagre increase in temperature and warm and moist conditions have led to phenomenal growth of various micro organisms, insects, pests and weeds. Moreover it creates drowsiness also. A general observation reveals that nowadays there are more number of mosquitoes, house flies, silver fish. bed-bucks and other insects/pests in the town. Growth of termites has been dangerously high in the years 1990 and 1991. The damage caused by the termites my reduce durability of the wooden structure and furniture of the town, a great loss is expected indeed. Altogether these changes are making life of the Shillongites hazardous and uncomfortable. The salubrious and benign character of the climate of Shillong is losing its charm and attraction day by day, and its restoration appears to be a difficult task for man. Pollution and degradation of environment of Shillong have further deteriorated the situation. Despite all the odds, genuine efforts can be made to ameliorate the environment and climate.

Acknowledgements

The author is thankful to the Director-General, Anthropological Survey of India, Calcutta for the kind permission to publish this paper. Profound thanks go to the authorities of the St. Edmund's College, Shillong, for providing the valuable climatic records. Thanks are also due to the colleagues who helped in preparation of the paper.

REFERENCES

1. Husain, Zahid, 1984. Some ecological observations on climatological data of Shillong, 1970-81. In *Shillong 1971-81* (ed.) B. Pakem, Research India Publications, Calcutta. pp, 11-20.

2. Indian Meterological Department (IMD), Government of India. *Climatological Tables of Observations in India (1931-60)*.

6

Status of Environmental Pollution in Shillong (1981-91) —An Overview

H. Nath
and
Abhik Gupta

Introduction

Shillong, the Capital of Meghalaya, was once famous for its selubrious climate and picturesque landscape, sparkling stream water, water falls etc., till the early part of sixties. Rightly this was called the Scotland of the East. However, within a span of two and a half or three decades, Shillong has lost most of its grandeur and importance due to degradation and pollution of its natural environment.

With the rapid growth of populatiou and urbanisation leading to an increase in various man-made activities, large quantities of pollutants/wastes are being released continuously into the city environment and thus in this race for progress and development, it is feared that the Shillongites might lose the race for healthy survival, if answers are not found to the twin spectres of over-population and environmental pollution.

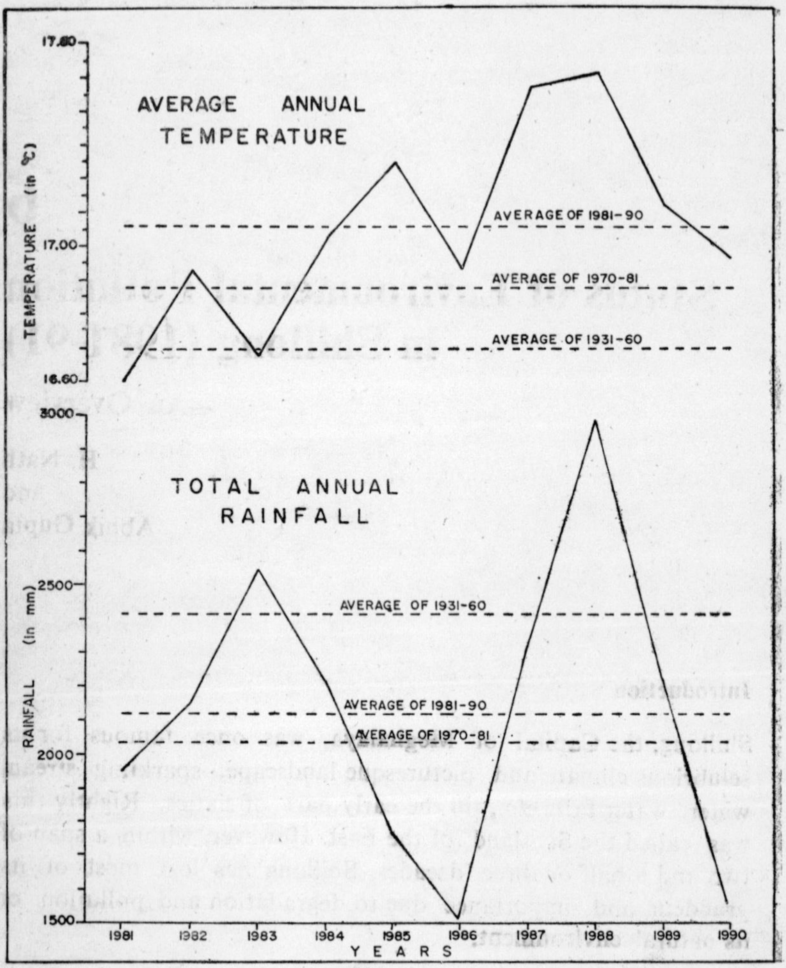
17.80
17.00
16.60
TEMPERATURE (in °C)
AVERAGE ANNUAL
TEMPERATURE
AVERAGE OF 1981-90
AVERAGE OF 1970-81
AVERAGE OF 1931-60
3000
2500
2000
1500
RAINFALL (in mm)
TOTAL ANNUAL
RAINFALL
AVERAGE OF 1931-60
AVERAGE OF 1981-90
AVERAGE OF 1970-81
1981
1982
1983
1984
1985
1986
1987
1988
1989
1990
YEARS

FIG. 1

Resources are shrinking as people are multiplying. A time has come when the political planners and economists have to think seriously about the adverse and drastic impact of human activities on the environment of Shillong and their planning policies and development programmes have to incorporate the insight and wisdom of ecologists with due regard to appropriate technologies. The development planning has to suit the conditions and expectations of people ensuring their participation and support. This paper gives an overview of some aspects of environmental pollution in Shillong.

2. STATUS OF POLLUTION

2.1 Air

The air that we breathe in Shillong is increasingly being polluted due to increased human activities. This impairment of air environment here is mainly due to emissions from:

—Chimneys used in coal fired boilers

—Automobiles

—Burning of coal in private houses, resturants etc., and

—Bakeries

Main pollutants from flue gases and other emissions are

—Suspended particulate matters

—Sulphur dioxide

—Carbon monoxide

—Oxides of nitrogen

Of the above-mentioned sources of emissions, vehicular emission is the major source of pollution of urban environment in Shillong. A large number of cars, buses trucks etc., including those from outside the State, ply in the city and release huge quantities of obonoxious and harmful gases into the city environment.

The Meghalaya Pollution Control Board made a preliminary study on the exhaust emissions from petrol driven vehicles during January and February 1990 and tested about 1228 vehicles. It was found that about 40% of the the fourwheel petrol vehicles were emitting such gases at levels higher than the permissible limits. Results of this study are shown in *Table-I*.

TABLE I

Vehicles emitting gases at higher levels than permissible limits

Type of vehicles	*No. of vehicles tested*	*No. of vehicles emitting CO gas beyond permissible limits*	*% of vehicles emitting gases permissible limits*
Petrol driven			
(a) Ambassador or Fiat cars	530	257	48.40%
(b) Maruti Cars Vans, Gypsis	258	123	47.60%
(c) Jeeps	227	59	25.90%
(d) Two wheelers	213	13	6.10%

Note: (1) CO-Carbon Monoxide

(2) Auto Exhaust Emission Standard for Carbon Monoxide from petrol driven four wheelers = 3% (by vol.)

(3) Auto Exhaust Emission Standard for Carbon Monoxide from petrol driven two and three wheelers = 4.5% (by vol.)

Similarly during 1990-91 another 1709 diesel vehicles (trucks and buses) were also tested. It was found that about 62.5% of them were emitting smoke more than the prescribed permissible limits as indicated in *Table-II*.

TABLE II

Vehicles emitting smoke at higher levels than permissible limits.

Type of vehicles	*Vehicles monitored*	*No. of vehicles complying with emission standards*	*No. of vehicles not complying with standards*	*%*
Diesel vehicles				
Trucks				
Buses	1709	641	1068	62.5%

Note: (1) Auto Exhaust Emission Standards = 65 H.S.U. under free acceleration method)

(2) H.S.U. = Hartridge Smoke Density Unit.

Thus vehicular emission is one of the major culprits in impairing the air quality of Shillong.

Ambient air quality

Air samples were collected and tested from two selected stations of the city in order to monitor the ambient air quality trends in Shillong. The results of the analysis are given in *Table-III.*

TABLE III

Ambient air quality (1990-91)

Location	*S.P.M.*		SO_2		NO_x	
	Range ($\mu g/m^3$)	*Standard* ($\mu g/m^3$)	*Range* ($\mu g/m^3$)	*Standard* ($\mu g/m^3$)	*Range* ($\mu g/m^3$)	*Standard* ($\mu g/m^3$)
1. State Central Library	42.1-115.5	100	* B.D.L-16.0	30	B.D.L.-92.6	30
*2. Moti-nagar	9.6-90.0	100	* B.D.L.-3.3	30	B.D.L.-71	30

Note: *(1) Plants absorb SO_2 and hence its value is low.

(2) The upper range of S.P.M. and No_x are higher than the permissible limits in some seasons.

The ambient air quality in other busy and congested areas can even the worse than the situatlon reflected in Table-III, especially during peak hours.

2.2 WATER

2.2.1 Drinking Water Quality

Different localities of Shillong receive drinking water supplies, though far below the actual demand, from various sources such as springs, streams, deep tube wells/hand pumps, and the Greater Shillong and Umkhen W.S.S. of the P.H.E. Department. In some localities, water from different sources, both treated and untreated, are now mixed in zonal reservoirs before distribution to consumers (which may be due to some constraints). This arrangement, sometimes-affects the quality of drinking water, especially the bacterrial quality needed for safeguarding the health of consumers and is likely to cause many water borne diseases. Although the analysis of some random water samples collected from different localities (given in *Table IV*) indicates that the quality of water supplied for domestic purpose now (August 1991) is by and large safe, it is advisable that the concerned authority should have a small unit of water quality monitoring of its own, (specially the bacterial quality) on a regular basis because water quality fluctuates. It may be estimated that about 80% of all diseases in the developing countries are caused by supply of unsafe water.

Meghalaya Pollution Control Board tested water of some private tuble well installations in the Police Bazar area of Shillong town and found the water of almost all the wells to be bacteriologically unsafe. Therefore, if this water is used for drinking (in households or in resturants) it is sure to cause different types of water borne diseases unless appropriate measures are adopted.

TABLE IV

Quality of Water (Tap Water) in different Localities of Shillong (August 1991)

Sl. No.	*Location*	*Turbidity NIU*	*Conductivity Unbo/em*	*pH*	*T. Alkalinity mg/L*	*Total Hardness Mg/L*	*Chloride mg/L*	*Nitrate-Nitrogen Mg/L*	*Nitrite-N mg/L*	*Iron mg/L*	*T. Coliform MPN/IQOml*	*F. Coli*
1.	Norgthymmi	2.0	50.0	7.0	24.0	22.4	22.7	86.0	Nil	0 05	Nil	Nil
2.	Nongrim Hills	2.4	15.0	7.0	20.0	8.0	19.8	6.0	Nil	0.07	Nil	Nil
3.	Bishnupur	2.4	10.2	7.0	6.0	3.2	15.6	36.0	Nil	3.03	Nil	Nil
4	Jaiaw	1.2	17.5	7.2	12.0	4.8	14.2	26.0	Nil	0.03	Nil	Nil
5.	Polo Hills	2.0	9.2	7.2	8.0	6.4	15.6	20.0	Nil	0.03	Nil	Nil
6·	Standard (ISI)	10.0	—	6.5-8.5	—	300.0	250.0	45.0	—	0.3-1.0	Below 10	Nil

NIL—may be taken as beyond detectable limits.

2.2.2 Surface Water Quality

2.2.2.1 Lakes/Impoundments

In order to assess the surface water quality of such water bodies, the M.P.C.B. carried out some investigations. The findings of these investigations are presented briefly in *Table-V*. The range

TABLE V

Water quality of lakes and reservoirs (1990-91)

Parameters (*Ranges of value, during 1990-91*)	*Word's lake*	*Umiam reservoir*
Temperature (°C)	15.0-24.0	17.5-25.6
Turbidity (NTU)	3.9-17.2	1.6-13.6
Conductivity (u mho/cm)	50-92	34-74
p^H	6.0-7.3	6.2-7.5
Total solids (mg/1)	54-121	45-136
Alkalinity (mg/1)	19.6-32.0	8-58
Hardness (mg/1)	6.8-60.8	5-38.3
Chloride (mg/1)	6.8-45.2	
Nitrate + Nitrite N	Trace-1.3	Trace-0.3
NH_3-N (mg/1)	0.6-2.0	1.3-3.0
Kjeldhal – N (mg/1)	1.4-5.6	1.1-9.2
Sulphate (mg/1)	10.4-53.0	3.4-14.4
Iron (mg/1)	0.4-1.0	Nil-1.2
Phosphate (mg/1)	1.4-9.0	0.3-0.6
Dissolved oxygen (mg/1)	3.0-6.2	3.7-8.4
C.O.D. (mg/1)	4.8-29.8	4.8-13.4
B.O.D. (mg/1)	1.0-4.2	0.8-6.0
Total coliform (MPN/100 ml)	22-2400	Nil-2400
Faecal Coliform (MPN/100 ml)	22-540	Nil-23

of values of different important parameters in the table thus give a picture of water quality fluctuations over a period of one year.

2.2.2.2 Streams/rivers

Extent of water pollution of streams passing through the city presents a grim picture. *Table-VI* presents the data on some important water quality parameters of River Umkhrah during rainy season when dilution of water is atleast ten times more than that during dry season. Hence dry season water quality is further degraded.

It is evident from the data presented that the water of the river has been so much polluted that it is unfit even for recreational use, bathing and laundering, not to speak of drinking.

2.2.2.3 Impact of water pollution on stream biota

Water pollution aided by Environmental degradation in the Umkhrah and Umshirpi catchments have adversely affected the flora and fauna in the Shillong streams. Organic enrichment of stream water and resultant increase in nutrient levels B.O.D. and C.O.D. values etc. have severely impacted the stream biota.

The results of some biomonitoring probes carried out in the Umkhrah-Umshirpi Catchments are summarized in *Table-VII.* It can be discerned from the table that pollution of streamwater and a general eco-degradation in the catchment (*Table-VI*) are accompanied by a concomitant reduction in the number of taxa of periphytonic algae, benthic macroinvertebrates and fishes and appearance of pathogenic organisms. Besides these quantitative changes. some qualitative changes in community structure were also revealed by the aforesaid investigations. Known 'Oligosaprobic' or clean-water forms of periphyton such as various diatoms were eliminated or reduced in diversity and density,. While 'Polysaprobic' i.e. polluted water forms like certain protozoans (*Didinium* etc.) and blue-green algae flourished with increasing levels of pollution. Similarly, innocuous benthic

TABLE VI

Water quality of Umkhrah River (1990-91)

Parameters	*Locations*		
	Near Polo	*Near Mawlai*	*Nongmynsong*
Turbidity (N.T.U.)	16.0	18.0	12.8
Conductivity (u. mho/cm)	105.0	183.0	14.3
p^H	6.9	7.0	7.1
Total solids (mg/1)	210.0	265.0	—
Total alk (mg/1)	50.4	100.8	8.0
Total Hardness (mg/1)	35.9	55.2	4.8
Chloride (mg/1)	14.9	31.5	14.2
Nitrate-N (mg/1)	6.8	8.0	26.0
Nitrate-N (mg/1)	0.4	0.5	Trace
Sulphate (mg/1)	12.8	16.0	—
Iron (mg/1)	0.7	1.0	0.02
D.O. (mg/1)	5.3	3.7	9.0
C.O.D. (mg/1)	147.8	162.0	40
B.O.D. (mg/1)	30.5	45.7	0.3
Total Coliform (MPN/100 ml)	9000	1,60,000	430
Faecal Coliform (MPN/100 ml)	2600	35,000	Nil

invertebrates like crabs, plecopteran most ephemeropteran, megalopteran and trichopteran nymphs were replaced by polysaprobic taxa like planorbids, planarians, chironomids and tubificid worms. Particularly alarming is the appearance of several pathogenic contaminants, for instance, the cysts of *Giardia intestinalis*, *Balantidium coli*, *Entamoeba histolytica*, eggs of *Ascaris* sp., and cercarial larval stages of schistosomes (blood flukes) (Roy and Tandon, 1990). At the same time, the total coliform bacterial populations in the stream water have been found to range between 28,000 to 1,60,000 MPN/100 ml (faecal coliform 17,000-35,000 MPN/100 ml) during the lean season when there is hardly any flushing by rain. These findings reinforce the contention that the hazard potential for human beings handling or using the stream water is indeed very high.

'Modus operandi' of polluting agencies:

It may be pertinent of briefly discuss as to how changes in community structure and composition in the Shillong streams are brought about by pollution aided by agencies of pollution and degradation.

(a) Quantitative and qualitative changes in vegetation cover: Extensive deforestation has taken place in the Greater Shillong area during the last two or three decades. Several factors like clearfelling for urban build up, timberlogging, the 'bun' method of potato cultivation, and quarrying for stone and sand have been chiefly responsible for decimating the forest cover in this area from about 3940. 6 ha 38 per cent) in the early sixties to a mere 1220 ha (11.76 per cent) by the middle or late eighties. About 37.9 per cent of this deforestation is estimated to have been caused by agricultural activities, the rest having been brought about by urban proliferation, road construction, timberlogging and quarrying. Consequently, almost the entire Umkhrah basin is denuded of any riparian (streamside) vegetation, except a few pockets of thin strands of pine. The Riat Laban Forest Reserve is the only green belt that has remained to protect a small part of the Umshirpi catchment. The reduction of vegetation cover along stream banks has also been accompanied by changes in floristic composition. While the original climax vegetation in this area comprises several broad-leaved tree species *Table-VII*), the secodary growth after burning and/or clearfelling is almost entireiy dominated by *Pinus Kesiya*, along with weeds like *Eupatorium* spp. and *Lantana camara*. It is known from several studies the world over that removal of riparian vegetation affects the stream biota in two major ways, firstly, by altering the light-shade and temperature regime in the streams which in turn serve as cuess for a variety of life-cycle responses, and secondly when mixed primary forests are replaced by monocultures such as that of pine, biotic diversity and biomass are drastically decimated (Woodall and Wallace, 1972, Newbold *et al*, 1980, Resh and Rosenberg, 1984).

(b) Particulate matter deposition; Yet another problem recognized to be associated with deforestation is the increased sediment load that goes into the streams. The rate of soil erosion from exposed slopes, stone quarries and potato 'buns' are estimated to be around 40-50 tonnes/ha/yr (Prasad *et al*, 1981). Consequently thick sand and silt deposits are found to coat the rocky substratum of the streams. This problem is further accentuated by the fine particulate matter originating from sewage and solid waste. Furthermore, substratum heterogeneity and complexity are grossly altered and reduced by stone and sand collection from streambeds. These factors have been held responsible for the elimination of several genera and species of Ephemeroptera (Gupta and Michael, 1991 b) and in increase in the numbers of burrowing and deposit feeding forms such as chironomida and oligochaetes (Resh and Rosenberg, 1984, Gupta and Michael, 1991 a).

(c) Organic enrichment/pollution: Finally, organic pollution from sewage disposol as evidenced by increased nitrite,

TABLE VII

Comparisons of community structure and diversity index values between protected and unprotected zones of Umkhrah and Umshirpi streams

	Protected		Unprotected	
Parameters	*Umkhrah*	*Umshirpi*	*Umkhrah*	*Umshirpi*
Major tree species in the catchment	*Pinus Kesiya Quercus SP.*	*Pinus Kesiya Quercus dealbata Q. Griffithii Schima Khasiana Acacia Sp.*	*Pinus Kesiya*	*Pinus Kesiya*
1	*2*	*3*	*4*	*5*
Number of taxa of periphytonicalgae and protozoans	21-35	20-28	5-17	5-12
Number of taxa of benthic macro-invertebrates	18-21	23-31	3-14	3-11

(Contd.)

1	2	3	4	5
Ranges of diversity index values	4.38-5.44	6.05-16.2	2.16-3.89	1.03-3.42
Number of species of fishes	7-9	7-9	0-2	0
Number of pathogenic protozoans and helminthes	0	0	3-5	3-5

Source: Gupta and Michael (1991 (a), 1991 (b), Roy and Tandon (1990)

nitrate, B.O.D. and C.O.D. values is also instrumental in reducing diversity by eliminating a host of taxa such as megalopterans, plecopterans, certain dipterans, coleopterans, trichopterans and most ephemeropterans from the enriched zones (Gupta and Michael 1991 a, 1991b). Similar conclusions were also drawn in other investigations (Wielgosz, 1979; Dudgeon, 1990),

3.0 DOMESTIC SEWAGE

Domestic sewage comprises human body waste (faeces and urine) and sullage (wastes from bathroom and kitchen). There is no proper system for domestic sewage collection and disposal in Shillong and its adjoining areas. This contributes to insanitary conditions and environmental pollution.

The residential houses here usually use septic tanks, service, tanks, service latrines and ordinary pit latrines for excreta disposal. Most service latrines, which are common in many localities of Shillong Municipality, are not properly cleaned regularly and as such their spillage very often finds access into nearby drains/nullahs. Sometimes even raw sewage is thrown into nearby water courses. Besides, the houses located on the banks of rivers/water courses discharge their domestic sewage (also solid wastes) directly into such water bodies through many toilets built over or near the water courses.

All these have contributed to severe pollution of streams in and around Shillong.

Conventional water borne sewage disposal schemes or sewerage systems may not be a practicable or appropriate solution for the whole master plan area beeause of various constraints and limitatians. But the present situation should not be allowed to remain as such. Concerned authorities should think seriously about this and adopt some low cost appropriate measures to abate or stop further sewage pollution of Shillong.

4.0 SOLID WASTE

Rapid urbanisation has resulted in creating numerous waste dumps in close proximity to human habitations and thus posing a grave threat to public health. These dumps automatically become the breeding sites of various disease vectors like flies, mosquitoes and rats which in turn can transmit diseases such as typhoid, cholera, infective *hepatitis* (Jaundice), tuberculosis and gastrointestinal disorders. It is, therefore, a dire necessity to undertake proper disposal of solid waste without polluting the environment.

4.1 EXISTING SYSTEM OF DISPOSAL

The Shillong cantonment Board and the Shillong Municipal Board which have some sort of waste disposal scheme collect about 3.8 t/d and 34.7 t/d of refuse respectively.

However, in other parts of Greater Shillong Master Plan area, the waste is composted/burned or just dumped by the roadside. Though voluntary cleaning is done by the citizens of certain localities, it is far from adequate. The refuse from Municipal as well as Barabazar areas are disposed off at a 3 acre trenching ground at Mawiong. The site has 65 trenches for disposal of refuse, night soil and carcases. However, the method is inaporopriate and insanitary, resulting in prolific breeding of flies, production of foul odour, and pollution of surface and ground water as well.

4.2 STUDIES ON SOLID WASTE OF SHILLONG

Studies conducted by NEERI, Nagpur, indicated that the total population of the Greater Shillong Master Plan area (viz. Shillong Municipal Board areas, Nangthymmai township, Mawlai township, Madantring, Pynthorumkhrah, rural components comprising 18 villages along with 22 slums and a floating population of about 30,000 of Barabazar) will be around 5,20,000 in

2011 A.D. This population is estimated to generate about 208 t of waste per day @ 0.40 kg/cap/day. The physical and chemical characteristics of the waste were analysed and the results are depicted in *Tables-VIII A* and *Table-VIII B*. The analysis reveals that:

(i) The organic fraction of the refuse goes up to 62% and the C/N ratio is usually above 30 indicating that it can be composted. This also has a biogas production potential of about 24.22 m^3/t.

(ii) Incineration will not be economically viable. As such, appropriate methods of disposal may include sanitary land-filling and/or composting.

4.3

For effective solid waste management, public awareness and active co-operation of local durbars/committees, NGOs as well as information media can play a vital role.

Local Durbars can also compel, if necessity arises, the house owners to dump such wastes in selected places or dustbins only and forbid them against dumping it in public drains or any other unauthorised places which causes environmental pollution and hazards.

In residential areas where vacant land is available, individual house owners may undertake composting within compounds and use the compost for growing vegetables etc. This practice not only keeps the compounds clean but also reduces the volume of wastes to be transported.

It needs no emphasis that waste removal is a valuable public service which has to be paid for as the public administration in third world countries lack the financial resources to pay for the entire waste management programme.

TABLE VIII-A

Physical analysis of Shillong City refuse Month of Sampling: November 1988
(All values are given in % and are calculated on weight basis received at source)

Sl. No.	Compostable matter	Coconut	Paper	Rubber and leather	Plastics	Rags/ textiles	Wooden matter	Coal	Metals	Glass and Crockery	Stones and bricks	Ash and fine organics	Moisture
1.	16.59	43.37	0.92	2.20	1.61	10.15	3.69	0.46	—	0.46	8.37	12.07	48.70
2.	62.40	—	3.38	2.82	0.53	3.26	—	0.56	0.58	4.23	6.79	14.68	45.60
3.	57.99	1.33	6.00	0.66	1,05	1.00	0.66	0.66	0.33	3.33	4.55	22.23	42.50
4.	45.74	0.54	8.30	1.09	1.74	2.29	0.56	1.92	0.55	4.36	3.82	29.08	32.60
5.	41.08	7.81	26.77	6.17	1.02	1.85	2.05	1.02	0.51	2.25	3.03	6.37	41.00
6.	37.08	2.87	23.76	0.59	0.86	1.78	2.37	1.18	2.62	1.77	8.72	16.29	43.90
7.	36.38	2.54	11.85	2.18	0.80	1.38	1.09	4.36	1.09	3.77	4.36	30.18	45.90
8.	11.97	3.98	12.05	0.46	0.64	3.24	1.38	1.38	1.84	1.56	34.90	26.57	60.00
9.	58.79	5.00	5.48	—	0.77	—	4.76	—	—	1.44	9.28	14.76	53.10

TABLE VIII-B

Chemical analysis of Shillong City refuse (All values are calculated on dry weight basis of Month of Sampling—November, 1988

Sl.	p^H value	Organic matter	Carbon %	Nitrogen %	Phosphorous as p_2 05%	Potash as K_2O %	C/N ratio	HCV in Kcal/Kg
1.	8.0	61.67	35.75	0.68	0.21	0.28	52.60	962.25
2.	7.5	57.85	33.53	0.74	0.27	0.22	45.30	799.57
3.	7.3	62.92	36.47	0.55	0.17	0.20	66.34	969.07
4.	8.0	63.50	36.81	0.56	0.15	0.15	65.76	1116.96
5.	7.8	69.53	40.30	0.83	0.16	0.19	48.62	1418.63
6.	7.5	50.36	33.83	0.54	0.23	0.31	62.89	949.09
7.	7.6	55.33	32.07	0.59	0.22	0.23	53.62	751.04
8.	7.8	65.86	38.17	0.54	0.19	0.22	71.28	768.75
9.	7.7	54.36	31.51	0.54	0.22	0.26	58.38	575.75

Thus it is evident from findings of all these investigations that:

(i) air quality in Shillong is increasingly being deteriorated.

(ii) by and large most surface water sources in and around Shillong have been grossly polluted due to various human activities

(iii) the environment is degrading rapidly, thereby accelerating environmental pollution.

These are happening mainly due to

— Inadequate control measures on vehicular and other particulate and gaseous emissions.

— Improper/inadequate disposal of domestic (sanitary) sewage and solid wastes.

— Inadequate general sanitation practices in residential and business areas (viz hotels, restaurants, market places etc).

— Indiscriminate discharge of liquid effluents from large number of garages, industrial establishments, clinics. hospitals etc.

— Indiscriminate man-made activities like various constructions, stone quarrying, tree felling etc.

5.0 CONCLUSIONS

Environmental pollution in and around Shillong is rapidly increasing. The situation will further worsen beyond rehabilitation within the next few decades unless appropriate preventive measures are adopted early to contain the situation. For this it, is desirable that concerned authorities and/or the Government should adopt some short-term and long-term measures.

Short-term measures may include

(a) Prevent or abate environmental degradation in and around city areas by stopping or restricting stone quarrying, tree felling, indiscriminate growth of hotels, restaurants and vehicle workshops; banning construction of any establishments or residential houses with or without toilets on the banks of river/stream courses;
dumping of solid wastes in any drains, streams etc., and introducing appropriate effective legal safe guards towards these objectives.

(b) Undertake a comprehensive solid waste collection and disposal scheme for Shillong Master Plan area in phases, adopting appropriate technology with people's participation.

(c) Take up sewage disposal (on-site and/or off-site) scheme which should incorporate simple low-cost appropriate mix of technologies with due considerations to customs and habits of users and constraints of maintenance etc.

(d) Develop peri-urban settlements/townships with minimum facilities for transport, education, medical care, markets, etc., in order to reduce congestion in the main city.

(e) Undertake early construction of by-pass road with road side plantations for diverting large number of diesel trucks and buses in order to limit air pollution from vehicles.

(f) Conduct vehicular exhaust emission tests regularly, penalise defaulters under the provisions of Motor Vehicles Act, 1988.

(g) Create a single and appropriate administrative authority covering all areas for effective management of different facilities.

Here it may be stated again that the most effective means of environmental management is through education which should aim at understanding the adverse effects of activities like directly discharging wastes into any sources of water, prevailing poor sanitation practices or releasing pollutants into air effecting its quality etc. This can best be done through mass media by incorporating this in the school education programme for which the Government should adopt some long term measures.

Long term measures

(a) Introduce conservation oriented education policy at appropriate levels and improve environmental education and training aspects.

(b) Adopt a natural resource conservation strategy.

(c) Incorporate environmental considerations into all public and private development planning.

(d) Develop comprehensive environmental information and data base.

(e) Strengthen programmes for environmental manpower development.

(f) Develop environmental management systems and implement environmentally sound sustainable projects.

REFERENCES

1. Dudgeon, D, (1990): Determinants of the distribution and abundance of larval Ephemeroptera (Insecta) in Hong-Kong running waters. pp. 222-232. In Mayflies and stoneflies (Ed. I.C. Compbell). Kluwer Academic Publishers.

2. GTZ: Solid Waste management with peoples participation.

3. Gupta, A and Michael, R.G. (1991 a): Benthic invertebrates as indicators of water pollution in Shillong streams. In: Environment Conservation and Wasteland Development in Meghalaya (Eds. A. Gupta and D.C. Dhar). Meghalaya Science Society, Shillong (in Press).

4. (1991 b): Diversity, distribution, and seasonal abundance of Ephemeroptera in a few streams in Meghalaya State, India. Hydrobiologia (in Press).

5. Meghalaya Pollution Control Board (1990-91): First Annual Report (Manuscript).

6. New bold, J.D., Erman, D.C. and Roby, K.B. (1980): Effects of logging on macroinvertebrates in streams with or without buffer strips, Can. J. Fish. aquat. Sci. 37: 1076-1085.

7. Prasad, R.N., Ram, P., Barooah, R.C. . and Raam, M. (1981): Soil fertility management in NEH region. Research bulletin No. 9 ICAR Research Complex for NEH Region Shillong.

8. Resh, V.H. and Rosenberg, D.M. (Eds.) (1984): The ecology of aquatic insects. Praeger Publishers, New York.

9. Roy, B. and Tandon, V. (1990): Occurrence of water borne, pathogens in Shillong Streams. Seminar on Pollution and and Env. Degradation. Centre for Distance Edn. NEHU. region, Shillong (Abstract).

10. Sastry, C.A. (1989): Environment and development. J. Ind. Associ. Env. management.

11, Urban Affairs Dept. Meghalaya: Draft report on planning for solid waste management in Shillong NEERI, Nagpur.

12. Wielgosz, S. (1979): The effect of wastes from the town of Olstzyn on invertebrate communities in the bottom of the River Tyna. Acta Hydrobiologica 21: 149-165.

13. Woodall, W.R. and Wallace, J.B. (1972): The benthic fauna in four small southern Appalachian streams. Am. Midl. Natur, 88: 393-407.

7

Population Trend in Shillong 1981–91

M.C. Pandey

Shillong has an area approximately 25.40 Square Kilometre which is about 0.11 percent of the total area of Meghalaya. The area is hilly with uneven topography. The Shillong town has been divided into 6 Agglomeration. As per 1991 census the population of Shillong was 2.22 lakhs which is about 13.0 percent of the total population.

After 1961 the population of Shillong has been growing at a very fast rate, the decadel variation from 1981 to 1991 has been approximately 27.23 percent. Approximately 12.6 percent (1991) of the population in Meghalaya lives in Shillong and constitute 33.8 percent of the population in the East Khasi Hills. In absolute terms an increase of 47570 persons from the 1981 Census (1.74 lakhs). Since 1961 the population of Shillong has gradually increased from 1.02 lakhs to 2.22 lakhs, an increase of 117.0 percent. During the same period the population of Meghalaya has increased by 128.8 percent, while the population of the country increased by less than 90 percent.

TABLE I

Population of Shillong Agglomeration 1961-91

Locality		*Area in Square Kilo-metres*	*1961*	*1971*	*1981*	*1991*
1	*2*	*3*	*4*	*5*	*6*	*7*
Shillong Municipality	Total	10.36	72438	87659	109244	130691
	Male		40550	47569	57092	69224
	Female		31888	40090	52152	61467
Shillong Cantonment	Total	1.84	11348	4730	6600	11075
	Male		7738	2679	2757	6646
	Female		3609	2051	2863	4429
Mawlai	Total	6.14	8528	14260	20405	30442
	Male		4350	7355	10716	15273
	Female		4178	6905	6989	15179

(*Contd.*)

1	2	3	4	5	6	7
Nongthymmai	Total	2.93	10884	16103	21558	26816
	Male		5443	8558	11271	13625
	Female		4461	7545	10287	13191
Madanrting	Total	2.11	—	—	6165	8927
	Male				3160	4535
	Female				3005	4392
Pathormukhrah	Total	2.20	—	—	10711	14322
	Male				5732	7908
	Female				4947	6414
Shillong Agglomeration	Total	25.40	102398	122752	174703	222273
	Male		58082	66161	91728	117211
	Female		44316	565591	82975	105062
Meghalaya	Total	22500.00	769380	1011699	1335819	1760636
	Male			520967	683710	904308
	Female			490732	652109	856318

Source: Census of India (1)

Table-1 summarises the population of Shillong since 1961 to 1991. Table-2 and 3 gives the sex ratio and decadel growth of Shillong Agglomeration.

TABLE II

Sex Ratio Shillong Agglomeration

	1961	*1971*	*1981*	*1991*
Shillong Municipality	785	842	913	888
Shillong Cantonment	466	765	762	666
Mawlai	960	938	905	993
Nongthymmai	852	881	912	968
Madanrting	—	—	950	968
Pynthorumkhrah	—	—	867	811
Shillong Agglomeration	762	855	902	896
Meghalaya	937	942	954	947

Population Trend

In absolute terms in a span of 10 years (1981-91) the population of Shillong has increased by 47570 which is not very high. The decadel growth rate has declined significantly from 43.32 percent during 1971-81 to 27.23 percent during 1981-91. However, the decadel growth is higher than 1961-71 (19.88 percent). The population figures presented on Table—1 are for Shillong agglomeration but, it may be noted that are concentration of population in patches around Shillong, which may have not been reflected in the Census figures.

Sex Ratio

Since 1931 the sex ratio in Meghalaya has been declining. Between 1951 and 1991 it has been fluctuating between 937 (1961) to 954 (1981). The sex ratio of Shillong agglomeration has been much higher than Meghalaya as a whole. It is interesting to note that the sex ratio in Shillong agglomeration has been increasing since 1961. Shillong Cantonment has the lowest sex ratio. It has significantly declined in 1991 as compared with 1981 and 1971 figures. One of the reasons for decline in sex ratio in the Cantonment area may be due to floating population. Decadel variation in growth rate is presented on table-3.

TABLE III

Decadel Growth Shillong Agglomeration

		1971	*1981*	*1991*
Shillong Municipality	Total	21.01	24.62	19.63
	Male	17.30	20.01	21.24
	Female	25.72	30.08	17.86
Shillong Cantonment	Total	—58.32	39.53	67.30
	Male	—65.37	2.91	141.0
	Female	—43.16	39.59	54.6
Mawlai	Total	67.21	43.09	49.19
	Male	69.08	45.69	42.52
	Female	65.27	1.21	117.18
Nongthymmai	Total	56.69	33.87	24.39
	Male	57.22	31.70	20.88
	Female	62.57	36.34	28.22
Shillong Agglomeration	Total	19.88	43.32	27.23
	Male	13.90	38.61	27.78
	Female	27.69	46.62	26.61
Meghalaya	Total	31.50	32.04	31.80

Source: Census of India—Provisional Population Totals Rural and Urban Distribution Series—I Paper—2 of 1991—(2)

Discussion

According to the 1991 census of India[1,2] the population of Shillong is 222273 persons. The increase over 1981 has been 47570 persons. During 1971-81 the population had grown by 51951 persons. While during 1961-71, the growth was 20354 persons. Thus there is decline in growth of population in Shillong during 1981-91. When compared with 1971-81 growth figure. However, since Independence the annual growth rate of population has been very high. During 1961-81, this rate was more than 5.0 per cent it has been reduced to 2.72 percent during 1981-91. If we continue to grow at 2.5 percent or more during the next decade, the population of Shillong will reach almost 4.2 to 4.5 lakhs by 2000 A.D.

The 1991 census results show that measures adopted so far in checking the population growth have not been very effective. There is no doubt that effective steps should be taken to check population growth in those States which have a high growth rate and have not shown significant decline during the eightees. There also should be appreciable decline in population growth where population pressures are tremendous on available resources. The pressure of population in relation to population density may appear low, particularly in the hilly areas,[3] but, environmental disaster due to pressure of population resulting in congestion and pollution has to be linked with the quality of life. Thus the rapid rate of population growth has to be reduced to conserve resources and maintain ecological balance.[4]

REFERENCES

1. Census of India 1991 Provisional Population Totals Paper 1 of 1991.

2. Census of India 1991 Provisional Population Totals Rural and Urban Distribution Series—I paper 2 of 1991.

3. Pandey M.C. 1990—Population and Population Pressure on Land NEHU J. Soc. Sci. and Hum. VIII (4) 13-30.

4. Puri R.K. 1991—Whither India's Population Hindustan Times August 19, 1991.

8

Demographic Profile of Shillong 1981-1991

R.P. Bhattacharjee

1. INTRODUCTION

Shillong, which lies at 25°34'N latitudes and 91°53'E longitudes at 1496 metre above m.s.l. is situated in the lap of Shillong hill range. It is a saucer-like undulating plateau surface flanked by hill ranges in all directions except north. The general slope is towards north-west and it is drained by Um Shyrpi and Um Khrah rivers.

1.1 Shillong—Its Origin

Before 1864, Shillong was an unknown nomenclature. Its present area was then covered by deep forest with Laban as a small Khadi Village under the then united Khasi State of Shillong. It was in that year that Shillong became the administrative village for Khasi and Jaintia Hills District. Two years later, in 1866, Col. Henry Hoopkin Son, Commissioner of Assam and Agent to the Governor General of India had strongly advocated in favour of Shillong as the future headquarters of Assam. Accordingly, on March 20, 1874 by a Government Notification (No. 49), Shillong was declared the capital of Assam province with effect from that date. Therefore Shillong is essentially the creation of British administration and its growth depends closely with the growth of administration.

1.2 The Capital of Meghalaya

Shillong served the administrative purposes of the British Raj in the pre-independence period. After independence, she served the Indian Government and the composite State of Assam and at present Shillong is the capital of Meghalaya (21st full-sledged state) since 21st January, 1972 after the North-Eastern (Re-organisation) Act of 1971.

Above all, Shillong is the ideal hill city of India.

2. DEMOGRAPHIC PROFILE OF SHILLONG 1981-91

2.1 Population Growth of Shillong Municipality

The provisional population of Shillong municipal area (M) as on 1st March, 1991 is 130,691 which is 21,447 persons, more than 1981 census having growth rate of 19.63% during 1981-91. During 1981 census, the population of Shillong (M) was 109,224. The results of 1991 census for Shillong (M) is reckoning due to the fact that for last 110 years of regular census, the growth rate during this decade is lowest (Table-1) and no-census decadel growth since 1881 census .had less than 20% growth rate like this.

Here the preposition is that, in Shillong Municipal area (M) there is no further room for residential expansion. It is known to all that Shillong (M) area is 10.36 sq. km. and a large chunk of this is occupied by State Government Offices, Central Government Offices and other administrative offices. The main business and other commercial centre are located in municipal area. The population growth of these areas are zero or constant. The people in the administrative offices are floating. The remaining residential areas has no further place for expansion in the present system of residential housing pattern. Therefore, the Population of residential areas of Shillong (M) will not have large scale growth rate in future to come until and unless the housing pattern is changed and more space for new houses or buildings provided. The population of Shillong (M) is shown in table-1 below:

TABLE 1

Population of Shillong (M) From 1881—1991

Year	*Population (in No.)*	*Decadel variation*	*Decadel growth rate*
1	*2*	*3*	*4*
1881	4,288	—	—
1891	6,720	+ 2,432	+ 56.72
1901	9,621	+ 2,901	+ 43.17
1911	13,639	+ 4,018	+ 41.76
1921	17,203	+ 3,564	+ 26.13
1931	21,300	+ 4,097	+ 23.82
1941	39,734	+ 9,434	+ 44.29
1951	53,756	+ 23,022	+ 74.91
1961	72,438	+ 18,682	+ 34.75
1971	87,659	+ 15,221	+ 21.01
1981	109,244	+ 21,585	+ 24.62
1991	130,691	+ 21,447	+ 19.63

2.2 Population of Shillong Urban Agglomeration (UA)

The provision population of Shillong UA as on 1st March 1991 is 222,273 consisting 117,211 males and 105,062 females Shillong sex ratio as 896. The Shillong UA contributes 67-54% of total Urban population Meghalaya which is 329,079 as per 1991 population census.

The population of Meghalaya in toto is 1 760,629 showing a decadal increase of 31.80% during 1981-91 and East Khasi Hills has population of 657,160 with a growth of 28.50% (Table-2).

The population of Shillong UA during 1981 census was 174.703 and the Shillong (M) had a population of 109,244. This shows that in the peripheri of Shillong (M), the population was 65,459 which has risen to 91,582 during 1991 showing a growth rate of 39.91% during 1981-91 while the growth rate of Shillong (M) during this decade is only 19.63%.

Therefore, we observe from this that the growth of population in the Shillong UA is mainly due, to population growth in the agglomeration areas in the peripheri of Shillong (M). And this is due to limited space in Shillong municipal area for a fresh housing stock and until and unless the housing pattern is changed in the municipal areas, the population will stagnate.

More clearly, the slow growth of Shillong (M) is due to the preposition of stagnation of residental accommodation in municipal area, in the present system of housing pattern. Due to this, we observe expansion of agglomerated townships and obviously the residential areas of today. the greater Shillong is expanding specially in the north direction even upto Umiam (Barapani) and Umshing. The population of Shillong UA since 1881 is shown in table-3.

TABLE II
Comparative Population of Shillong

S. No.	*City District/ State*	*Population (in No.)*		*Decadel Growth (%)*	
		1991 (P)	*1981*	*1981-91*	*1971-81*
1	*2*	*3*	*4*	*5*	*6*
1.	Shillong UA	222,273	174,703	27.23	42.32
	(a) Shillong (M)	130,691	109,244	19.63	24.62
	(b) Mawlai	30,442	20.405	49.19	43.09
	(c) Nongthymmai	26,816	21,558	24.39	33.88
	*(d) Pynthprumkhran	14,322	10,771	33.71	—
	(e) Shillong Cantt.	11,075	6,620	67.30	39.96
	*(f) Mandarting	8,927	6,165	44.80	—
2.	East Khasi Hills Dist.	657,160	511,414	28.50	34.35
3.	Meghalaya	1,760,626	1,335,819	31.80	32.04

*These two areas agglomerated after 1971-census.

TABLE 3

Population of Shillong UA From 1881

Years	*Population (in No.)*	*Decadel Variation*	*Decadel Growth (%)*
1	*2*	*3*	*4*
1881	4,288	—	—
1891	6,720	+ 2,432	+ 56.72
1901	9,621	+ 2,901	+ 43.17
1911	13,639	+ 4,018	+ 41.76
1921	17,203	+ 3,564	+ 26.13
1931	26,536	+ 9,333	+ 54.25
1941	38,192	+ 11,656	+ 43.93
1951	58,512	+ 20,320	+ 53.20
1961	102,398	+ 43,886	+ 75.00
1971	122,752	+ 20,354	+ 19.88
1981	174,703	+ 51,951	+ 42.32
1991 (P)	222,273	+ 47.570	+ 27.23

2.3 Population of Shillong by Sex

According to 1991 census, (Provisional), the number of females in Shillong UA are 105,062 numbers compared to male population of 117,211 showing sex ratio as 896 while during 1981 it was 905. There is a short fall-by 9 in sex-ratio which can be attributed to lower-sex ratio in Shillong Canttonment area as 666 (1991) compared to 762 (1981). In the Shillong (M) area number of females recorded as 61,467 against male numbers of 69,224 showing sex-ratio as 888 (1991) against 913 (1981). The sex-ratio of other-agglomerated areas are, (i) Mawlai, 993(1991) and 904 (1981); (ii) Nangthymmai, 968 (1991) and 913 (1981); (iii) Pynthorumkhrah 811 (1991) and 869 (1981); (iv) Shillong Cantt; 666 (1991) and 762 (1981); and (v) Makanrting as 968 (1991) and 951 (1981). The comparative population by sex of Shillong is shown in Table-4 below.

2.4 Density and Literacy

The density of Shillong UA as per 1991 census is estimated (by the author) as 5751 compared to 6878 (1981). The Shillong municipal area has a density of 12,615 (1991) compared to 10,544 (1981). The density of other agglomerated areas are Mawlai 4958 (1991) and 3323 (1981); Nongthymnai, 9152 (1991) and 7357 (1981); Pythorumkhrah, 7090 (1991) and 5302 (1981); and Madanrting as 4231 (1991) compared to 2922 (1981). In the East Khasi Hills district the density is estimated as 126 (1991) compared to 98 (1981), while in whole of Meghalaya, the density is 78 (1991) compared to 60 (1981).

This is to be noted that in a hilly-city, the increasing density with a constant total area leads to the increasing demand for housing-stock. But until the housing pattern is changed in Shillong UA area specially in Shillong municipal area, there is no room for further population expansion and increasing demand of housing stock Vis-a-Vis further residential accommodation. The density of Shillong during the decade 1981-91 is shown in Table-5 below.

The total number of literates in Shillong UA (1991) along with number of literates in East-Khasi Hills and Meghalaya is also depicted in table-5. Due to non-avaliability of total numbers of population in the age group 0-6, the percentage of literacy could not be calculated. But we have an estimate of proportionate literacy to total proportionate population in Shillong UA as per provisional population totals of 1991.census.

TABLE IV
Population by Sex

Sl. No.	City District/State	Total Population 1991 (P)		1981		Females per 1000 males	
		Males	Females	Males	Females	1991 (P)	1981
1	2	3	4	5	6	7	8
1.	Shillong UA	117,211	105,062	91,728	82,975	896	905
	(a) Shillong (M)	69,224	61,467	57,092	52,152	888	913
	(b) Mawlai	15,273	15,169	10,716	9,689	993	904
	(c) Nongthymmai	13,625	13,191	11,271	10,287	968	913
	(d) Pythorumkhrah	7,908	6.414	5.732	4,974	811	869
	(e) Shillong Cantt.	6,646	4,429	3,757	2,863	666	762
	(f) Madanrting	4,535	4,392	3,160	3,005	968	951
2.	East Khasi Hills	341,216	315,944	262,952	248,462	926	945
3.	Meghalaya	904,308	856.318	683,710	652,109	947	954

TABLE V

Density and Literacy

City/District State (Area km²)	*Density*		*Total Literates (No), 1991*			*Share of Literates in Shillong UA (1991)*		
	1991 (P)	*1981*	*Persons*	*Males*	*Females*	*Persons*	*Males*	*Females*
1	2	3	4	5	6	7	8	9
1. Shillong UA (25.40)	8,751	6.878	157,950	88.235	69,215	100.0	100.0	100.0
(a) Shillong (M) (10.36)	12,615	10.544	96,873	54,638	42,235	61.5 (58.8)	61.9 (59.1)	61.00 (58.5)
(b) Mawlai (6.14)	4,958	3,323	19,008	9,905	9,103	12.1 (13.7)	11.2 (13.0)	13.2 (14.4)
(c) Nongthymmai (2.93)	9.152	7,357	19,994	10,569	9,425	12.7 (12,1)	12.0 (11.6)	13.6 (12.6)
(d) Pynthorum-khrah (2.02)	7,090	5,302	8,296	5,117	3,179	5.3 (6.4)	5.8 (6.7)	4.6 (6.1)

1	2	3	4	5	6	7	8	9
(e) Shillong Cantt. (1.84)	6,019	3,598	7,725	5,023	2,702	4.9 (5.0)	5.7 (5.7)	3.9 (4.2)
(f) Madanwriting (2.11)	4,231	2,922	5,554	2,983	2,571	3.5 (4.0)	3.4 (3.9)	3.7 (4.2)
2. East Khasi Hills (5,196)	126	98	319,878	172,659	147,219	—	—	—
3. Meghalaya (22,429)	78	60	689,419	377,281	312,138	—	—	—

N.B. Figures in brackets (COL, 7,8,9) indicates share of total population in Shillong UA as per 1991-Census (prov).

Source; Census of India, 1981 and 1991

Shillong UA shares 49.2% of total literates in East-Khasi Hills and 22.8% in Meghalaya. But in respect of total population Shillong UA shares only 33.8% of total population in East-Khasi Hills and 12.6% of total Meghalaya, population. This shows more literate urbanites in Shillong compared to share of population in East-Khasi Hills and Meghalaya.

Within Shillong UA (Col. 7,8 and 9 of Table 5), we find that Shillong (M) and Nongthymnai shares more literate than the total share of population both for males and females. In the Shillong cantonment area, the male folk shares proportionate number of literates to their population in Shillong UA. All other localities in Shillong UA, proportionatly there is less literates in respect of total population. This is another factor for less percentage of growth in Shillong municipal area specially during the decade of 1981-91. The high percentage of literacy specially in females deters the population growth as we see in the case of Kerala (1991). More literacy specially among females engage woman-folk in different types of job and awareness of a small-family norm predominates. The other reasons for stagnation in Shillong (M) may be due to slower natural-growth (NG). But due to lack of data in respect of birth-rate and death-rate in Shillong area, the same could not be examined here. But the NG (simple average) of Urban areas in Meghalaya during 1976-80 and 1981-87, which is estimated as 1.17% and 1.57% respectively indicates a positive increase over these two periods. If this is true for Shillong (M) than there should have been more, population growth in Shillong specially in Shillong (M) area instead of slowing down.

3. Conclusion:

From the above demographic analysis it can be concluded that the population growth of Shillong municipal area is near-stagnation. This is due to (a) present housing-pattern which results expansion of Shillong UA mainly towards North and in other agglomerated places: (b) decrease in number of females per 1000 of males 1913 to 888 during 1981-91). (c) Steadly increase in density of population (10,544 to 12,615 during 1981-91) vis-a-vis shortening room for further expansion of housing stock in Shillong municipal areas; (d) more literates in Shillong (M) and (e) increasing member of administrative and commercial establishments further squeezing residentional accommodation and resultant factor of more floating-population in the shillong municipal areas.

REFERENCES

1. Zahid Husain—"*Some Ecological observations on Climatological Data of Shillong, 1970-81* (P. 11, 12).
   Published in Shillong. 1971-81 Ed. by B. Pakem.
2. B. Pakem—*Shillong 1971-81*; *An Introduction* (P. 1), Ibid.
3. L.S. Gassah—*Shillong as an Administrative and Political Centre* (*1971-1981*), [P. 26, 27) (Book Ibid].
4. J.N. Choudhury—*The Khasi Canvas* (P. 323-331).
5. Dr. D.N. Majumdar—*Tribal occupational Mobility* Research
   Dr, B. Datta Roy India Publications, Calcutta (P. 71, 73).
6. Census of India, 1991, series 16, Meghalaya paper-I of 1991, provisional population Totals (Corrected Copy).
7. Census of India, 1971, Series-3, Meghalaya, Part-IIA General population Table.
8. District Census, East Khasi Hills, Meghalaya, 1981.
9. Dr. B. Datta Roy (Ed)—*Patterns and problems of population in North-East India* (1986).
10. Directorate of Economics, Statistics and Evaluation, Govt. of Meghalaya, Shillong-1.

    (1) Statistical Hand Book, Meghalya, 1981 (P. 8, 9).

(2) Statistical Hand Book, Meghalaya 1984 (P. 17, 18).

(3) Meghalaya Economy in Figures 1990.

(4) District level key Statistics Meghalaya, 1989, 90.

(5) Meghalaya State's Economy in Figures, 1984.

(6) Statistical Abstract, Meghalaya, 1983.

11. Basic Statistics of N.E.R. 1990-NEC, Shillong. (P. 18-19)

12. Basic Facts, Meghalaya, D.I.P.R., Meghalaya.

13. Peter R. Cox.—*Demography* (1979) Vikas publishing House Private Limited, New Delhi-20.

14. M.G. Nanumappa—*Urbanisation Trends in India* (1981) Ashish Publishing House, New Delhi-27.

15. G. Viswanadham—*Urban Demography and Ecology*, (1979) Light and Life, Publishers, New Delhi-9.

16. Census of India, 1991, Series-1, India, Paper-1 and Paper-2 of 1991.

9

Change of Settlement Pattern in Shillong City Through Decade A Micro Analysis

P.K. Guha*

Introduction

In the pre-historic time the human being lived in caves, trees and other natural shelters. But as the time changed with the process of ongoing changes the human dwellings have also been changed according to their own requirements depending on the regional ecology and availability of the materials. Say for e.g. marsh dwellings where the huts were constructed on the high raised platforms on the water level. Pile dwellings were constructed on the high raised platform in the jungle to save themselves from the hostile animals. The nomadic people used to live in the tent before the introduction of permanent houses or huts. The

* Shri P. K Guha, Anthropological Survey of India, North-Eastern Regional Centre, Shillong-793 001, Meghalaya.

conception of permanent houses came only after the introduction of cultivation. With this background an attempt has been made to write this paper.

In India the first effort was made on house types by Subramanyam (1938). He studied on four main house types in South India. Singh (1957) studied on house types in the Middle Ganga Valley in the eastern Uttar Pradesh. Dikshit (1965) described the rural house types in Dehra Dun Valley. Tewari (1966) studied the house types of Jaunsar Himalaya. He had shown the human dwellings in Sonpar region. Mishra (1969) studied the application of geographical methods in the analysis of house types. Gosal (1972) in his review work on rural settlement geography, had mentioned the theoritical approach on Indian house types, Chauhan (1971) studied the house types of the Upper Yamuna Khadar region of western Uttar Pradesh along with other dimensions.

Geographical Condition of Shillong Municipal Area

Shillong 91° 28'E and 25° 30'N) was important headquarter of formar Khasi and Jaintia hills districts in 1864 and became the capital of Assam in 1874. But on 21st January, 1972, Shillong was made the capital of Meghalaya. It was destroyed by earthquake in 1897 and rebuilt. Its area is 25.40 sq. km. Physiographically, Shillong is situated in the central upland zone of the Meghalaya plateau. It contains remmants of seven peneplanned surfaces, ranging in height from 1500 m to 2083 m, thus preserving the several traces of erosion cycles in this part. The Shillong hills lowering peneplaned surface tending East South East to West North West over which streams meander before plunging into the deep valleys of the Umiam and the Umkhen. In and arround Shillong city many rapids and waterfalls are seen which shows that this region has a youthful topography and was formed to a recent uplifts. The Shillong Peak (1961 m) situated south of Shillong proper, is in fact a hill top rising above the gentle range of such hills which on the northern side disappear into the Laitkor plateau, where Laitkor peak is another similar hill top. There is a hill top named Diengiei (1823 m) which is situated at the west of Shillong.

The temperature of Shillong is moderate. The winter is very cold, the temperature goes down to 1 °C in the month of December-January when one experiences frost in Shillong. In the summer the temperature rises up to 26 °C in the month of May-June. The mean annual rainfall is 7,196 mm.

Population

The total population of Shillong according to 1981 Census is 1,74,703 individuals of which 91,728 males and 82975 females. So, the density per sq. km. is 6990. The total tribal population is 85,838 of which 40886 males and 44947 females. Total scheduled caste population is 1063 of which 658 males and 405 females. The population growth rate of Shillong has been calculated and it is found that in 1971 (Total population 122,752) the decadal growth rate was (19.88) and in 1981 the decadal growth rate is 42.32.

Sex-Ratio

According to 1961 Census the sex-ratio was 763 but in 1971 census, it is raised to 857 and in 1981 Census, it is found 905 in Shillong urban area.

Number of Households and Space Occupied by the Individuals

According to 1981 Census the number of households is 33,978 in Shillong urban area. Average population per household is 5 (five) and 1360 households are found in one square km. area. In Shillong municipality area the number of household is 2129 in per square km. area, in Mawlai the number of household is 599 in per sq. km., in Nongthymmai the number of household per sq. km. area, is 1445, in Pynther Umkhrah the number of household is 1123 per square km. area. In Shillong Municipality area per household population is 5 (five) in Mawlai per household consists 5 (five), in Mawlai per household, consists 5 (five) persons in Nongthymmai 6 (six) person are found in per household and in Pynthor Umkhrah per household population is 4 (four) on average.

House Types

It has been mentioned earlier that in the past, the human being used to construct dwelling depending on the materials which were locally available. Hunter (1975) mentioned that the dwellings of the rich people were generally constructed of masonry, with thatched roof and plank floor and divided into two or three rooms. The ordinary and poor people used to construct their houses of stone, mud or plank walls, with a thatch or cane roof. These are fitted with wooden platforms or loose planks placed on the ground to serve as beds. These materials were collected from nearby hills and jungles. So it has been observed that in the past the people used to cut jungle to bring wood and bamboo for their construction of houses.

Changes in Housetypes Through Decade

Presently in Shillong, we find a completely different picture in house types. Through many decades the changes had taken place. It has already been mentioned that the people started deforestation since long either to use it as firewood or for the construction of house. As a result the quantity of wood and bamboo becoming less. So, to procure the aforesaid materials people had to go for long distance, as a result the carrying cost of the materials are becoming high. Moreover, the houses of these types have to repair after few years. So, the people of Shillong now-a-days had stopped of constructing these types of houses. At present the people are constructing modern types of pucca multistoried in a limited space and these are made out of brick, cement, iron rod etc. This tendency has grown among the people of Shillong irrespective of caste and creed is due to:

1. Due to higher cost of wood and bamboo and it is not easily available.

2. Today, the cost of construction of brick building and wooden houses are almost same.

3. Brick building is permanent and it is not required to repair frequently like the wooden houses.

4. Brick building is the effect of composite culture of the people of plains and hills.

5. To-day, the population is growing in Shillong in a faster rate but the space is limited. So, within the limited space it is presumed that the multistoried building of the city area can accomodate the maximum number of individuals in better further condition. It has been observed that, in Laitumkhrah areas several brick buildings, have been constructed within past ten years. Similarly in Dhankheti, Malki, Police Bazar, Pynthor Umkhrah, Nongthymmai, and other localities of the city several two-three storied residential buildings have been constructed. This is mainly due to the increase of population in Shillong, at large and decrease of space in general.

Conclusion

From the limited available data and observation it has been possible to show the change of housetypes in Shillong. From the above discussion it can be opined that the geo-social conditions have influenced the change of house types in Shillong. People from different regions came to Shillong either for service in Government, Private sectors or for the business. As a result the population had increased to a great extent, so to accomodate them the local people are constructing building within a limited space. The building materials can easily be brought to Shillong from distant places as this place is well communicated with neighbouring states. From the primary analysis of date it can be stated that the inter-mixture of the society had caused the change of house types. Moreover, the overpopulation and the change in climatic condition has also taken place during this period and these brought the changes the settlement pattern of Shillong at large.

Acknowlegement

The author is grateful to Dr. S. S. Dutta Choudhury, R. A. (P). Anthropological Survey of India, Shillong for his unmitigated Zeal in the completion of the whole paper.

REFERENCES

1. Census of India 1981. East Khasi Hills District, Census Hand Book. Part XIII-A and B Village and Town directory.

2. Chatterjee, S. P. 1968. *India : A Physical Geography* Publication Division, New Delhi.

3. Chauhan, V. S. 1971. 'Rural settlements in upper Yamuna Khadar region in India' in *21st I. G. C. Selected Papers. Vol. 3.* pp. 49-59.

4. Das, H. P. et. al. 1971. 'Meghalaya-Mikir Region' in India: *A Regional Geography* N.G.S.I. Varanasi. pp. 676-697.

5. Dikshit, R. D. 1965. 'Rural House Types in Dehra Dun Valley' *Deccan Geographer* 3 (1) pp. 43-51.

6. Gosal, G. S. 1972. 'Geography of Rural Settlement'— A trend report in *A Survey of Research in Geography*, ICSSR. New Delhi. pp. 188-202.

7. Hunter, W. W. 1975. *A statistical Account of Assam* Vol. II. Delhi, pp. 220. (Reprint).

8. Mishra, S. N. 1969. 'Human Dwellings in Sonpar Region (U.P.): A Geographical. Analysis'. *National Geographical Journal of India Part I.* pp. 8-23.

9. Singh, R. L. 1957. 'Typical Rural Dwellings in the Upland of Bararas (India)' *National Geographical Journal of Indian* 3. Part 2. pp. 51-64.

10. Subramanyan K. M. 1938. 'Four Main House Types in South India' *Journal of Madras Geographical Association* 8 (2) pp. 168-175.

11. Tewari, A. K. 1986. 'A House Type in Joumsar-Himalaya' *The Australian Geographer*, 10 (1) pp. 35-47.

12. — 1960 *Notes and Queries on Anthropology* London. Routledge and Kegan Paul Ltd. pp. 236-237.

10

Population Increase and Road Traffic Problems of Shillong

A. Saikia

While in the Occident, urbanisation follows industrialisation, in the Indian context, urbanisation is more the result of 'push' factors operating in the rural areas and forcing the population to migrate to urban centres in search of employment. Since urbanisation has a poor industrial base in many Indian cities, the migrant population gets absorbed in the tertiary sector.

Indian cities grow more due to urban accretion than urbanisation. Thus it is clear that: (i) cities in India will continue to grow, unless employment opportunities outside of agriculture are developed; and (ii) cities are tertiary oriented in terms of employment structure. As a result of rapid population increase in cities, shortfalls in urban services, amenities and infrastructure such as housing, water supply, transport, educational facilities, recreational. health and welfare facilities gradually creep in. In effect, as population increases, the effectiveness of the urban centre's amenities decreases.

The city of Shillong conforms to the above scenario and as a result of rapid population increase, the city is facing a variety of problems ranging from shortage of drinking water supply to traffic blockage. An attempt is made to gauge the magnitude of the city's traffic problem in the light of its population increase and to forward measures to ameliorate the same.

Location and Physiography: Occupying an area of 25.40 sq. kms., Shillong is situated at 25° 34 N latitude and 91° 53'E longitude in the central part of the East Khasi Hills district. The Shillong Urban Agglomeration comprises of the six townships of Shillong Municipality, Shillong Cantonment, Mawlai, Nongthymmai, Madanryting and Pynthorumkhrah with the last two towns being added to the Agglomeration in the 1981 Census.

It occupies the Shillong Valley of the Meghalaya Plateau. The Valley is flanked by the Shillong Peak (1961 metres) of the Shillong range in the south and Mawpat Peak (1957 metres) of the Mawpat Hills to the north-east and is drained by the tributaries of the Umshypri and Umkhra rivers. The relative relief of Shillong varies considerably over different areas, ranging from over 300 ft per furlong in the southern and north-western borders of the city to over 200 ft in the north-eastern, north-western and southern parts of Shillong municipality, 50 to 100 ft in most of the remaining area of the municipality, between 0 to 50 ft, and 100 to 200 ft in Nongthymmai, to 100 to 200 ft or 300 to 400 ft in the northern parts of Mawlai and less than 100 ft for most of the Cantonment area[1]. For the present study, the topography of the city has not been considered as the city lies largely in a Valley area and road traffic is determined more by the functional attribute of an area than its relief.

Growth and Present Status: Shillong has had a meteoric growth to its present proportions. This is true in its historical perpective, as well as its growth in the part few decades. Historically, the importance of Shillong grew quickly from the weekly market of Iewduh[2], and its history started roughly in 1864, when the British selected Shillong as the site for the district headquarters. Since then, the history of Shillong has been a continuous process of steady and sustained accretion of population, as a result of the sequential enhancement of its administrative status.[3]

Separation of Assam from East Bengal saw Shillong being made provincial headquarters of Assam in 1912. This resulted in a large number of government offices, quarters for government staff, medical centres etc. coming up in the town, along with a large influx of population into the town. This trend of immigration associated with the growing importance of Shillong as an administrative centre continued after independence and an inflow of population from high density areas like the Brahmaputra Valley, Bihar, Bengal and U.P., took place. Like-wise, the emergence of Shillong as the capital of Meghalaya and the establishment of NEHU at Shillong accelerated the growth of Shillong.

The major functions of the city are administrative, educational and commerce and trade, not necessarily in order of importance; with the city continuing 'to be an administrative link par excellance'.[4] It is not only the capital of Meghalaya, but also the administrative centre of the Autonomous Khasi Hills District Council and its Court, and the administrative headquarters of the Syiem of Mylliem and his Court.[5] The city also hosts a number of Central and State Government offices, regional offices of public sector undertakings, Banks, etc.

As an educational centre, Shillong is one of the best in the entire north-eastern region, and until the previous decade it was stated to have four times more educational institutions per sq. kms. than any other town in India.[6] It offers a wide range of wholesaling and retailing facilities, with the major commercial area clustered around Bara Bazar—Police Bazar.

Along with the functional diversification of the city, the city's population has correspondingly increased. And since urban migration from outside the state is one of the most important streams of migration[7], it would not be wrong to hold a view that of the population of Shillong, the middle class segment is an important one; and along with the more affluent sections of society they account for a major share of vehicle ownership. Also, ownership of motor vehicles (particularly two wheelers), among students during the academic session tends to increase the vehiclcs plying on roads of Shillong. Moreover, since the road connections to Agartala and Aizawl and Silchar pass through Shillong, this adds immensely to the heavy vehicular traffic passing through the city's main roads. Ofcourse, all this is in addition to the traffic between Shillong and Guwhati, Cherra and Dawki via national highway No. 40, and between Shillong and Jowai via national highway No. 44. Table 1 shows the number of registered motor vehicles in Shillong and their annual increase. As evident from the table, the number of vehicles registered in Shillong[8] has increased sharply over the years 1985 to 1989, to reach the 20,000 mark in early 1989. It shows a rate of growth of a staggering 92% during this period. Disturbingly enough, it appears unlikely that such a growth will decline significantly, and even a marginal increase would add to the city's traffic problem. Shillong is experiencing frequent traffic blockade along its major traffic routes. The roads affected are from Nongthymmai/Umpling Bazar—Laitumkhra-Dhan-kheti-Malki enroute to Police Bazar and Burra Bazar, with their offshoots (i.e. feeder roads) to Laban Bazar, Garikhana Jaiaw.

It may be noted that the city of Shillong was at the beginning, planned for a few thousand people only. With many newer areas having already brought under Shillong, the scope for expansion of roads or construction of roads in the heart of the city is extremely limited. Given such circumstances, the aim must be in maximising the carrying capacity of the existing system[9]. Before attempting to suggest palliative measures a look at the

TABLE I

Annual Increase in Registered Vehicles in Shillong

*Year	Trucks & Tractors	2-Wheelers and 3 Wheelers	Bus	Cars, Taxis, Jeeps & Trailers	Others	Total	Annual increase (in %)	Total incrcase (in %)
1985	2036	2516	571	5617	95	10835	—	
1986	2452	2925	639	7058	110	13184	21.68	
1987	2710	3643	674	7627	112	14766	12.00	
1988	2960	4020	732	8312	117	16141	00.31	
1989	4339	4771	1005	10558	144	20817	28.96	92.13

* Year ending 31st March.

Source: District Transport Officer, Shillong.

intensity of the traffic problem of Shillong is in order. A traffic count conducted by the author during 1990, at important road intersections, calculated the traffic flow for the morning and evening peak periods. At each of these road intersections a traffic count for a minimum period of fifteen minutes, at morning/evening peak periods, was taken. These quarter-hour estimates were converted into hourly estimates. Generally, the morning peak period was identified as being between 8.30 a.m. to 10.30 a.m., with the evening peak traffic being counted between 3.30 p.m. to 5.30 p,m. Such a peak period would vary from area to area depending on its prime function. For instance, the evening peak period around Don Bosco or Dhankheti, both educational areas was taken to be around 2.45 p.m. to 3.15 p.m., while the same was between 5.00 p.m. to 5.30 p.m. for Police Bazar, a commercial area. In order to iron out any irregularities that may have crept into the traffic count, the surveys were conducted twice for each peak period. If the evening survey on day I was conducted proceeding from point A towards point E during 3 p.m. to 5 p.m., the survey order was reversed on day 2, proceeding from point E to point A, during the same period. At busy junctions where traffic load was too heavy to be accurately counted by one person, three or four onumerators counted traffic flow on different roads emanating from the junction.

Table-II shows the peak hour traffic volume at select intersections during 1990.

At some intersections like Police Bazar and Kachery, more than 2,500 vehicles pass in an hour. Due to lack of parking space on-street parking is allowed in most roads and this decreases the width of the road. Normally 2,503-3,000 vehicles would flow easily, but the irregular width of the roads combined with on-street parking and halting of taxi-cabs/buses in the middle of the roads creates the ever-increasing problem of traffic blockadge. Since travellings, vehicle ownership and population are interrelated, the traffic problem of Shillong has to be seen in terms of its population size. In 1981 its population was 174,703—an

TABLE II

Peak Hour Traffic Volume at Select Road Intersections of Shillong, 1990

Sr. No.	Name of the Intersection	Peak Hour Volume Morning	Peak Hour Volume Evening
1.	Nongthymmai	620	1024
2.	Fire Brigade	1392	1208
3.	Laitumkhrah Police point	1230	1192
4.	Dhankheti	1696	1968
5.	Malki	1552	1628
6.	Kachery	1704	1408
7.	Police Bazar	2564	2128
8.	Bara Bazar	1520	1860

Source: Field Study.

increase of 42.32% over the previous decade. If the same growth rate persists, than Shillon g's population could be in the vicinity of 248,000. In fact, the po pulation of the Municipality has been estimated at 113,138 persons in 1991[10]. However, the population of the agglomeration could well be close to the 2.5 lakh mark, in spite of the low growth rate of the Shillong Municipality during 1981-1991, (of 3.56%), as the other townships of Shillong Cantonment, Mawlai and Nongthymmai had much higher rates of growth during the 1971-81 decade at 39.96%, 43.09% and 33.88% respectively, compared to 24.62% of Shillong Municipality[11]. Even if the growth rate of the six townships were to decline sharply to 32.32% during 1981-1991, the population of Shillong would amount to no less than 230,608 persons.

The situation is now clear: Shillong is a city with 2.3 to 2.5 lakh people and over 20,000 vehicles ply the roads—but traffic is concentrated along a few main routes of the city's road network. The C.B.D area is around Police Bazar—Bara Bazar, and other commercial/market areas ar secondary in importance and have poor self-contained levels, and this increases trips and traffic to the C.B.D. area. Added to this is the 1500-2000 odd trucks[12] that pass through Shillong every day to from Guwahati, Silchar and Aizawl. Rapid increase in population, travel-trips and traffic volume is creating incessant problems of smooth traffic flow, and if Shillong's road network is to function as a viable transportation medium, then measures to improve its functioning are required. It is suggested that[13] :

1. Road-width widening be taken up in the major traffic routes of the city to facilitate traffic flow. If necessary, acquisition of land for this purpose, has to be taken up as soon as possible. Delay in this regard will only aggravate matters as acquisition of land could be, legally, a long-drawn affair. It may be noted that road-widening is, howevers, a ahort term palliative, yet it is an imperitive measure if any dent is to be made in ameliorating the problem of road traffic blockadges in Shillong.

2. Since traffic flow is generated by the C.B.D. and commercial areas, the self-containment levels of the origin areas needs to be increased so as to minimise the traffic flow between such areas.

3. There is a deed for dispersal of administrative and commercial areas to other parts of the city to decrease traffic along the axial transport routes of the city.

4. Innovative traffic management techniques are necessary. These could range from improving the public bus service system, to introducing new bus routes or preventing unscheduled stops by buses. Innovations such as creating

pedestrian-only zones around bazar areas or shopping centres need to be tried out.

5. Since the traffic problems of Shillong are aggravated by through-traffic to neighbouring states, the construction of the Shillong-by pass road should be taken up on a priority basis.

Refernces and Notes

1. Singh, J.P. (1980), Urban Landuse Planning in Hill Areas: A Case Study of Shillong, Inter India Publications, New Delhi, p 40.

2. Initially, Shillong was no more than the locality of Laban and its few settlements, and the weekly market of Iewduh.

3. Saikia, A., (1990), Road Network and Traffic Density in Shillong, M. Phil. Dissertation (unpublished), Deptt. of Geography, NEHU, p 73.

4. Datta Ray, B., Shillong as an administrative Centre, in B.B. Goswami (ed) Cultural Profile of Shillong, Anthropological Survey of India, Calcutta, (1979), p. 52.

5. Gassah, L.S., Shillong as an Administrative and Political Centre (1971-1981), in B. Pakem (ed) Shillong 1971-81, NEICSSR, 1981, p. 27.

6. Das Gupta, N., Educational profile of Shillong, in B.B. Goswami (1979), op. cit. p. 32.

7. Urban Migration to Shillong is important in the sense that a large chunk of its working population employed in the government service sector, (white collar professionals), comes from other urban centres. Likewise, the seasonal student migration to Shillong.

8. The number of registered vehicles is taken as representative of the total vehicles plying in Shillong—although this is an

approximation. However, it has been considered as more or less accurate and is used in view of the difficulty involved in procuring data on the number of vehicles paying road-tax in Shillong.

9. Patankar, P.G., Urban Transportation Systems: Problems of Planning in Gopal Bhargava (ed), Urban Problems and Policy Perspectives, Abhinav Publications, New Delhi (1981), p. 84.

10. Census of India, 1991, Meghalaya, Paper-I of 1991, Provisional Population Totals.

11. Census of India, 1981, Meghalaya, Series XIV. Part II A and B.

12. State PWD, Meghalaya, December, 1990.

13. Saikia, A., op. cit., p. 110.

11

Traffic Congestion in Shillong

Sazidual Alam

1.0 Introduction

(a) Shillong the capital city of Meghalaya situated at an altitude of 4908 feet above sea-level and an outstanding hill station with a population of around 1.75 lakhs (1981), has become one of the most important urban centres in the entire north-eastern region. The city has experienced a steady urban expansion and substantial increase in government, semi-government, trade and commerce and educational activities which have resulted in a significant shift of population from its neighbouring areas.

(b) Shillong with an ever increasing population and activities has also led to an increase of traffic on the roads. Traffic congestion in the town today has assumed such acute proportion that it warrants immediate attention. The problem is further aggrevated due to the mixing of local and long distance traffic espacially on National Highway 40 which connects Shillong to Guwahati and National Highway 44. In the absence of arterial by-pass the G.S. Road is functioning as a major link for Tripura,

Mizoram and Cachar District of Assam and large volumes of passanger and goods movement is taking place through the heart of Shillong city.

2.0 PRESENT SCENARIO

(a) Restricted road width and adequate parking places are the most acute problems facing the city today. The problem has become acute because of the fact that the city with its infrastructural facilities were initially laid with a view of sustaining a few thousand population but Shillong today has grown to over two lakh population;

(b) Characterised by a high rate of vehicle ownership narrow roads, concentration of activities and unavailability of additional vacant land, parking too has become a serious problem especially in the central, commercial and administrative areas and also along the major corridors of the city. Unavailability of organised parking space has led to unwanted on street parking creating innumerable allied problems of traffic congestion traffic jams, delay injourneys and accidents.

(c) Even though the city has witnessed remarkable progress in all fronts but the road network has practically remained stagnant over the years. Some of the causes leading to traffic congestion are:

(i) Lack of parking places, specially near the commercial centres;

(ii) Absence of adequate pedestrian facilities on the major roads;

(iii) Mushroom growth of commercial activities specially along the road side;

(iv) Narrow roads and lack of parallel corridors within the city;

(v) Mixing up of local and through traffic on national highway;

(vi) Lack of proper terminal facilities for mini/city buses and goods vehicles.

(vii) Lack of proper traffic control and management measure.

(viii) Poor geometrics of road intersections etc.

(d) The areas which suffer most are the older parts of the city which are comparatively built up, have no scope for any further development and are catering to vehicular volumes much beyond their capacities, thus resulting in congestion and confusion.

(e) With each passing day, traffic congestion in Shillong is becoming increasingly hazardous giving rise to certain vexing problems like increased journey time due to increased traffic bottlenecks especially near the commercial areas.

(f) As per the report on comprehensive Traffic and Transportation Studies for Greater Shillong Area prepared by National Transportation and Research Centre, it has been estimated that peak hour flow of traffic is the highest at Police Bazar followed by Sweeper lane-Motphran intersection. Table 1 shows the estimated peak hour traffic flow on different sections.

3.0 PLANNING STRATEGY

In order to tackle the problem of acute traffic congestion in the city the planning strategy may be as follows.

(A) Improvement of existing infrastructure within the city.

(B) Traffic management.

(C) Reliving the present city congestion through development of a new township.

(A) Improvement of Existing Infrastructure Within the City

(a) *Improvement of road junctions and intersections*: Road junctions and intersections have been recognised as a major source creating traffic problems. After taking due cognisance of land and other physical constraints, steps should immediately be taken to improve the road junctions and intersections where ever it is practically feasible.

(b) *Widening of existing roads and construction of new roads*: The scope of road widening does not seem to be an appropriate solution on major arterial roads. Wherever feasible, development/upgradation of link roads may be examined. In other areas, subject to availability of land, widening schemes should be undertaken to achieve the desired space standards: In addition to the existing network, few additional road links are to be provided to ensure that some of the bottleneck locations in different area of the city are avoided.

(c) *Construction of Parking Places*: Parking has been considered as an integral part of overall traffic requirements. Growth in commercial activities and increase in vehicle ownership have resulted in increased parking demand especially in the central area of Shillong. The peak parking demand at several places being far excess of the parking capacity, adequate measures need to be taken to provide required parking facilities. Immediate requirement of Shillong city is the location of parking lots at convenient spots near the commercial centres:

(i) At the central area level since land is more scare, the problem can be better tackled by going for multi level parking lots and outside the central area level, it will be adequate to go for single or double level parking lots.

(ii) Considering the fact that the situation is already bad and it can only turn worst, the schemes must be taken up and implemented on priority basis and land made available as early as possible.

(iii) The Urban Affairs Department, has been doing a remarkable job in this regard. Two parking lot scheme one at Mawlong Hat and the other at the S.C.E.R.T. premises has already been completed. and a few more is expected to be taken up during the Eight Five Year Plan.

(d) *Construction of National Highway By-pass*: The problem of traffic congestion in Shillong is further aggravated due to mixing of local and long distance traffic mainly on National Highway 40 which connects Shillong to Gauahati and National Highway 44. In the absence of any arterial by-pass link the G.S. Road is functioning as the major link for Mizoram, Tripura, Silchar and large volume of passanger and goods movement takes place through the heart of Shillong city causing confus-sion, congestion, Pollution and accidents. With the construction, of the National Highway by-pass it is hoped that the problems will be eased considerably.

(e) *Facilities for Goods Vehicles*: Road transport plays a very important role in the economy of the region. The roads in Shillong city are narrow, parking areas are not adequate and the terminal areas are not properly designed to keep pace with the ever increasing demand. At present truck parking is taking place in Bara-Bazar, Garkhana and its surrounding areas and this leads to choatic conditions in the traffic circulation in that area. It is therefore urgently felt to locate the truck terminus outside the city limits. The site should be chosen in such a manner that it should not only have adequate space for provid-ing the required facilities but should also be nearer to the main city and where some of the basic facilities exists.

(f) *Mini Bus/City Bus terminal*: At present, there is only one city bus terminal located at Mawlonghat. It is to be noted that traffic in and around this point has been growing at a fast rate chocking up the channels of movement. The traffic congestion in and around Bara Bazar is mainly due to the following reasons:

(a) Lack of parking spaces.

(b) Narrow roads.

(c) Haphazard growth of shopping activities.

(i) The terminal located at Mawlonghat is not able to meet the present day requirements mainly due to inadequate circulation area and consequently there is a great deal of choas all around.

(ii) Since bus Services form an important mode of transport in and around Shillong. the terminal area requirement is likely to become substantial in the near future. The present terminal area will be far too inadequate to meet the total requirements, it is being felt necessary to have more bus/mini terminal areas in places like Mawlai, Nongmynsong, Happy Valley, Umpling, Madanriting and Upper Shillong. The present bus terminal at Barabazar needs to be removed to ensure a smooth flow of traffic in that area.

B. Traffic Management

(a) *Curb Side Parking*: Curb side parking control should be enforced on the major arterials. The entire area from Garikhana to Police Bazar intersection should be converted into parking free zone. This will provide additional space for movement of vehicles. Since land available for accommodating the increasing demand for parking spaces may not be sufficient attempts must be made to use most optimally the small panels of land already available for this purposes.

(b) *Traffic regulation measares*: Since road widening may not be possible in all city roads, the only option under the existing circumstances is to go for traffic regulation measures in the form of one way system wherever alternate corridors are available or can be created, this will ensure smooth traffic flow conditions.

(c) *Re-routing of mini/city buses*: The mass transportation in Shillong is primarily road based. The mini/city bus services is provided mainly by the private sector operating on selected corridors.

(d) It can be anticipated that the future mass transportation system i.e. mini/city buses will capture large share of traffic. Keeping this in view, a proposed re-routing pattern has to be planned so that all work centres are connected to the residential areas.

(e) Presently the city buses ply mostly on the Bara Bazar—Police Bazar—Laitumkhrah—Nongthymmai route. Even the buses going to Happy Valley follow the same route, though shorter route from Bara Bazar via Arunachal Pradesh Secretariat—Civil Hospital—St. Edmund's College is available. This will enable some of the traffic load to be diverted from the narrow roads of Laitumkhrah through the National Highway thereby easing congestion on Donbosco—Laitumkhrah stretch.

(f) Further the buses should not start and terminate at Mawlonghat. but should come for a short term to pick up/drop passengers. In this context immediate steps should be taken to create ncw mini/city bus terminals at locations mentioned above to case the traffic pressure on Mawlonghat.

(g) *Underground Pedestrian Subways*: Construction of underground pedestrian subways may be considered for four junctions viz. Police Bazar, Motphran, Dhankheti and Laitumkhrah. Subways are more economical and space saving in comparison to fly overs. Pedestrians subways will help in the separation of pedestrian movement from vehicular movement thereby easing congestion to some extent, However the possibility to go for underground padestrian subway may be examined further by the concerned authority.

(C) Releiving the Present City Congestion Through Development of a New Township

(a) The traffic growth on the city network can be reduced considerably if some of the activities are located in the periphery of the city. The most ideal thing would be to go for a Satellite township with all services and facilities made available where the additional population can be accommodated. This will lessen the traffic burden of Shillong city to a considerable extent and things are expected to improve.

(b) The Department of Urban affairs has selected a site for a new township which is approximately 13 Kms from Shillong city centre. The National Highway by-pass is likely to pass between the existing and the new township.

(c) In the above context, it may be necessary to discourage the establishment of all future industrial and wholesale activities in Shillong and encourage their establishment in the new township, at the same time, making attempts to shift the existing wholesales activities from Shillong city centre to the new town by giving proper incentives. This will not only relive population pressure on Shillong city but will also relieve the traffic congestion of Shillong to a considerable extent.

TABLE I

Estimated Peak Hour Flows on Different Road Sections

Sl. No.	*Name of the Stretch*	*Estimated volume in PCUS (Peak Hour)*
1.	Police Bazar-Katchery intersection	2462
2.	Katchery intersection Rajbhavan	1578
3.	NEC Secretariat-Rajbhavan	957
4.	Katchery intersection I.G.P.I. intersection	1587
5.	I.G.P.I. intersection I.G.P. II intersection	2054
6.	I.G.P. II intersection Barik intersection	1158
7.	I.G.P. II intersection Civil Hospital intersection	780
8.	Barik Malki intersection	1690

Contd.

1	*2*	*3*
9.	Malki Dhankheti I Intersection	1754
10.	Dhankhati I intersection Dhankheti II intersection	1797
11.	Dhankheti II Don Bosco intersection	1077
12.	Don Bosco-Laitumkhrah intersection	936
13.	Barik Garrison Ground (Civil Hospital II)	743
14.	Civil Hospital II Civil Hospital intersection	1367
15.	Civil Hospital I NEFA Secretariat intersection	1060
16.	NEFA Secretariat intersection Anjali Cinema	636
17.	NEFA Secretariat intersection Military Hospital	927
18.	Laitumkhrah-Nongthymmai	1125
19.	Nongthymmai-Band Stand intersection	665
20.	Police Bazar, Butcher Lane intersection	2167
21.	Butcher Lane intersection Sweeper Lane Junction	2322
22.	Sweeper Lane Junction Bara Bazar intersection	1756
23.	Bara Bazar intersection District Council Junction	1688

Source : National Transportation Planning and Research Centre, New Delhi.

4.0 Conclusion

The city growth in the last few decades has been phenomenal but physical constraints and limited road network has greatly hindered the overall development. The urban sprawl has been evident in all dirctions with many new localities coming up in the Shillong Urban Area. With the continous increase in population and corresponding increase of vehicles the road network had come under heavy strain. Besides continuous increase in commercial activities and lack of proper terminal facilites and parking spaces have created a very hazardous situation and unless appropriate traffic engineering and management measures are taken immediately, the situation is bound to worsen. It is therefore suggested that the recommendation made above may be considered for future detailed studies.

12

Changing Townscope of Shillong

Mr. H.K. Mazhari

1. Shillong the Capital City of Meghalaya has shown higher Growth of population in the last decades, Shillong Municipal area which had a population of 87804 thousand in 1971 increased to 1,09,244 lakhs persons in 1981. As per 1991 Census the population has increased to 1,30,691 lakh; the township of Nongthymmai, Mawlai, which had only 21,558 persons and 20,405 persons in 1981 shot up to 26,816 persons and 30,442 persons respectively in 1991. The other two townships of Madanriting and Pynthorumkhrah has also shown high increase in population.

1.1 The increase rate of Urbanisation has resulted in over straining of urban infrastructure, traffic congestion and deterioration in urban environment; the situation aggravated in the past in absence of any frame work for development of these town. There was no legislation in the State which could be used effectively to deal with the sudden growth and mushroom development.

1.2 A part from deterioration in the level of services in the city, there has been acute pressure on land. During the last few decades, due to non-availability of buildable land within the Shillong Municipal areas, there has been sprawling development of the town in all the three directions namely towards Mawiong, Upper Shillong and Laitkor. Even unbuildable land was cleared for development of residential and commercial areas, and forest cover was removed to meet the growing demands of the city population.

1.3 Shillong which was once known as 'Scotland of the East' was under tremendous presure of urbanisation during the past decades, could not protect its scenic environment. The direct consequence of urbanisation was the boon in construction and building sprang up in locations which were inaccessible and civic amenities costlier to provide.

1.4 In addition to its sprawling development, the other effect of urbanisation was that, within the core areas of the city, land utilisation became intensive and high rise building became order of the day. The other factor which contributed mainly in the development of high rise building and sub-division of plots was the applications of Meghalaya Transfer of Land (Regulation Act) 1971.

1.5 According to the above Act, land cannot be transfered to non-tribal, except through inheritance. Subdivision to smaller plots and there by encouraging maximum coverage of land and high rise construction was the direct result.

2. Townscape of Shillong.

2.1 Shillong in the past was only a seat of Administration and functionally on Administrative town. It had also characteristics of a hill resort and townscape was blending with the natural surrounding. The town consisted of some of the Administrative residential building and the Bazar to meet the requirements of the small population. Most of the building were single storyed with pitch roof and corrugated iron sheets. The building were known as 'Assam Type'. These were very light structure and suited and blended with the environment very well. Since the structure were very light no special measure were necessary to provide seismic forces in the structure. As there was not much pressure on land, even administrative offices were located in single storied stucture.

2.2 After the creation of Meghalaya State, the increased pace of development resulted in great pressure on land and the consequence was that not only Administrative and Commercial activities moved into multi-storyed R.C.C. structure but even the residential buildings were more than one storied. Initially due to non availability of many skilled labour required for R.C.C. construction, the number of high rise building were limited. During the last decade there has been sharp increase in construction of high rise building in the city for reason indicated above.

2.3 The entire townscape has been affected, R.C.C. construction with flat roof looks alien and does not blend with the surrounding. Some of the areas in the town particularly the commercial areas have similarities with that in the towns of plains.

2.4. Such development has been noticed more in areas which were lying in between the commercial centres. One such areas in the town which undergone complete change is Dhankheti-Malki stretch which lies in between Barabazar, the main wholesale and retails centres and Laitumkhrah and up-coming commercial centre. The residential areas have been converted into commercial use and high rise structure have come up, housing the office and commercial establishments.

2.5. Similar changes have occured all along the main road from Laitumkhrah to Nongthymmai in the South-East and also from Barabazar towards North. This type of development did not take place towards Upper Shillong due to the presence of Cantonment.

2.6 Even in and around Laitumkhrah and Barabazar many high rise building have come up by dismantling the existing low structures.

2.7 Police Bazar has witnessed a sea change and almost all single storyed buildings has now been replaced by Multistoryed structure. The rest are in the process of this change.

2.8 Even the State Government Administrative Complex at Lower Lacheumiere has Undergone change. Three single storyed Assam type buildings have been replaced by R.C.C. buildings with minimum of four storyed. Many are in the process of reconstruction.

2.9 Direct conflict of this development has been increased strain on infrastructure like water, drainage, roads etc; Increased traffic congestion near commercial areas is reflection of this change in the townscape.

3. The future townscape.

3.1 This change can be regulated if appropriate actions are taken to develop other commercial areas with better civic amenities to attract new business and trade. This may be possible if new commercial establishments are planned with higher accessibility. This may substitute lower attraction of new centres and reduce pressure on the old established commercial areas and also those residential areas lying in between these centres.

3.2 As mentioned above changes in the townscape have occured mainly due to increase in economic activities and existing legislations. Absence of proper building by-laws only added to the force of change. Shillong though a hill station has lost its main characteristics and its old townscape and the process of change is on. The question is can it be stopped and is it desirable to stop this change?.

13

Slums in Shillong Analysis of its Impact

W. Syiem

1. Introduction

1.1 The Shillong urban area has been one of the oldest, largest and fastest growing hill areas in the country. Initially developed to sustain a few thousand population, Shillong has grown to nearly two lakhs of people today. This high growth rate is mainly attributed to the tremendous migration of poor sections of the rural population to the capital city in search of better economic opportunities and quality of life. The pace and magnitude of such rural-urban migration leaves the urban authorities lagging behind in providing the resources to meet the minimum, needs of the migrants for living space and other basic amenities.

1.2 Over a period of time, this process has culminated into the emergence of slums in the heart of the city which poses serious hurdles in its planned development. With urbanisation of Shillong progressively increasing over the years, there has been greater influx of rural population swelling the number of slum dwellers. There are now slums in almost every ward of Shillong.

2. Slum Population

2.1 At present no comprehensive data on the number of slum dwellers, and slum characteristics etc. are available as the survey by the Department of Urban Affairs is still in progress. But based on rough estimates made by the Department, the total slum population in Shillong would be about 42,000 persons.

2.2 There are 22 identified slum areas in Shillong but beyond the identified ones there are also a few more slum areas which have emerged of late.

3. Problems of Slums

3.1 The main problems of slums are their insanitary environment and over-crowding. Insanitary conditions have arisen out of the lack of civic facilities like lower drainage system, sanitation facilities, footpaths and the like. Over-crowding is due to faulty arrangement of roads, maximum utilisation of space for cheapness etc.

3.2 To solve these problems in the slums of Shillong, the Government had introduced in the Fifth Plan the Slum improvement Schemes under the Minimum Needs Programme which later on formed an integral part of the 20 Point Programme.

3.3 Over the succeeding five-year plans, the scheme has been playing a significant role in ameliorating the socio-economic conditions of the slum dwellers through the provision of basic amenities like drinking water supply, santitation facilities, street light, drains, footpaths, road paving etc. in the slum areas.

3.4 This approach to solution of problems has another important aspect. The slum dwellers are invariably consulted through the local durbars before taking up any work of improvement in their areas. Such outlook of the administration has created awareness amongst the slum dwellers encouraging community participation. Gradually, some civic responsibilities may be passed on to the slum dwellers under the new pattern of administration to be evolved.

4. Characteristics of existing Slums in Shillong

4.1. Over a period of 10 to 15 years, the location of slums have acquired area specific characteristics that vary from one area to the other. Shillong, being a hilly area, the slum areas may be located at hill tops, on hill slopes or in low lying areas. Ever the socio-economic characteristics of these slum areas differ from those of other slums areas in the country. For instance, in a particular slum area there is a mixed composition of slum population comprising of both the Middle-Income Group and the Lower Income Group. Though a majority of the slum population consist of Scheduled tribe population, the socio-economic conditions may vary from one section to the other. Ours being a casteless society, a slum area represents an amalgamation of all income groups,

4.2 The beneficiaries of the slum improvement programme may, therefore, not necessarily be the urban poor as the benefits are being percolated to all sections of the society. In the dichotomy of distribution of wealth, there is invariably a co-existence between the higher income and the lower income groups. Thus, while improving the living conditions of the slum dwellers it has become inescapably necessary to provide the basic infrastructure of the economy and comfort of the well-to-do. This socio-economic pattern of the city life has therefore given birth to the co-existence of pucca building with slum dwellings.

5. Impact of the Slum Improvement Programme on the quality of life of the Slum Dwellers

5.1 The impact of the scheme on the slum dwellers of Shillong vary from one area to the other. Out of the 22 identified slum areas, improvement works have been taken up in 16 areas. The provision of the facilities as specified under the scheme has brought about a marked improvement in the living conditions of the slum dwellers.

5.2 In Qualapaty, Naspatighari, Mawlong Hat where improvement work have been taken up during the Fifth Plan, the impact is not much seen as most of the assets created have deteriorated due to lack of maintenance by the local bodies who are not in a position to maintain these assets for want of adequate funds. Moreover, the slum dwellings are so congested that perhaps only improvement works are not adequate enough to sustain the improved amenities. Here, perhaps it would be more suitable if the much dilapidated buildings and cluster of huts are cleared and rehabilitate the slum dwellers elsewhere. This would not, however, be feasible on account of the reluctance of the slum dwellers to shift from their original place of residence which would mean more serious hurdles for the government to overcome.

5.3 On the contrary, in other areas like Lumparing, Riat-Laban, Madan Laban, Wahingdoh, Mawprem, etc. the efficacy and impact of the investment in these slums can be appreciated in terms of the con-commitant benefits of the amenities as provided percolating to the slum dwellers. This can be attributed to the co-operation of the slum dwellers. This can be attributed to the co-operation of the slum dwellers and the local durbars while implementing the scheme and their active involment in the programme.

5.4 After all is said and done, the malady of over-crowing would continue in the slum dwellings but this is a thing best left to the slum dwellers themselve. Since there has been an increased awareness of the slum inhabitants about the existence of the slum improvement scheme, it is anticipated that there would be better community participation in the slum upgradation and the problem of maintenance would thus be minimised.

5.5 The appreciation of the quality of services provided in the slum areas shown by their inhabitants have encouraged even the other slum dwellers not covered under the scheme to come forward for inclusion under the improvement programme. The available statistics (about 80% of the slums) show that the slum dwellers are aware of the operation of the scheme by giving response in the affirmative.

6. Analysis of the facilities provided in the slum areas

6.1 The scheme of Environmental Improvement of Urban Slums has envisaged the provision of seven basic amenties i.e. drinking water supply, community baths and latrines, storm water drains, sewerage, street lighting, footpaths and road paving.

6.2 It is not possible to provide all the seven items in all the slum areas. In general, the selection of amenities to be provided in a particular slum area depends on its particability and is guided by the availability of funds and the pressing problems being faced by the slum dwellers.

6.3 The provision of Community baths and latrines has not found favour with most of the slum population and hence, has not been taken up on average scale. This is so because of the difficulty in maintaining these assets for want of adequate water supply, lack of regular cleanliness and non-availability of land in the slums for construction of such latrines. Such units constructed in the past have either been abandoned or converted into dry latrines such as toilets constructed during the 5th Plan at Qualapatty and Naspatighari.

6.4 The provision of water supply and street lights has not been given due priority as they are regarded as the responsibility of the local bodies as their normal function. Even then, some public water points and street lighting facilities have been provided in some slum areas like Malki, Lumparing, Laitumkhrah, etc.

6.5 Other facilities which have been provided in the slum areas on a large scale are drains, footpaths, approach road and retaining walls. Though construction of approach roads and retaining walls are not covered under the scheme, these facilities are found necessary to be provided due to the adverse physical features of the slum areas. Retaining walls have been provided to protect footpaths, lanes and drains without which the improvement work would have been infructuous. Approach roads, on the other hand, are very important from the point of view of accessibility of a slum area being located at odd places like hill tops or in low-lying areas. Moreover, approach roads serve as linkage between a slum area and the main town for easy availability of emergency services.

6.6 Even construction of small bridges, culverts etc, which are not specified under the scheme, have been taken up in some slum areas like Pynthorumkhrah, Mawprem etc. These are necessary due to the presence of small streams etc. and have been constructed either over the pavements, footpath or approach roads.

7. Conclusion

7.1 Thus, as has been seen in the foregoing paras, there is variation in the efficacy and impact of the slum improvement scheme on different slum areas of the City; it is therefore, felt that the problems faced by the slum dwellers of different areas be looked into.

7.2 Slum problem is really a problem of poverty and has to be tackled accordingly. With the primary jobs of removing insanitation from the slums, the guideline of slum improvement now embraces comprehensive improvement of slums. In other words, economic upliftment through education facilities, medical care and employment generation is to be under taken. Recently such comprehensive improvement approach has been launched by the National Government through the schemes of Nehru Rozgar Yojana and Urban Basic Services for the poor.

7.3 In order that maximum benefit is derived out of the scheme the slum dwellers may be involved in preparation of the plans and their execution by setting up their own local committees. The plan should be evolved from within the community and should not be imposed from above. This should be the people's programme and not that of the State Government or the Municipal Board.

7.4 It is also imperative that slum dwellers should be involved in maintaining the civic amenities provided in their slum areas and managing the flow of other benefits meant for them as mentioned above.

14

Umbra Behind the Beauty of Shillong : Some Observation

S. S. Datta Choudhuri

Generally, it is said, that the darkness always prevail below the lamp. Similarly in this beautiful region there lies some darkness which sometimes may create a problem in respect of health and hygenic condition of the population in micro and macro dimension. This unhygenic conditions are manyfold in nature. This town of eternal beauty is growing very fast in respect of its population size, cultural activities, in education and in developmental aspect. But unfortunately, the problem related to civic amenities of the Township area has resumed with greater proportions, and, this has so happened, due to the rapid growth of the population within the region. Therefore, in this paper a micro analysis were made by the present author for its rectification for greater interest of the population in general.

In Shillong municipal are the number of population are increasing very fast. Its number as per 1971, 1981 and 1991 census are 87659, 107673 and 1,13,138. The sex ratio in the aforesaid decinnial period as observed are 855, 902 and 843 respectively per 1000 males (C.F. census provisional figure, 1981 and 1991).

The state of public health has to be understood merely from the incidence of diseases, maladice and ailments, but it is to be understood from general physical environment in which the population live. The term environment is defined as "the totality of the external condition and influences that affect man" (Winick, 1956: 187 of Hasan 1979 : 45). However, to visualize the same the existing civic amenities were discussed below to have some panoramic view.

Water distribution: In Shillong municipal area the drinking water is distributed either from the service reservoir (SR) or from the over head tank (OHT) and from these reservoirs through pipe it is distributed to the different houses. The distribution is not done by the pump but through gravitational forces. Most of the pipe connections of this region are age old and they are lying over the surface. The water reservoirs of the greater Shillong Water Project, distribute water in the same procedure as it was adopted in case of over head tank. If we look into this matter very carefully, it could be observed that most of the pipe connections of the houses are not properly maintained, either it lies within the drain or it is badly placed on the surface. In some places the condition of the pipes are such, that it may cause accident too. Wastage of water is a regular feature while in some areas the water scarcity is acute. The broken pipe lines within the drain and in some dirty places may act as a pivot for contamination of diseases.

Very recently, at the time of SAARC conference, with the deployment of maximum man power and man hour, the Government of Meghalaya took much pain to repair the pipe lines of the Mahatma Gandhi Marg, and they put some of the pipe lines within the tranchoo. Even to-day by the side of the Assembly House the broken pipe lines are there, which encircle the area like octopus. Similarly, in G. S. Road, Garikhana, Lachumiere, Laban, Jail Road, Mowlong Hut area and in some other regions there we find some tempered water connections through which maximum wastage of water take place and the chances of contmination can not be denied.

On the other hand, this water which is a source of life, carries maximum sand and dissolved dust particles along with it and these may cause many deterious effect on of the people. As it is well known that all organic matter decays rapidly in water. It provides food for pathogenic bacteria, amoeba, infusoria and saprophytic bacteria (Hasan 1979: A9) and these ultimately may cause various types of ailments like dysentry, diarrhoea, gastro-enterities and geodiacis etc. The lack of proper filteration and unscientific way of water distribution are the root causes of all these diseases. This can partially be avoided if the water reservoirs are cleaned periodically and disinfactant are sprayed to kill the germs at regular intervals.

In the last decennial period, Government of Meghalaya under the supervision of Public Health Engineering have initiated Greater Shillong water project to provide maximum supply of water within the town and to facilitate the work some overhead tanks has also been constructed. As regards, the distribution of water, the geographical condition of the area though acted as a barrier but our scientific and technological advancement can do best to rectify some of the prevailing situations and it is to be done on emergency basis. The immediate repair of the pipe line is very much needed to avoid the aforesaid health hazards and to make this region a beautiful one.

In Shillong, the drinking water is distributed through tap and the total capacity of these tanks and reservoirs are approximately 60 lakh (±) liters. If the wastage of water is minimised then it can feed many more lives in future and to avoid this irregularities public awareness is very much needed.

Drainage: Of all the reasons of environment pollution, the drainage system holds the main role to pollute an areas. In Shillong township area, there exists two types of sewerage namely, open surface drain (OSD) and Box surface drain (BSD). In rainly season all these drains are cleaned through natural process. But in other seasons, due to the lack of insufficient water there lies all the decomposed garbages and if it was not cleaned properly then it may cause on unhygenic situation and pollute the environment of the region.

As it is well known that the stragnent dirty water of the drain is the suitable place for the propagation of various types of germs and insects including mosquito and these ultimately causes various types of ailments like fever of unspecified nature, malaria etc. The lack of civic sences of the people in general is the vital cause which makes the environment polluted. Therefore, the constant awareness of both the people, Municipality and other related organisations are very much needed. The Mawlong Hut area (near the Shillong city bus stand) is so dirty, that it is very difficult to think that we are living in the Switzerland of the East. The open surface drain and the deposited garbage on way to market is an acute problem within the area.

In this area it can be noticed that the broken pipe lines also lies within the drain. No doubt, the area is congested due to traffic and floating population but, if we together pay little attention about its cleanliness then some problem can be solved. The lifting of the broken pipe lines from the drain are to be made immediately and the drain are to be covered to avoid nuisence.

Disposal of street garbage: The sweeping of the roads are done regularly and the street garbages are cleaned by the conservancy department of Shillong Municipality. This cleaning part of the town are mainly done by the Sikh scavengers and by some Nepalis. The Municipality at present having three tractors and seven trucks which carries all these garbages and they dump it to the Mawlai tranching ground. The total number of employee who are engaged for this cleaning work are 159 and most of them work as casual worker. Presently, Government of Meghalaya adopted some proposal to utilize these garbages as manure.

Habit of Defecation: The proper disposal of human faecal material is important for environmental sanitation. In Shillong, during the year 1968-69 there existed 3766 service latrins and 981 water barrie latrins in 1979 there existed 1990 water borne latrin and 4695 service latrins and 13 other types but in 1991 there exists only 3000 service latrins. Presently Govt. of Meghalaya is not giving any permission for the construction of service latrin, and they are trying to convert all the existing service latrins into sanitary latrins with septic tank facilities. In this connection Mazahari (1984: 35) opined that the "Water pollution in Shillong is mainly due to the existence of many service latrins. The night soil is ultimately thrown into the streams which have been converted into open sawers". However, this system is gradually decreasing.

Recently, Govt, of Meghalaya has taken up a project in collaboration with HUDCO and they are expecting a loan of Rs. 82 lakhs soon, to facilitate the construction of sanitary latrin, within the area. Under these scheme for construction of sanitary latrin, the higher income group people will not get any benefit, the middle income group people will get certain percentages of the total expenditure incurred for the construction of sanitary latrin, whereas the lower income group will get a long term loan with maximum benefit. But how much amount will be paid at its initial stage that has not yet been decided and for that reason certain laws and by-laws will be made to facilitate the work soon.

Toilet Habits: The toilet habit of the people in general is very poor in nature. In the township area very seldom we get any public urinals. Whatever the existing urinals are there it is very badly maintained. Therefore, the public awareness is very much essential for its proper maintainance. In this connection Municipality has taken some proposal for the construction of certain Public urinals in different parts of the town and it is expected that the common nuisence in the township area will be partly rectified in course of time and this will prevent many more diseases in future.

Role of Shillong Municipality: The role of Municipality for better health condition is immence in nature. There stimulated activities can do best in future if the people of the region, other government agencies and social workers of the region come forwards with the ideology that we will make our homeland a beautiful one, then and then only all these existing microproblems can be solved within a twincle of eye.

In the Plan project of 1991 Shillong Municipality has adopted certain measure in this regard to provide maximum facilities to the people of the region. They as follows:

1. Construction of Public urinals.
2. Development of existing road as far as practicable.
3. The foot paths will be made to avoid accident.
4. More and more drains will be made either box type or open surfaced one to facilitate the disposal of dirty water.
5. The existing old and broken bridges will be repaired and small and new bridges will be constructed Where ever it is necessary.

Maximum attention will be paid for the augmentation of drinking water.

Conclusion: In the present study some of the problems related with the health condition and certain basic need of the people of the region were discussed. It is well known that the sufficient supply of pure drinking water, sanitary disposal of human

Appendix:

Distribution of civic amenities in Shillong Municipal area
(c. f. sources Census of India and others)

Year	*Total income*	*Total expenditure*	*TYPES OF CIVIC AMENITIES*					
			Types of drain	*Number of Latrin*			*Method of disposal of night soil*	*Sources of of supply of drinking water*
				Water bourn	*Service*	*Others*		
1968-69	1,100,750-00	1,006,665-00	KD BSD OSD	981	3,766	—	WB	SR., T
1981	3,900,100-00	2,975,000-00	SD BSD	1990	4,695	13	WB/ST	SR/CHT; T
1991	10,300,000-00 (anticipated)	—	OSD BSD	—	3,000	—	WB/ST	SR/OHT., T

Abbreviation:
KD=Kutcha drain
BSD=Box surface drain
OSD=Open surface drain
WB=Wheel Barrows
ST=Septic tanks
SR=Service reservoir
OHT=Over head tank
T=Tap Water

excreta are very much essential to avoid some of the diseases either water bourn or caused by insects and germs can be eliminated and on the other hand they can facilitate decent standard of living. If the water supply and waste disposal are properly attended then the fever (Both specified and unspecified) and various types of gastroenties can be eliminated and these inturen will help the people in general and the infants of the state in particular.

REFERENCES

1. Jala, J. M. 1971. Census of India, *District Census Hand book, Pt. XA and XB, Village and Town Directory of Meghalaya.*
2. Hasan, K. A. 1979. *Medical Sociology in Rural India.* Ajmon, Sachin Publication.
3. Mazhari, H. K. 1984. Shillong the fast growing city (In) *Shillong 1971-81* (ed.) B. Pakem, Calcutta Research India Publication for NEICSSR, Shillong.
4. Tayeng, J. 1981. Census of India: *Meghalaya Provision Population totals.*, Paper-I of 1981 series 14.
5. — 1981. District Census Hand Book., Pt. XIII A and B village and Town directory, East Khasi Hills.
6. Winick 1956 C.f. Hasan, K. A., 1979: 45.

15

Water Supply of Shillong : Its Problem

Subrata Chakravorty

A city in order to sustain itself must have an adequate water supply for its ever growing population. The demand for more water both for domestic and Industrial use increases as its population increases. The necessity for tapping the water resources both surface and under-ground becomes essential as well as a proper management and distribution of the water supply is also needed.

It is seen that 'urbanization and man's development of water as a resource distort many aspects of the land-water ecosystem, a subject that falls within the realms of the geomorphologists.'[1]

Thus various studies as to how Geomorphology can perhaps solve the problems of water supply has been conducted in the developed nations. Similar studies in our country too may solve the problems of water supply especially in a hilly area like Shillong where topography perhaps tends to play rather a negative role in the distribution and management of the water resource of the city.

In the study 'Hydrology for Urban Land Plannint—A Guide book on Hydrologic effects of Urban Land Use' (L.B. Leopold 1968)[2] the author has identified four effects of land use changes on the hydrology of an area, which are 'changes in peak flow characteristics, changes in total run-offs, changes in quality of water and changes in the hydrologic amenities. Of all land-use changes affecting the hydrology of an area, urbanisation is by far the most forceful'.[3]

Similarly urbanisation of Shillong at a rapid speed has affected both the quantity and quality of water resource. Shillong inspite of receiving very high rainfall of about 2400 mm per year on the average, yet is known as a water scarcity area.

The area is drained by the rivers Umshirpi, Umkhrah which joins together near Beadon, Biship falls to form Wah Roro a tributary to the river Wah Umiam. Shillong is faced with water shortage for domestic purposes to the tune of 30 lakh gallons per day when compared to the total population of 201577[4] as per 1981 census having a requirement of 100 gallons per person per day. Water resources in Shillong includes a number of water springs and a few low discharge streams.[5]

Since the study area is situated very close to the water divide around the highest elevation of the Meghalaya Plateau viz. Upper Shillong and Laitkor peak having an elevation of about 1800 m to 1920 metres above mean sea level, the discharge of water in the streams are meagre to very little. Moreover the streams are mainly of low order with very shot length thereby having low discharge.

'The volume of run-off is governed primarily by infiltration characteristics and is related to the land slope and soil type as well as to the type of vegetation cover.[6] But in Shillong due to the pressure of population on land the steep slopes have come under settlement activating, constructional activities which have promoted indiscriminate felling of trees thereby reducing the infiltration and percolation capacity which in turn has increased the rate of runoffs thereby causing water scarcity.

In fact it has been observed during recent years that at least seven springs in Laban-Lowsohtun area and Upper Nongthymmai having an average slope of 15°-20 has dried up perhaps because of the felling of trees for constructional purpose in these catchment areas. Thus the problem may necessiate a Geomorphological understanding of the area.

The quality of water for drinking purpose is deteriorating which comes from the streams and springs of Shillong which are fed directly into the piped distribution system and stored in tanks to be distributed by the Shillong Municipality and the Public Health Engineering Department, Government of Meghalaya.

The deterioration of the quality of water in the streams is mainly because of the fact that often there is dumping of waste and garbage in these streams. Moreover, a number of stone quarries which are located over the steep slopes and by the sides of streams viz. stone quarries at Nongthymmai, Rynjah, Pynthorumkhrah, Mawlai which are located on banks of the Demthring and Wah Umkhrah have added to the pollution of water due to siltation. Atleast four, public latrines are located by the side of the Umpling nala within 30 metres up-stream of be intake of Umpling water supply.[7] All these having an adverse effect on the quality of drinking water of the city and perhaps Geomorphology can play role in minimising the problem for proper slope management and selection of site for waste disposal at the Pediment or waning slope rather than on the waxing slope which may solve the problem to a large extent.

Table 1 gives an account of the main water sources of the Shillong Municipality and the township of Mawlai.

TABLE 1

Source of Water Supply of Shillong Municipality and Public Health Engineering Department (1991 approximately)

Source	*Capacity in gallons per day*	*Installed by*
Wahrisa	1 lakh	SM*
Wahjalynnoh	1 lakh	SM
Umjasoi	2 lakh	SM
Crinoline	.80 lakh	SM
Wahdiengheng	.50 lakh	SM
Madan Laban	.50 lakh	SM
Patta Khana	.25 lakh	SM
Mawprem Tank	4,40.000 gallons	PHED
Barabazar Tank	2,90,000 gallons	PHED
Lachaumiere	3,70,000 gallons	PHED
Mawlai Mawroh	1,30,000 gallons	PHED
Jail Road	10,000 gallons	PHED
Ganesh Das Hospital	40,700 gallons	PHED
Upland	60,000 gallons	

*SM = Shillong Municipality

PHED=Public Health Engineering Department.

Source: Official Records of Shillong Municipality and Public Health Engineering Deptt., Govt. of Meghalaya, Shillong

An analysis of the table 1 shows that the Shillong Municipality covering an area of 10.36 sq. km. catering to population size of

109244 as per 1981 census received around 16 lakh gallons of water per day. However, all the localities within the municipality do not received an equal amount of water.

Though mismanagement and wastage of water through leaking pipes and water logged pools is responsible for the unequal distribution of water perhaps Geomorphology too has had a role in this unequal distribution. It has been observed that the localities of Rilbong, Kechstrece, Bishnupur, Lumparing receives around 34 liters of water per head per day when compared to localities of Laitumkhrah, European Ward, Police Bazar, Barabazar, Mawkhar etc. which receive around 50-52 liters of water per head per day. This may be because of the former localities are situated at a higher altitude and steeper slopes (15°-20°) when compared to the latter. Perhaps the steep slope may have had an adverse effect on the distribution of water on the former localities.

In the selection of site of the water tanks it is perhaps necessary to have an understanding of the local topography of the area for a location of a tank on the waxing slope or the upper part of the slope may help in the easy distribution of water with in the city.

In tapping the underground water it has been observed that the valleys and topographic lows are suitable for the construction of large diameter bore wells as well as open wells for these areas viz. Pologround, Mawroh, Pynthorumkhrah, Valleys of Mawpat. Mawlynrei have highly clayey deposits which have poor permeability and transmessibility[8] of water.

An understanding of the geomorphic features along with the underlying geology may be helpful in selecting sites for tapping underground water resource of the Study Areas. Infact the Geological Survey of India, North East Circle had carried on two exploratory drillings at Rynjah where the two bore holes of 62.55 metres and 72.30 metres respectively were dug up which penetrated the confined acquifers in fractured quartzites and turned out to be flowing wells, which recorded around 7540 litres to 5150 litres of auto flow of water per hour during the wet season and 720 to 306 litres per hour during the dry season.[9]

Hydrological studies by CGWB* have revealed that the water level varies between 1 metre to 3 metres in topographic lows and within 10 metres depth in Upland areas with seasonal fluctuation to the tune of 3 metres and 8 metres respectively.[10] Thus Geomorphological characteristics of the area may help in selecting the sites for tapping the ground water resource of the area besides the distribution which shall perhaps be beneficial in minimising the problem of water supply faced by the city.

However thc problem needs a further micro level studyin order to find the exact location of the tanks and distribution of water so as to minimise the negative role of the terrain in the supply and tapping of drinking water. Here the attempts is general which needs further investigation at a micro level to find how far the topography plays a role not only in regard to water supply but also in relation to distribution of settlements and population of the Shillong characterised by rugged topography and steep slope:

REFERENCES

1. D.B. Coates (1974) *Editors Comment on Papers 4 Through 9* Benchmark Papers in a Geology, Environmental Geomorphology and Landscape Conservation, Vol. II, Urban Areas, pp. 58-68.

2. L.B. Leopold (1968) *Hydrology for Urban Land Planning —A Guidebook on Hydrologic Effects Urban Land Use,* U.S. Geol. Surv. Urc. 554, Govt. Printing office Washington D.C., pp. 1-18.

*Central Ground Water Board.

3. *Ibid.*
4. Census of India 1981, Series 14, Meghalaya Part II A and B.
5. Report from Urban Development office, Govt. of Meghalaya.
6. L.B. Leopold (1968), *op. cit.*
7. Report from Urban Development Office, Govt. of Meghalaya.
8. *Ibid.*,
9. Report from Geological Survey of India, North East Circle Shillong.
10. Report from Urban Development Office, Govt. of Meghalaya, Shillong.

16

Planning Strategy for Development of New Town for shillong

BK. Panda

INTRODUCTION

Shillong, the state capital, located at an attitude of 1500 meters above the sea level, is one of the oldest, largest and fast growing hill town in the country. With the shifting of administrative headquarter of Assam in 1864 by the British administration, the insignificant village grew as a newton in size, magnitude, significance and its face lift continued unabated.

The status of being a state capital, influx of population for commercial activities and development function over the years gave tremendous boost to the expanison of the town and it has become a populous and proliferating city. The outward extension has physically engulfed five other towns into its fold.

Growth Trend

Shillong Urban Agglomeration consisting of six townships i.e. Shillong Municipality, Mawlai, Nongthymmai, Cantonment Board, Pynthorumkhrah and Madanryting cover an area of 21.27 sq. kilometers with population of 1,75,180 in 1981 whereas Shillong Municipality alone accounts for 1.07.673 persons.

After the bifurcation of the State of Assam and Meghalaya in 1972, the urban agglomeration recorded an unprecedented increase of 40.99% against the growth of 19.89% during 1961-71. The reason may be attributed to the initiation of and concentration of setting up regional functions, Central Government organisation, institutions of public and semi-public bodies. However, the growth of Shillong Municipality is only 22.83% which was much lower than the urban agglomeration. The reason may be attributed to congestion within Municipal area and sprawl of population in the peripheral of fringe area.

Problems Identification

Shillong had basically developed as an administrative centre but in due course, it has outgrown to become a regional commercial centre of North-Eastern India. The tremendous growth unplanned and unco-ordinated due to lack of and inadequacy of proper legislation has resulted in haphazard growth desecrating the urban landscape and degrading the living conditions.

Concentration expansion an of various administrative functions and institutional establishments of State and Central Government offices, regional research and academic centres in the last few years within the city has aggravated the congestion and overcrowding as most of these centres availed private sector housing.

Haphazard development of whole-sale activities and trade and commerce, without any basic facilitates. has resulted in creating slum and traffic congestion.

In increasing traffic on National Highway, which cuts across the central area and increasing number of internal vehicular traffic without any scopc of increasing the road width has resulted in frequent traffic congestion and traffic jam.

The resultant increase in concentration of activities and rapid population growth poses the following problems in the city.

1. Almost all the buildable land available for development has already been built up creating a shortage of serviceable land to accommodate future population and activities.

2. Increasing demand of land and houses against scarce stock has tremendously increased the land value and house rent.

3. Scarcity of housing stock and absence of buildable land posed tremendous strain leading to undesirable vertical extension of structure and overcrowding. It may be mentioned that there is an insignificant per cent of Government housing facilities available as a result, most of the construction activities are private sector effort and investment.

4. Mushrooming of haphazard development in the fringe area and also housing activity in undevelopable land leading to environmental degradation.

5. Over crowding due to the intensification, overburdened the infrastructural facilities, as a consequence, inadequacy of water supply and sanitation leading to growing slums. Absence of proper legislation and agency to guide and regulate the development of the urban area in toto is a major constraint. The existing building bye-laws is operative only within the Municipal limit but it is ineffective and the machinery responsible for its enforcement is also sluggish.

6. Construction and development of building and activities in the fringe areas are uncontrolled and unregulated leading to an overburdening and un-economic extension of infrastructure.

7. The scarce financial resources and low allocation in providing the infrastructure for meeting the demand is another constraint leading to slum development. The unplanned and uncontrolled accelerated growth has generated increasingly serious economic, social and environmental problems.

The problems, if not tackle at this stage, the living environment will deteriorate beyond an unmanageable proportion which will adversely affect the economic development of the city as well as the state as a whole.

Why a New Town?

Past a experience in creating new towns shows that it requires the assembly of large scale land, a large initial investment, a large gestation peri od from initiation to achieving a positive cumulative cash flow. Moreover, the risks involved can be considerable and short run returns and equily capital are either, non-existant or extremely low. Then, the question comes, why to create a new town instead of expanding the existing one?

Shillong, being situated in a plateau of undulating terrain, growth and expansion of activities have been guided by the physical terrain features and not much of continuity is observed. Out of the total Master Plan areas. The developable land has been identified as undevelopable area. The developable land has been almost utilised and in the central part of the city, the intensification of uses has been well marked. A recent study by 'Geological Survey of India' indicates "the building activities at undesirable sites are increasing rapidly".

Extension of the existing township would have been preferred but due to the physical constraint. The fringe area, mostly undevelopable land, has to be preserved for environmental implications. It is envisaged that whatever quantity of developable land are still available, cannot therefore provide a reservoir of new development and unless provisions are made for accommodating the increasing wholesales, commercial and transportation activities, which are creeping gradually into the residential areas, there may be a disastrous situation.

Hence, the approach is to tackle the problems in two ways. As a curative measure, improvement of infrastructure facilities should be taken up within the existing city and as a long term measure, a new town should be developed to acommodate and facilitate the future population and economic activities.

Future Demand

The growth land of population and acceleration in economic activities over the years in the city gives ample evidence and dynamic growth. It is expected that this trend will persist until it is influenced by negative spatial policies and financial disincentive policies. The estimated population of Greater Shillong by 2001 A.D. and 2011 A.D. will be 3,80,000 and 5,00,000 persons respectively. On the other hand, even by intensifying the land-use and density, the present city will accommodate around 3,50,000 population. Hence to accommodate the spillover 1,50,000 population, approximately 2,000 hectares of additional land will be required to mitigate the scarcity. Hence effort has to be made at right earnest to syphon the additional population without affecting the economic growth of the city.

Locational Consideration of Township

A choice might often be offered between building new town near the existing city or a remote area, and vacant site or by expanding small or medium size existing settlements. In a developing region; often considered, building a new town in the remove area act as a catalyst to the economic development of hinderland by subserving as a 'growth foci'. But in a hilly area like Meghalaya, where the economic base is at a subsistence level and potentiality of new avenue of economic activities are gleam, infrastructure facilities are almost non-existent and where the prime city has overwhelming influence, isolated new town would not serve the purpose as has been experienced in the past after settling so many new administrative centres.

Hence, in a state like Meghalaya with limited resources and conflicting claims of priority, it is considered important to locate new town within commuting distance which offers appreciable advantages as every facilities may not required to be provided at the initial stage, employment period and also, the overhead cost of development will be lower due to availability of skilled lavour force and material at a cheaper rate.

Thus, the site should be identified and proposed at close proximity of Shillong city, keeping in view, the conceptual advantage as well as other planning consideration such as existing growth tendency, size conditions, availability of large stretch and high percentage of developable land at cheaper rate political sensitivity in acquire land, availability of existing and potential sources of water in close proximity, accessibility and environmental impact etc.

Objectives

The primary objectives of developing the township are detailed as follow:

(i) To absorb 'overspill population' of Shillong and to facilitate the growth.

(ii) To prevent destructive land use from a concentrated urban structure on the fringe area of the already congested area.

(iii) To improve the economic structure by facilitating future expansion and promotion of economic activities and growth.

(iv) To create a desirable urban living environment.

Policy Issues

A comprehensive planning approach should be adopted integrating the distribution of productive forces and population recognising the spatial and locational aspects of economic growth, and desirable physical environment for human need and welfare.

The township should have a diversified economic base which is an essential means of promoting the development of any town and should be developed as a self-contained unit.

Decentralisation of administrative function, particularly district level officer to the new town and channelising those investment of such infrastructure to the new town for creation of the same. All other new development activities should also be diverted and directed to the new town as all new commercial (wholesale, warehouse), transportational industrial and institutional activities should be discouraged in the existing city.

A 'Development Authority' should be set up for developing the township with wide range of development, financial and management power in order to avoid the complexity and creating ineffective gamot of functional agencies.

Increasing private sector investment should be tapped and encouraged. Public sector investment should be minimised and restricted only to create the initial impetus and providing affordable serviceable land for the poor.

Since building a new Born is a complex process, involvement of various agencies are inevitable and essential through out the process of development. Hence high power 'Co-ordination and Monitoring Committee' should be set up for the purpose.

The responsibility of creating the new town belongs to the public authority, thus, Government finance is imperative and should provide for the initial capital investment during the early planning and development period.

Strategy of Development

Building of new town successfully depends on the development strategies to a greater extent as well as determines the financial involvement and implication. An attempt has been made to indicate the strategies to be adopted.

As a decentralise measure, the district level administration should be shifted to the new town. Since mostly the district level offices are functioning in private building, the same may be shifted along with housing provision for the employees. This will not only lay an initial impetus but also be the functional base of the town.

A 'Transport Centre' should be developed with necessary infrastructure such as serviding, repairing activities, filling station, parking space and hotel etc. to promote transportation which will act as an impetus of development.

Further, a regional wholesale commercial centre should be established with necessary provisions of warehousing facilities. The 'Transport Centre' will provide the basic source of attraction for development of the market centre. New small scale industries such as saw mills, fabrication units and hallow block making industries which are increasing day by day should be accommodated and encouraged in the new town.

It is proposed that the township should be developed in phases but the physical plan should be prepared in such a way to facilitate scope of expansion and as an integrated unit. The first phase development should be initiated at the beginning by acquiring the land and the land required for development in subsequent phases should be left as 'differed planning zone.'

The land required in the first phase should acquired by Government and after developing, the land can be parcelled out either by outright sale or lease hold basis. This system will give continuous control over urbanised area making easier the provision of public facilities and enable to capture land value and help to prevent land speculation.

The authority should predominently confine to land development scheme with minimum level of construction and should restrict itself to provide peripheral services and recreational facilities. However, are from other agencies should be pulled together for income development and construction of essential building for the poorest section.

All types of development activities should be initiated at the same time so that each activity will support the others. More specifically the development of offices, houses and retail shops should start at the same time.

In Shillong, the private sector investment, mostly individual investment accounts for major share of housing development. Hence once the public sector investment is made and development process initiated, private sector investment will follow suit without any exception.

Financial Strategy

Project appraisal on new town in both developed and developing countries are abundant where in public sector and private sector investments were applied either in isolation or in combination of the both. The degree of success and failure in each case varies widely. However, in general, the finding emerged out of these projects is public sector and private sector investment alone; often, leads to the failure of the projects primarily because of non-availability of required finance as per time schedule in case of public sector investment while in the later speculative forces defies the need of market force. Hence, the financing of the new town should preferably be the blend of the two.

Finance on an adequate scale for the whole project, both from public and private sources. should be assured for firmly in prospect before new town programme is launched.

In case different sources of finance are involved, the division of responsibilities and arrangement for cooperation between them and for timely availability of funds by all concerned should be clarified to the maximum extent possible at the outset.

In order to ensure that decisions to proceed with new town are taken in the knowledge of their financial prospects, economic appraisal should be undertaken to establish their economic viability, taking account of any concessions, or other special financial conditions that may be applicable. Financial objectives and investment criteria should be defined and apprepriate mechanism developed to enable financial performance to be monitored and investment controlled throughout the period of development.

Suitable investment and financial control machinery will also be of importance from the piont of view of assessing comparative financial benefits between particular projects, and in relation to different phasing of development.

The substantial public sector investment in the new town can generate increased values throughout. Special measure may therefore be required to ensure that part of these increased values are drawn off for the benefit of public sector.

The satisfactory resolution of the special financial problems that arise in connection with the development of newtown is crucial to their successful realisation.

Conclusion

Keeping in view the problems, need, strategy of development and financial intricacies and complexities of developing new town, the issues still open to be addressed are should we venture for a new town? Are we heading towards the right direction ? If so, looking at the public financial constraint and resource crunch, should not the private sector (People as a whole) be a helping partner in the development process shaping the city?

Bibliography

1. T.C.P. Department Government of Meghalaya, 1986, *Need for Extension of Shillong; A case for setting up a New Township*. Report unpublished.

2. U.S. Department of Housing and Urban Development, *Financing New Communities*. Washington.

3. United Nations, 1966, *Planning and Development of New Towns*. Report on the Symposium on Planning and Development of New Towns.

4. Organisation for Economic Cooperation and Development 1979 *Implementation of Urban Plan* Published by OECD, Paris.

5. Linn Johannes F. 1980 Cities in the developing world: *Policies for their Equitable and Efficient Growth* Published for the world Bank for Oxford University Press. New-york.

17

Meghalaya Urban Development Authority Shillong

"Its Role and Function in Relation to Implementation of Shillong Master Plan"

H. K. Mazhar
and
B. Jones Dhar

1.0 The Shillong Master Plan was prepared in the year 1976 and the recommendations contained there in are valid till 1991. Immediately after the Plan was prepared, the same was not approved by the State Government as the Meghalaya Town and Country Planning Act, 1973 was not enforced in the entire State. The Assam Town and Country Planning Act, 1959 which was adopted had its limited applications in the three normal Wards of Shillong City namely, the European Ward, the Police Bazar Ward and the Jail Road Ward. Hence, the Master Plan which was prepared after carrying out various detailed studies for a period of twenty years remained only a paper document.

1.1 It was during 1989 that the State Government extended the application of Meghalaya Town and Country Planning Act, 1973 to the entire State and also constituted the Town and Country Planning Advisory Councils as per Chapter II, Section 3 of the Act. The Advisory Council in its first meeting held in September, 1989 examined the proposals and approved the same in its second sitting held in August 1990.

1.2 As per Section 8 of the Act' Development Authority was constituted in March, 1990. The main function of the Authority being the development of the town in accordance with the recommendations of the Master Plan. While discharging its duties, the Authority is expected to carry out any other function which is suplemental, incidental and consequential to the above.

1.3 The Shillong Development Authority immediately after its constitution in 1990 took up the function of granting building permission which is one of the tools to ensure that recommendations of the Master Plan is not violated. However, its operation is still limited to the areas within Shillong Municipal limits. Outside the Municipal limits the Authority has not been able to exercise its power. The Rangbah Shnong who have been exercising this power may agree to assist the Authority in the above function if the Syiem have no objection, Syiems have not yet given their consent. This has resulted in haphazard growth even after the notification of the Master Plan in October, 1990 and constitution of the Development Authority.

1.4 The other Factor which has prevented the Authority to exercise its functions in the Non-Municipal Areas is the shortage of technical hands and the inspecting staff. The consequence of this policy of the Authority is clearance of building construcrion within the Municipal area, while the Areas which developed in the past without any control still remains untouched. This had led to dual control of building permission within Municipal Areas and mushrooming of structure outside.

1.5 If the current census figures (1991) is any indication of the growth of the city the population increase has been more in areas outside the Municipal limit. Shillong Municipal area has shown the least increase (19.63%). Increase of population for all the towns is given below.

Population of Urban Agglomerations, 1991

City/Towns	*Population 1991*	*Growth Rate 1971-81*	*Growth Rate 1981-91*
1. Shillong UA	222,273	42.32	27.23
(a) Shillong M	130,691	24.62	19.33
(b) Mawlaiyamai	30,442	43.09	49.19
(c) Nongthymmai	26,815	33.08	24.39
(d) Pynthorumkhra	14,322	—	33.71
(e) Shillong Cantt.	11,075	39.96	67.30
(f) Madanryting	8,972	—	44.80

Source: Census of India, 1991 (Provisional).

1.6 It is, therefore, imperative that the control on development is to be more on non-Municipal Areas. However, the situation is just the opposite. Unless Meghalaya Urban Development Authority, takes adequate steps in this direction, the situation may be out of control in times to come.

1.7 As pointed out above, the Authority, limited its operations only to granting building permission and has not taken over any other function of development including real estate schemes as has been the case in all other development authorities in the country. Most of the Authorities including Delhi Development Authority and Calcutta Metropolitan Development Authority have got themselves converted into executing agencies thereby taking large scale development of residential, commercial and office development. In that process, the main function of enforcement of Master Plan has been given back seat. Not only that' the existing executing agency like the Public Works Department, the Public Health Engineering Department and Municipal Boards are deprived of these jobs, it at times leads to unhealthy competitions and peofessional rivalry.

1.8 The question, there, is what should be the role and function of the Authority. If the Authority goes strictly by the provisions of the Act, functions are unlimited and can encompass any activity in the city.

1.9 Hence, the provisions of the Act may not be the guiding factos in deciding on the functions to be assigned to the Authority.

2.0 As pointed out above, the Development Authority has to perform three main functions and these are (a) Planning, (b) Enforcement and (c) Implementation.

2.1 As per the Meghalaya Town and Country Planning Act, 1973 the Master Plan is to be prepared by the Director of Town and Country Planning. However, the Authority has to prepare the scheme in areas notified as scheme areas under Section 15 of the Act. Hence, Planning functions of the Authority is restricted to Planning and preparation of scheme within the scheme areas. Scheme area can be any area within the Master Plan boundary and even virgin area could be notified as scheme areas. In otber words, all action plans and project planning are to be the main function of the Authority.

2.2 In regard to enforcement of Master Plan. all powers vest with the Authority. According to Section 171 of the Meghalaya Municipal Act, 1973 (Assam Municipal Act, 1956 as adopted by Meghalaya), the power of giving sanction to erect materially, after or re-eract any building shall vest in the Authority and the sanction of the Municipal Board. It is, therefore, clear that once the Authority is set-up, it takes over the fuctions of the Municipal Board relating to granting of building permission. This is necessary to ensure that no construction takes place in violation of the Provisions of Master Plan.

2.3 As per Section 12 of the Meghalaya Town and Counry Planning Act, 1973 the implementation of the Master Plan is the responsibility of the Authority. However, no details have been indicated that either in the main Act or in the rules framed under the Act as to how the Authority is to implement the Master Plan. In some cases, the Authority have directly taken up the execution of various scheme thereby converting itself into another Public Works Department of the State Government and reducing its importance as an agency for monitoring and co-ordination. The World Bank report has commented adversely of the functioning of the various Authorities in the country which have taken the role of builder. In the Urban Development Project report for the World Bank assisted Programme, it has been suggested that the Calcutta Metropolitan Development Authority should gradually shed its functions of implementation and pass on these to the existing executing agencies in the City of Calcutta. It is better to learn from the experience of Calcutta Metropolitan Development Authority, Delhi Development Authority, and other development authorities who have gone for massive construction schemes. Madras Metropolitan Development Authority has however restricted this activity and by and large played the role of co-ordinating agency.

2.4 In case of Shillong, at present, there are five agencies which are operating in the field and these are the Public Works Department, Public Health Engineering Department, Meghalaya Government Construction Corporation, Meghalaya State Electricity Board and the Municipal Board. These agencies have in-house expertise for construction and that should be utilised to the optimum level instead of creating similar expertise in the Authority. Not only that, this will add to the over-head of the Authority and it will also increase problems of co-ordination between the existing agencies and the executive wing of the Authority.

2.5 The Authority has to function as an Umbrella body and should be responsible mainly for co-ordination, sanction and monitoring of schemes. It may be ideal if the entire funding of the City is done through the Authority so that it can keep a watch on the progerss of the scheme and ensure that these are in accordance with the Master Plan.

18

Need for Low-Cost Sanitation in Shillong

Amres hPriya

First of all I would like to give my views on the need for adopting low cost sanitation system as a whole. As the name suggests, it is the cheapest system of sanitation among the many other systems developed so far. The technology adopted for constructing such latrines is also very simple. It is most suited to Indian conditions and for many other developing countries. The most important aspect of this system is that it does not contaminate or pollute the atmosphere or surface soil. Although pollution of ground water cannot be prevented but with proper precaution the ground water source can be utilised for domestic use safely. On site sanitation with a pour flush two pit latrine, popularly known as Sulabh Shauchalaya, is acceptable, affordable and easily available. The requirement of water is also much less in comparison to other sanitation systems. Now a two litre flushing cistern has been developed, which can be fixed to the pour flush system. Thus it has been possible to overcome one of the factors that led to the non-acceptance of low-cost pour flush system by the middle and high income group population. These latrines are also very easy to maintain and do not entail any expenditure on maintanence. It can be maintained by the users themselves. Therefore, this system is not only a break through in sanitation technology, but also a meaning-ful step towards abolition of scavenging (an age old practice of carrying night soil on the head).

It was Mahatama Gandhi, Father of our Nation, who was the first to serve the cause of scavengers and struggled for liberating them from cleaning night soil. The concern of Mahatma Gandhi for scavengers/Bhangis is clear from the following words he said once:

"I may not be born again and if it happends, I will take to be born in a family of scavengers so that I may relieve them of inhuman, unhealthy and hateful practice of carrying head loads of night soil."

The importance of Mahatma's thought was realised by many persons of whom Padma Bhushan Dr. Bindeshwar Pathak, a renowned action sociologist, is the one who gave a realistic structure to these thoughts. He started Sulabh movement in 1970 with the foundation of Sulabh Shauchalaya Sansthan (now known as Sulabh International), a voluntary social organisation. A twin programme of construction of individual toilets along-with the liberation of scavengers was under-taken by the organisation in Bihar with the co-operation of the Govt. of Bihar and other concerned urban local bodies. His work was appreciated not only in Bihar but in many other states of India and the world as a whole. Now Sulabh International is successfully working as a link between the Government., local bodies and the public in different states of India. It has so far constructed/converted 6 lacs of individual dry toilets in different parts of India into pour flush ones and is also looking forward to providing sanitation facility in each and every corner of India. Recently the founder of Sulabh International has been honoured with the 'Padma Bhushan' award by the Hon'ble President of India, for his great dedication and thoughts in the field of sanitation and liberation of scavengers. So far 30,000 scavengers have been liberated and rehabilitated by Sulabh International. Presidently, Sulabh International renders its services not only in the construction/maintenance of Sulabh Shauchalayas but also in other diverse fields such as pollution control, bio-energy generation from human excreta, low-cost housing construction, collaboration with national and international agencies, scientific and tecnical research, rural reconstruction and training of human development.

Many other national (both Govt. and non-Govt.) and international organisations such as UNICEF, W.H.O., HUDCO etc. are also playing an important role in the development of low-cost sanitation (LCS) system through various programmes in different parts of the country. They are providing assistance to the public through the state Governments so as to enable maximum number of households in the country to be in a position to construct a pollution free latrine, instead of dry, pit or bucket latrine.

Regarding Shillong, the recently conducted survey shows that there are 7,487 holdings out of which 2,184 holdings have either dry/pit latrine or directly connected to the drains and 816 holdings do not have any type of sanitation facility.

Shillong, 'Scotland' of the east, a place of tourist interest, has to be neat and clean and as far as possible should be pollution free. This will add to the interest of the people visiting Shillong alongwith the improved health of the persons residing there. In order to achieve that position, it is very essential to convert the existing dry, pit or bucket latrines and the others connected to the drains in-to hygeinic system of sanitation. For that, LCS system is best suited to the interest of both the public as well as the Government of Meghalaya. Being a hilly area, it has got its own advantages of adopting the LCS system. The ground water pollution could be prevented by taking proper precaution. The waste gathered in pits will get converted into high quality manure in a short period. The manure could then be used to increase the fertility of the soil for higher agricultural production. In addition to that the Government of Meghalaya could be benefited by the "Integrated scheme for liberation of scavengers" through Low-Cost Sanitation. Under this scheme, there is a subsidy of 45% for Economically Weaker Section and 25% for Low Income Group and loan of 55% for E.W.S., 60% for L.I.G. and 75% for Middle and High Income Groups. There is no subsidy for Middle and High Income Groups. The Local unemployed youths could also be engaged in the work as motivators after proper training at Dist. levels. They could motivate the local public regarding the utility and importance of Sulabh Shauchalaya. Thus the problem of unemployment could be reduced to a certain extent. However, there is a section of people in every town whose houses have no space for private toilet and thus they defecate in open. For them the only feasible alternative is a properly maintained community toilet. Sulabh International constructs and maintains community toilet-cum-bath complexes in co-operation with respective Municipalities of the towns. These complexes (popularly known as Sulabh Complexes) play an important role in keeping the town clean and reducing the pollution. For a town likc Shillong, where tourists are a regular feature, such complexes are essential. Construction of Sulabh Complexes cannot be an end in itself. The objective is to wean people away from open defecation and ultimately to promote hygienic practices to improve community health and environment so that the complexes constructed are used by the public and are operated and maintained well. Motivators shall have to visit the households which do not have latrines in their house-holds to educate them about the health benefits of using the community toilet complexes and pay for the services.

The maintenance of toilet complexes has been tried by local bodies through their own staff/contractors but these experiences have not proved successful to keep them clean and adourless.

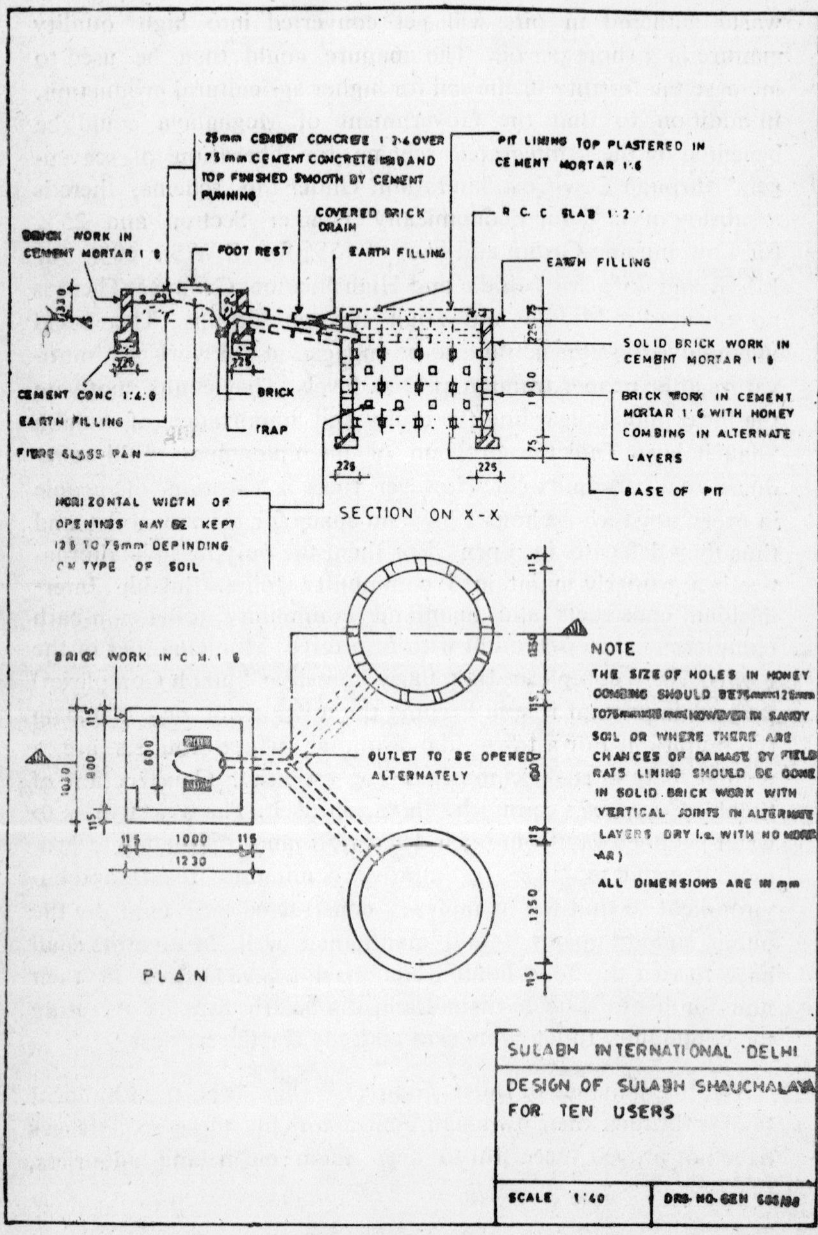
25mm CEMENT CONCRETE 1:2:4 OVER
75mm CEMENT CONCRETE AND
TOP FINISHED SMOOTH BY CEMENT
PUNNING
PIT LINING TOP PLASTERED IN
CEMENT MORTAR 1:6
COVERED BRICK
DRAIN
R. C. C SLAB 1:2
BRICK WORK IN
CEMENT MORTAR 1:6
FOOT REST
EARTH FILLING
EARTH FILLING
SOLID BRICK WORK IN
CEMENT MORTAR 1:6
BRICK WORK IN CEMENT
MORTAR 1:6 WITH HONEY
COMBING IN ALTERNATE
LAYERS
CEMENT CONC 1:4:8
EARTH FILLING
FIBRE GLASS PAN
BRICK
TRAP
BASE OF PIT
HORIZONTAL WIDTH OF
OPENINGS MAY BE KEPT
125 TO 75mm DEPINDING
ON TYPE OF SOIL
SECTION ON X-X
BRICK WORK IN C.M. 1:6
OUTLET TO BE OPENED
ALTERNATELY
NOTE
THE SIZE OF HOLES IN HONEY
COMBING SHOULD BE
HOWEVER IN SANDY
SOIL OR WHERE THERE ARE
CHANCES OF DAMAGE BY FIELD
RATS LINING SHOULD BE DONE
IN SOLID BRICK WORK WITH
VERTICAL JOINTS IN ALTERNATE
LAYERS DRY (i.e. WITH NO MORTAR)
ALL DIMENSIONS ARE IN mm
PLAN
SULABH INTERNATIONAL DELHI
DESIGN OF SULABH SHAUCHALAYA
FOR TEN USERS
SCALE 1:40

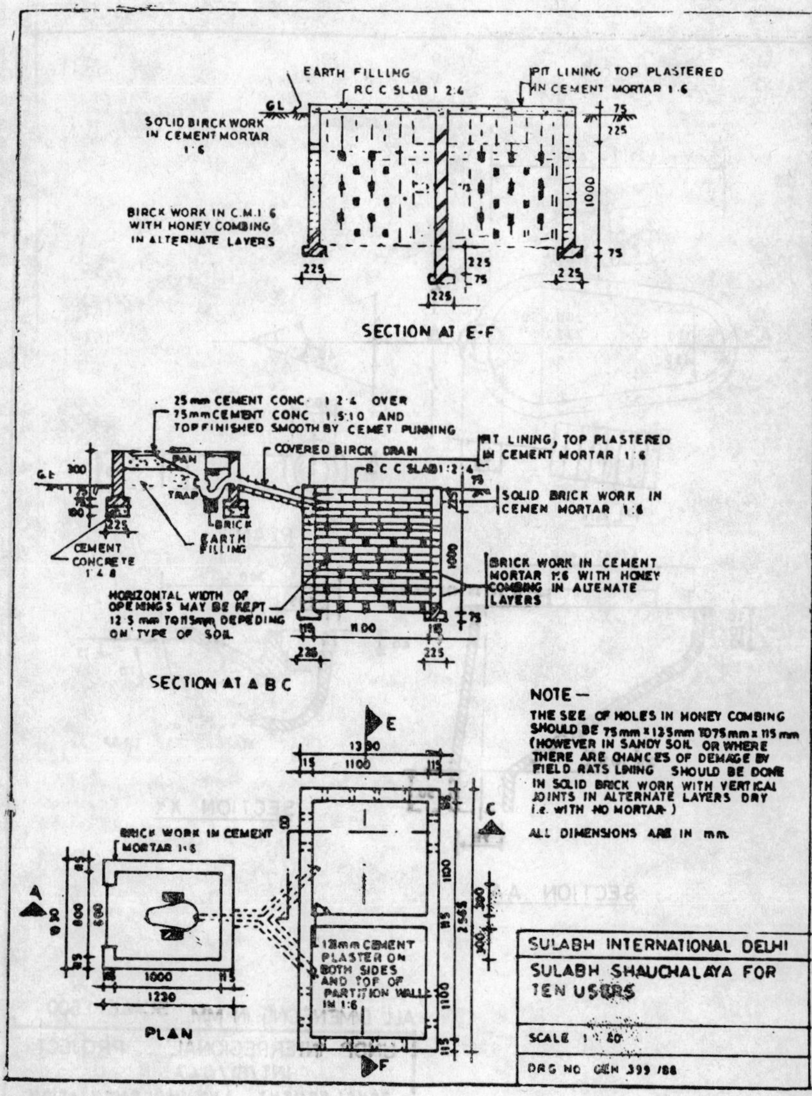
EARTH FILLING
RCC SLAB 1:2:4
PIT LINING TOP PLASTERED IN CEMENT MORTAR 1:6
SOLID BIRCK WORK IN CEMENT MORTAR 1:6
BIRCK WORK IN C.M.1:6 WITH HONEY COMBING IN ALTERNATE LAYERS
SECTION AT E-F
25 mm CEMENT CONC. 1:2:4 OVER 75 mm CEMENT CONC. 1:5:10 AND TOP FINISHED SMOOTH BY CEMET PUNNING
COVERED BIRCK DRAIN
PIT LINING, TOP PLASTERED IN CEMENT MORTAR 1:6
R C C SLAB 1:2:4
PAN
TRAP
BRICK
EARTH FILLING
CEMENT CONCRETE 1:4:8
SOLID BRICK WORK IN CEMEN MORTAR 1:6
BRICK WORK IN CEMENT MORTAR 1:6 WITH HONEY COMBING IN ALTENATE LAYERS
HORIZONTAL WIDTH OF OPENINGS MAY BE KEPT 12.5 mm TO 115 mm DEPEDING ON TYPE OF SOIL
SECTION AT A B C
NOTE —
THE SIZE OF HOLES IN HONEY COMBING SHOULD BE 75 mm x 125 mm TO 75 mm x 115 mm (HOWEVER IN SANDY SOIL OR WHERE THERE ARE CHANCES OF DEMAGE BY FIELD RATS LINING SHOULD BE DONE IN SOLID BRICK WORK WITH VERTICAL JOINTS IN ALTERNATE LAYERS DRY i.e. WITH NO MORTAR)
ALL DIMENSIONS ARE IN mm.
BRICK WORK IN CEMENT MORTAR 1:6
12 mm CEMENT PLASTER ON BOTH SIDES AND TOP OF PARTITION WALL IN 1:6
PLAN
SULABH INTERNATIONAL DELHI
SULABH SHAUCHALAYA FOR TEN USERS
SCALE 1:40
DRG NO GEN 399/88

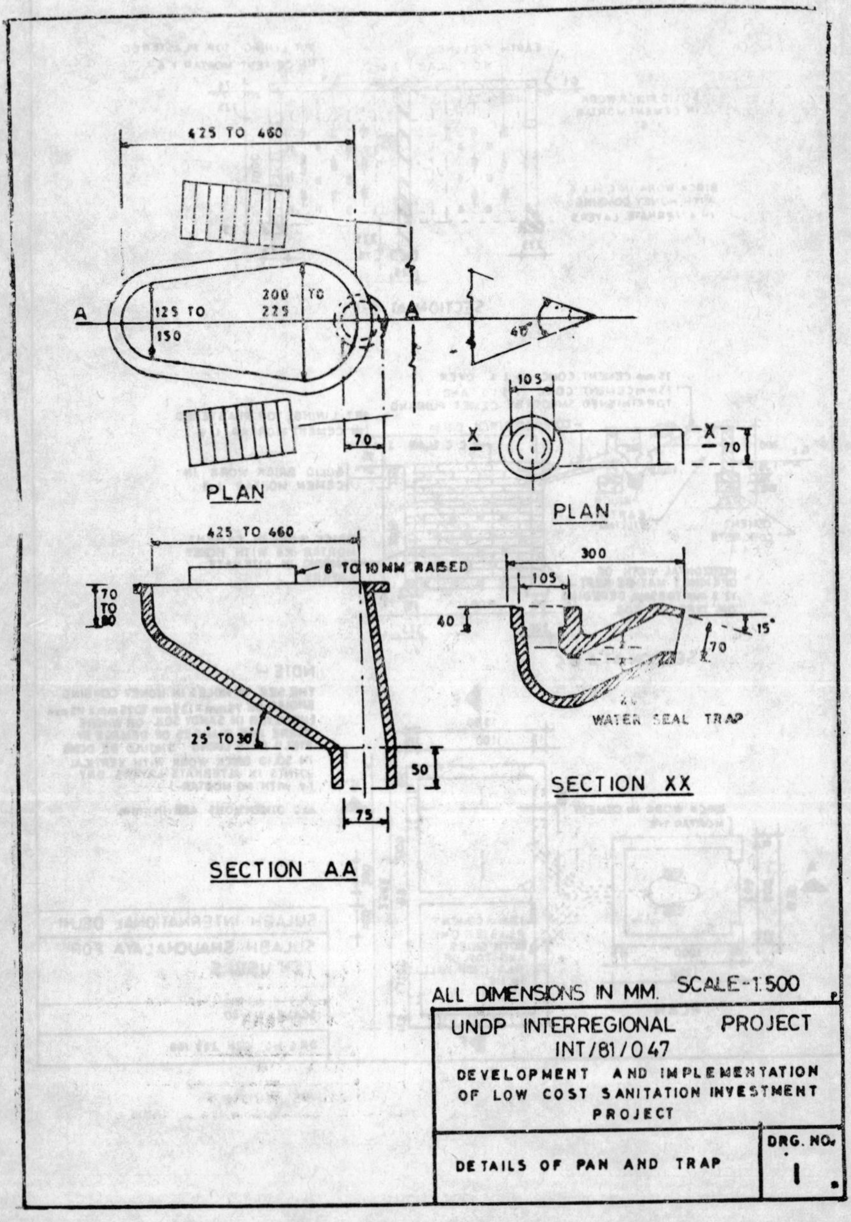
425 TO 460
200 TO 225
125 TO 150
A
40°
70
105
X
70
PLAN
425 TO 460
8 TO 10 MM RAISED
70 TO 80
25° TO 30°
50
75
SECTION AA
300
105
40
15°
70
WATER SEAL TRAP
PLAN
SECTION XX
ALL DIMENSIONS IN MM. SCALE-1:500
UNDP INTERREGIONAL PROJECT
INT/81/047
DEVELOPMENT AND IMPLEMENTATION OF LOW COST SANITATION INVESTMENT PROJECT
DETAILS OF PAN AND TRAP
DRG. NO.
1

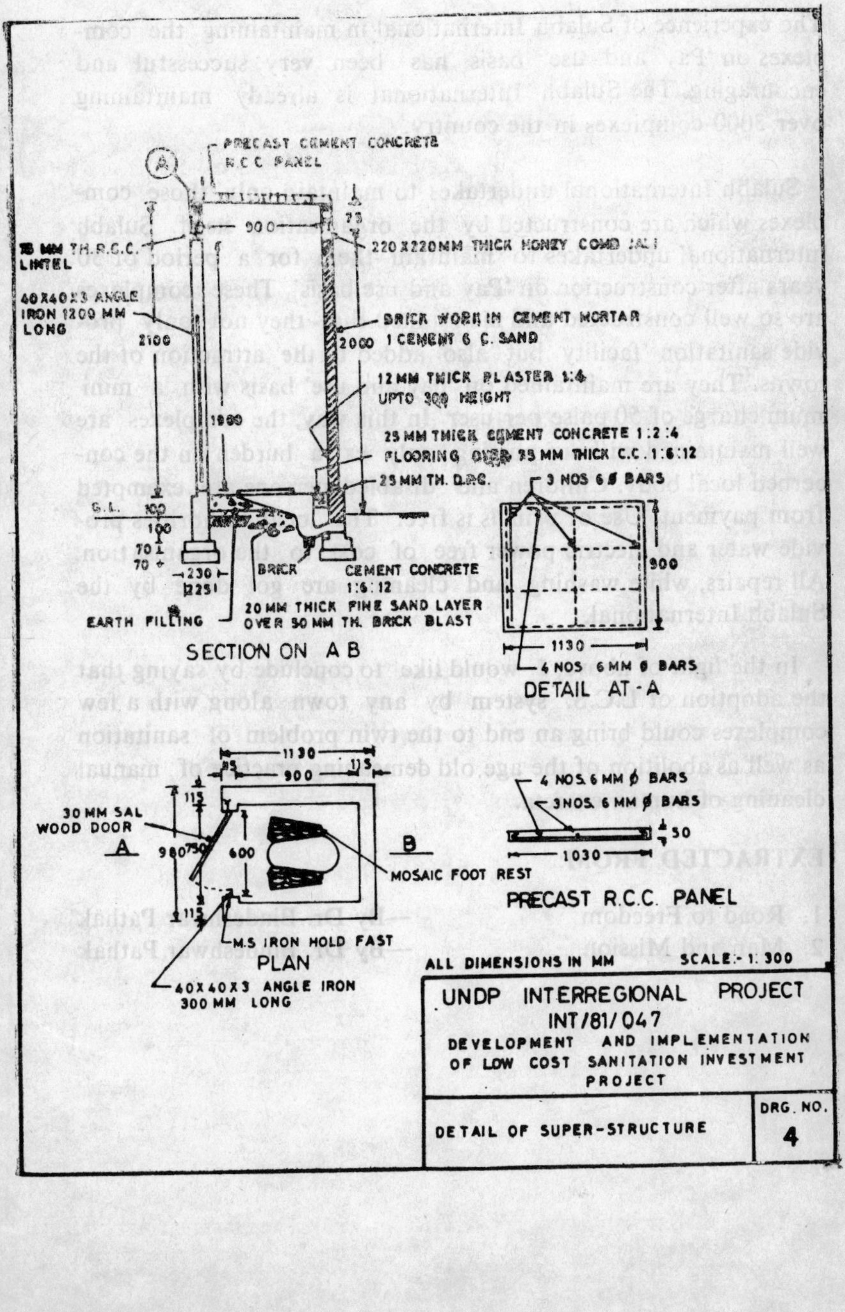
PRECAST CEMENT CONCRETE
R.C.C PANEL
75 MM TH.R.C.C. LINTEL
220 X 220 MM THICK HONEY COMB JALI
40 X 40 X 3 ANGLE IRON 1200 MM LONG
BRICK WORK IN CEMENT MORTAR 1 CEMENT 6 C. SAND
12 MM THICK PLASTER 1:4 UPTO 300 HEIGHT
25 MM THICK CEMENT CONCRETE 1:2:4 FLOORING OVER 75 MM THICK C.C. 1:6:12
25 MM TH. D.P.C.
G.L.
BRICK
CEMENT CONCRETE 1:6:12
20 MM THICK FINE SAND LAYER OVER 50 MM TH. BRICK BLAST
EARTH FILLING
SECTION ON A B
3 NOS 6 Ø BARS
4 NOS 6 MM Ø BARS
DETAIL AT - A
30 MM SAL WOOD DOOR
MOSAIC FOOT REST
M.S IRON HOLD FAST
PLAN
40 X 40 X 3 ANGLE IRON 300 MM LONG
4 NOS 6 MM Ø BARS
3 NOS 6 MM Ø BARS
PRECAST R.C.C. PANEL
ALL DIMENSIONS IN MM
SCALE:- 1: 300
UNDP INTERREGIONAL PROJECT
INT/81/047
DEVELOPMENT AND IMPLEMENTATION OF LOW COST SANITATION INVESTMENT PROJECT
DETAIL OF SUPER-STRUCTURE
DRG. NO. 4

The experience of Sulabh International in maintaining the complexes on 'Pay and use' basis has been very successful and encouraging. The Sulabh International is already maintaining over 3000 complexes in the country.

Sulabh International undertakes to maintain only those complexes which are constructed by the organisation itself. Sulabh International undertakes to maintain them for a period of 30 years after construction on 'Pay and use basis'. These complexes are so well constructed and maintained that they not only provide sanitation facility but also added to the attraction of the towns. They are maintained on 'pay and use' basis with a minimum charge of 50 paise per user. In this way, the complexes are well maintained without putting only extra burden on the concerned local body. Children and disabled persons are exempted from payment. Use of urinals is free. The local authorities provide water and electric power free of cost to the organisation. All repairs, white washing and cleaning are got done by the Sulabh International.

In the light of above, I would like to conclude by saying that the adoption of L.C.S. system by any town along with a few complexes could bring an end to the twin problem of sanitation as well as abolition of the age old demeaning practice of manual cleaning of human excreta.

EXTRACTED FROM:

1. Road to Freedom —By Dr. Bindeshwar Pathak
2. Man and Mission —By Dr. Bindeshwar Pathak

19

Housing Strategy for Shillong

A.K.M. Karim

1. The Problem and its Magnitude

Although housing is considered as a basic human need after food and cloth its problems, especially for the poor, are becoming more and more acute day by day. Not only the quantitative shortage is increasing alarmingly in the urban areas due to large scale rural urban and intra urban migration but the qualitative degradation of the existing housing stock is greately aggravating the problem. The poorer is the country the bigger is the problem. Even in the developed countries the problem is showing its urgly face.

As on 1st March 1981 the estimated urban Housing shortage in India is 7 millions and that in Meghalaya is about 5000 units. 6 (six) lakhs households were absolutely houseless in the country in 1981.

In 1991 out of 840 million population in Indian an estimated 51.2 million live in slums and squatter colonies and 50% urban households live in over-crowded one-room tenements.

The estimated shortage of dwelling units for Shillong urban agglomiration in 1991 is over 3000 units taking into account quantitative shortage, multi-family oecupancy and unserviceable houses.

2. Causes

The main causes of urban housing shortage are:

(i) Developed urban land and buildings cost very high and are beyond the reach of many.

(ii) Scarcity or suitable vacant developed urban land of appropriate size.

(iii) Shortage of appropriate cheap [durable local building materials.

(iv) Housing is capital intensive and many people do not have the large sums of money needed for housing at the initial stage.

(v) Shyness of the investors in Real Estate for fear of income-tax and wealth tax and loss of rental houses to tenants under the prevailing tenancy Acts favouring tenants.

3. Various Programmes being Implemented by Various Agencies

Government of India introduced ten types of Housing Schemes since 1952 which were regrouped into six categories in July, 1982. By and large these are the six schemes being implemented by the State Governments out of [Plan funds. They are the Housing Schemes for the—

(i) Economically Weaker Sections

(ii) Low Income Groups

(iii) Middle Income Groups

(iv) Rental Housing Scheme for State Government Employees

(v) Subsidised Housing Scheme for Plantation Workers

(vi) Rural Housing Scheme-cum-Construction Assistance.

4. The Present Agencies Involved in Housing

The Agencies involved in the field of Housing are:

I. *Housing Department*—It provides—

(i) Subsidy of roofing materials under Rural Housing Scheme and for EWS/LIG Loan-cum-subsidy programme

(ii) Rental Housing Scheme for State Government employees

(iii) Cluster Demonstration of Low Cost Housing Colonies for E.W.S. Houseless Villagers

(iv) Night Shelter for the poors visiting the towns

II. *Community and Rural Development Department*—Executing the Indira Awaas Yojana.

III. *Housing Building Advance to the Employees by Government Departments (State and Central) and various Agencies.*

IV. *State Apex Housing Co-operative Society*—They cover the members of the Primary Co-operative Societies.

V. *Meghalaya State Housing Board*—

(i) Loan to all categories on HUDCO norms for construction, renovation and extension of houses.

(ii) Proposed Schemes include sale on Hire Purchase of ready built houses.

The All India Level Organisations Are

VI. *Housing Development Finance Corporation (H.D.F.C.)*

VII. *Nationalised Banks*:—Recently decided to give loan at 17% (seventeen per cent) interest.

VIII. *Life Insurance Corporation*:—Offer loan to policy holders under "Own your Home" scheme @ 80% of insured polity at 11% interest.

IX. *H.P.F.C.*—Housing Promotion and Financing Agency, a subsidiary of the State Bank of India.

X. *N.H.B.*—National Housing Bank a Subsidiary of Reserve Bank of India operating by now the well-known 'Home Loan Accounts Scheme'.

Many houses are being built by the Urban Development Authorities, Self Financing Housing Societies, Real Estate Agents and Other Non-Governmental Organisations.

5. Bottlenecks/Problems

(i) Deserving families cannot take advantage of various schemes as most of them do not possess suitable land for mortgaging against loan.

(ii) Many do not come forward due to ignorance and inability to comply with the formalities involved even in filling up of forms.

(iii) Housing Loans, like commercial loans have high rates of interest and short periods of repayment. So people are not very keen to take them.

(iv) In Meghalaya the Meghalaya Land Transfer Act restricts purchase of land even by other Government and Semi Government agencies and restricts financing institutions from taking land in mortgage against housing loans advanced by them.

Therefore, the only Housing Agencies in Meghalaya that can give loan to any eligible individual without much difficulty are the State Housing Board, Meghalaya Co-operative Apex Bank and Apex Housing Financing Society.

6. Actions taken so Far

The Government and the organised sectors help in constructing houses within the six Schemes mentioned earlier. But their action is so limited that majority of the houses are built by individuals in the unorganised sectors.

Apart from introducing various housing schemes after independence the Government of India also set up the National Building Organisation and the Central Building Research Institute, the former to disseminate information on housing and the later for research on housing. Various other National research laboratories are also working in this field eg. the Regional Research Laboratories.

In 1972 the Housing and Urban Developed Corporation was set up as a prime institute for channelising institutional finance for housing and urban development and for giving technical guidance in this direction. The HUDCO became the Central Nodal Agency in India for Housing Finance and for setting up National Norms. Slowly many other Institutions like H.D.F.C. etc. were set up.

Various concepts that were used for providing affordable houses are:

(i) Aided self help where (a) Loan/grant is given (b) basic materials are supplied (c) Prefabricated units are supplied

(ii) Incremental Housing with core units

(iii) Inducement for using local materials directly or in modified forms.

(iv) Inducement for using low cost housing technology.

In 1976, Government of India circulated the Urban Land Ceiling Act to be adopted by various State Governments with the basic objective of taking away the surplus vacant urban land from individuals for utilising it for public housing. Some States including Meghalaya did not adopt this Act.

Housing for the poor also were included in the Minimum Needs Programme and 20 Point Programme.

On May 12th 1988 the Government of India adopted the National Housing Polity in the Parliament with its objective to:

(a) motivate and help all people and in particular, the houseless and the inadequately housed, to secure for themselves affordable shelter through access to land, materials, technology and finance;

(b) encourage investment in housing in order to achieve a sustained growth of the nation's housing stock, and its proper conservation, renovation and upgradation;

(c) create an enabling environment by eliminating constraints and developing an efficient and accessible system for the delivery of inputs to maximise housing efforts;

(d) improve the environment of human settlements with a view of raising the quality of life through the provision of drinking water, sanitation and other basic services;

(e) Promote vernacular architecture and preserve the nation's rich heritage in the field of human settlements.

Its Priorities Are:

(a) the Scheduled Castes and Scheduled Tribes and freed bonded labour;

(b) rural landless labour, including artisans;

(c) widows, single women and women-headed house-holds;

(d) economically weaker sections;

(e) low-income-groups;

(f) victims of natural calamities

The National Housing Polity emphasised that the various agencies should not act as builders but as facilitators by providing developed plots, housing finance, low-cost building materials and technical guidance. As its follow up action the National Housing Bank was set up for housing finance and Building Centres are being set up for low cost building components produced on co-operative basis using indigenous materials. The Policy also highlights the role of Non-Governmental Organisations and of streamlining legal and administrative procedures.

In Meghalaya, a State Housing Polity was adopted in the Assembly on 29.4.88 where the main thrust was laid on Housing for the poor especially in the rural areas by advancing highly subsidised soft loans and building materials subsidy to the poor, exemption of stamp duty, facilitating the preparation of land documents and providing single window service. As per the polity all bottlenecks are to be removed to facilitiate smooth flow of Institutional Finance for Housing for all the categories.

As follow up of this Policy we have already exempted EWS/LIG beneficiaries from Stamp Duty, supplying C.G.I. sheets as grant and susidy to 5822 families since 1988.

7. Suggested Strategy for Shillong Urban Agglomeration

To meet the immediate shortage of over 3000 units of Shillong urban agglomeration of 1991 we need over Rs. 30.00 crores at an all-inclusive cost of Rs. 1.00 lakh per units for land, services, infrastructure and housing; majority in single and two roomed tenements. Many of them will have to be in the form of rental accommodation. We will also have to embark upon sites and services programme coupled with cash loans.

This will need concerted effort of all concerned agencies.

20

Hapazard Growth of IEWDUH (Barabazar) Shillong

(A Case Study)

P. C. Biswas

Since the shifting of the military Head Quarters of the Chief Commissioner of Assam from Saidsophen (Cherrapunji) to Shillong a tiny village (Laban) with only 1363 inhabitants in 1872, in the year 1864, the town grew centering round this military Head Quarters. When the seperate state of Assam was formed, Shillong was made the capital of Assam in 1874 and remained so except for an intervening period from 1905 to 1911, when the capital was had been shifted to Dacca. The town developed in the later years as the administrative centre and as a sanatorium. The British rulers took care to build it as a beautiful town for their comfortable living. They had their military establishment in a vast area, known as Cantonment, in the centre of the town itself. The civil administration comprised the three areas: Jail road, where settlement was given to the Government employees, Police bazar, where businessmen were accomodated and Lachumiere (European Ward), residence of the European officers. These areas were known as normal areas or British area. Naturally there was some syrt of planned development of these areas. Following the growing activities of the military and the civil administration, people from the rural areas and also from outside the district were increasingly coming to settle in the town and the town grew beyond the said three normal areas, which remained under the jurisdiction of Tribal Chiefs (Syiems).

When the Shillong Municipal Board was formed in 1910 under the Bengal Municipal Act, 1884, it comprised only the normal area. However lateron for the purpose of rendering municipal pervices, the Syiem ceded his power on these areas to the Municipality. With the growth of economic activities amongst the local people, for selling their surplus product and purchasing the daily essential commodities, IEWDUH started developing as the main business centre, but it remained outside the British administration.

IEWDUH was considered, not only as a weekly market but as a sacred place, where the Syiem used to offer Pujas near the monoliths, invoking God's blessing for the welfare of the people.

Originally there was no permanant shop in IEWDUH and the people assembled there once a week for marketing and after the days business, they dispersed. The main outlet for transporting the local products, fruits, vegetables, minerals etc. was through sylhet district and the business extended upto Dacca and the commercial goods also came from this channel. As a result wholesale businessmen had their centres near the bordering areas of Sylhet and common markets developed. It was through such interconnection that outside businessmen, particularly from Sylhet district and also Dacca since 1840 and Rajasthan were attracted to start their business at IEWDUH and with the permission of the Syiem, started constructing permanant shop buildings in the area, which augmented the coffers of the Syiem and benefited the local people also. Even though it was averred in the court of Law that originally Barabazar was included within the Shillong Municipality, being Holding No. 1, there being no proof of it, the Court did not accept this contention. There was neither any proof that the Syiem ever had ceded his power to the Municipality for administering Municipal services. So the area remained under the exclusive jurisdiction of the Syiem. Neither the State Government not the Municipality had any authority over Barabazar and it grew spontaneously without any body to look after its planned development. The Syiem had no paraphernalia and the necessary financial resources at his disposal in administering essential civic services like drianage, garbage clearance, sanitation, roads etc. to this area and the mushrooming growth of shop buildings went on without any control whatsoever, to the point of suffocation. After the independence, when the District Counil was formed with jurisdiction over the tribal area including Barabazr, there was no indication that it took any interest over the haphazard growth of Barabazar or in respect of the vital necessity of providing the essential civic services to the area. Neither did it exercise its authority in laying some guideline to the Syiem for settlement of shops and the specification for the same and providing necessary finance etc. for the administration of the bazar. So in the midst of the socalled "Scotland of the East" and the "shining patch of beauty" as Shillog was described by Prof. G. G. Swell in one of his election manifesto, Barabazar projects an ugly spot in the panorama of Shillong.

It is really an enigma that while Barabazar is under the jurisdiction of the Tribal Institutions, i.e. the Syiem, the District Council and the State Government in the head, dominated by the Tribal representatives themselves, why is it that it has been long neglected, allowing its mushroom growth without any semblance of planning whatsoever.

There was no reliable figures as regards the number of permanant shop buildings, set up by the Tribals and the non-tribals, how many were built with the approval of the Syiem, how many stalls and pedlars sitting on the sides of roads and byelanes and how many tribals transferred their shops to the non-tribals etc. However from some years past awide-spread feeling is sought to be created that the non-tribal traders are dominating and the tribals are being deprived of their traditional right over the bazar. Even though the District Council passed an Act (The Khasi Hills Autonomous District Trading by Non-Tribals, Regulation) was passed in 1954, the Rules laying down the proccdure for securing the necessary licence by the non-tribals, were framed in 1959 and even after that, the provisions of the same were not implemented. When the Regulation was sought to be implemented, the matter was taken to the High Court. In the mean time there were several amendments, making the provisions more rigid, giving rise to legal complications and generating social and political tension.

According to the version of the Barabazar Merchants Association (comprising the non-tribal traders) they had 1139 members in their list. There might be more non-tribal traders who were not members of the Association, but still carring on their business in the bazar. Out of these 1139 members, 694 applied to the District Council in prescribed form seeking licence in 1987. But only a few of the applicants were given licence, keeping other applications still pending. According to the Mylliem Durbar, 542 cases of the non-tribal trader's applications were recommended by them. In the mean time more than two thousand applications are said to have been accumulated in the office of the District Council. The problem has assumed serious dimension and no body knows how to settle the matter to the satisfaction of all concerned. While it cannot but be admitted that there must be reasonable restriction to the increasing flow of non-tribal traders into Barabazar, the demand for clearing the Barabazar the "sacred market place of the Tribals" of all the non-tribal traders could not be accepted to any rational man and it is not to the interest of the tribal themselves, as it would seriously dislocate the whole economy of the state itself and it is also not possible to push the history two hundred years back and make Shillong a tiny village again or only a military centre as in 1864, However the root cause for recurring disturbances centering round Barabazar i.e. the uncontrolled growth of Barabazar, with ever increasing flow of non-tribal traders, creating social and political tension, must be faced by the authorities concerned.

Two years back there was talk of establishing an alternate Bazar for removing the congestion of Barabazar and accomodating the intending Tribal traders. But nothing has yet come out of it. Now that the Defence Ministry is said to have agreed to leave a portion of the Cantonment at the disposal of the State Government an alternative marketing complex may and should be established in a planned way, which apart from minimising the cause of discontent and tension amongst the tribals, would given a face lift to and beautify Shillong. At the same time ways and means must be found how to renovate the existing Barabazar complex, with adequate civic services, bringing it under the perview of Greater Shillong Mater Plan and execution of the adopted scheme, should start with Barabazar.

The following suggestions may be placed before the authoritie concerned for consideration.

1. The State Government while not interfering with the day-to-day management of the Barabazar, must intervene through its Tribal Affairs Deptt., for cordination and adoption of a scheme to rationalise the settlement of shop buildings in Barabazar to both tribals and non-tribal traders.

2. The Syiem of Myliiem who is the traditional owner of Barabazar, should be given sufficient resources for updating the civic services, particularly drianage system and garbage clearing etc. with sufficient staff and equipment at his disposal.

3. A local Body under the Municipal Act may be formed with the Syiem at the head, under the overall guidance of the District Council for management of the bazar.

4. Immediate steps should be taken to dispose of the pending applications for licence.

21

The Muslims of Shillong : An Observation

Saifun Nessa

This study does not remain confined only to the decade 1981-91, but depicts a picture of the Muslim society in Shillong in its historical perspective. Secondary source materials relevant to the subject, were consulted. Besides this, data were collected by interviewing a few persons, experienced in the field.

In order to know about 'Shillong and her Muslim relation', one needs to hark back to the history of Cherrapunji during pre-British and British period. Cherrapunji is that historical spot of Khasi hills which had experienced Muslim contact earlier than the advent of the British. Ofcourse, recorded history is available only after the British annexation.

It is learnt that the Khasis and the Bengali Muslim traders entered into trade relation in the pre-British days. This resulted in the migration of a few families in the border areas in both the directions. In 1841, Robinson recorded about a Muslim setlement in the Khasi hills.[1] In 1871; 49.7 per cent of the total population of the district of Sylhet were Muslims.[2] Trade and commerce in the Khasi hills were mainly carried on the southern part (present Bangladesh), Trade relation extended upto Calcutta, which was made possible through river traffic.

In the Statistical Account of Assam, Hunter mentions in detail that the hills possessed the monopoly of supplying Bengal with lime, potatoes and oranges. Other articles of export included bay leaves, betal nut, 'pan', black paper, honey, fruits, tember, bees wax etc. Hunter writes, "The local trade is entirely in the hands of the Khasis themselves, and the larger portion of the produces is despatched direct to Calcutta".[3] Imported articles included brass pots and pans, crushed rice, cloth of sorts, pulse, fish and dry fish, oil, salt, sugar, tea, coffee, tobacco, wines, wheat flour etc. There were no Marwari or Jain Merchants. "There are a few Bengali traders from Dacca, who do not take up a permanent residence in the hills'.[4]

Khasi hills were never under any Muslim rulers nor there entered any Muslim preachers. They entered in search of avenues for survivals and as traders. The Khasis like many other tribes preferred an independent life and so neither wanted to be exploited nor wanted to establish contact with outsiders. M'Cosh mentions, "They are proud of their mountains, and look down with contempt upon the degenerate race of the plains . . . . warlike and brave in actions".[5]

The Khasis strongly resisted British penetration and went to the extent of killing British officers Bedingfields and Burlton and nearly fifty native sepoys. almost 160 years ago.[6] In 1835 Nongklao was made the headquarters of British administration and continued till 1854. From the year 1854 to 1864, Cherrapunji remained as the headquarter. During 1864-66, the station was shifted to Shillong—a small village. When the Provice of Assam was created in 1874, then Shillong was made the permanent seat of local administration and in 1905 with the creation of the Province of Eastern Bengal and Assam, Dacca was made its capital and Shillong remained as its summer capital.

The British officers bewitched by the natural beauty and salubrious climate of Shillong named this land as a "Little England', "Queen of the hills in India" and as the 'Scotland of the East'. They took keen interest and trouble for planned development and beautification of Shillong. They generously accepted the helping hands of the Muslims in those matters.

Shillong remained as the capital of Assam till 1971. During the last two decades (since January 1972) Shillong has been making significant progress but by retaining her traditional charm. Since 1972, Shillong has been the capital of Meghalaya. Being an administrative centre for more than a century Shillong has been attracting a large number of people from other parts of the country.

The Muslim-Khasi Relation

Few Muslim traders from Bengal were known to have entered Cherrapunji in the middle of the 19th century. They entered with the support of the East India Company. Due to the transfer of capital, along with the European officers those Muslims shifted to Shillong in 1860's. This group of Bengali Muslims can safely be considered as the early Muslim settlers of Shillong. Their fourth and fifth generation descendants are scattered in Laban and Police Bazar areas of Shillong. They purchased land from the British government and became the owners of considerably larger Estates.

In the middle of the 19th century trader Gulam Hyder and his son Kasimuddin from Hoogly district of Bengal entered Cherrapunji through the Goaland-Chattak route. The distance was first covered by boat and then on foot. J. N. Choudhuri comments about Gulam Hyder,—"He came in quest of business and earned the nickname of *Bakshawala* as he carried his merchandise in large boxes. With the shifting of the civil station from Cherrapunji, he migrated to Shillong in 1864".[7] In Shillong the purchased the Rook Wood compound and Snowy View area in Police Bazar from Mr. D. Inglis. They also purchased the land where the present Bijou Cinema, Broadway complex, Islamia school, Mohini Store complex, Muslim Union Guest House etc., are located. The other areas which were purchased by other early settler are mentioned under the section 'The Muslim Trust' of this paper.

Gulam Hyder and his son were the pioneers in Shillong in several fields. Besides being General Merchants and Bankers they opened Departmental Stores in Police Bazar, Oilman's Store and Boots and shoes. They sold patent medicine and opened stationaries. They took up haberdashery, millinery and perfumery. They were the crockery merchants, confectioners and Soda Water manufacturers. They were the proprietors of the Imperial Dairy, Shillong and also started a printing press. Thus, they introduced new economic activities and have been contributing significantly towards the economic and socio-cultural development of Shillong.

The British government was highly satisfied with the works of Kasimuddin and felicitated him with the 'Khan Bahadur' title in 1915, In 1888, Kasimuddin Molla secured a contract from the British government to begin the first Shillong-Gauhati Daily Passenger (horse drawn) Tonga Service. That used to cover 64 miles up and down in a day. Earlier to that people were carried on *Thapa* (a basket), mainly in the Bholaganj-Cherrapunji route. Then developed the Bullock cart. In the Shillong-Gauhati route, it continued side by side with the Tonga service.

The first Shillong-Gauhati Motor car service, on commercial basis started in 1906. Kasimuddin took the initiative and he was permitted to ply the first two passenger buses named 'Ranee' and 'Maha Rani' in the Shillong-Gauhati Road. A young Muslim lady, Begum A. N. Mowla Buksh was the first Indian lady to travel in an 'Albion' passenger bus on the inauguration of the Shillong-Gauhati service which stated an era in the motor transport in this region.[8]

Initially, there were two Anglo Indian drivers; they were Mr. Pokos and Mr. Douglas[9], and then on advertisement drivers from Bengal were inducted. Remembered among them are Harihar Banerjee, Haridas Das and Banku Bihari Ghosh.

The first Electric Dynamo for the workshop in Shillong was brought around 1906. The Gulam Hyder building in Police Bazar was the first building in Shillong to have electric lights. The building had collapsed in the devasting earthquake of 1897 and it was reconstructed in 1906 (again gutted in 1989). Kasimuddin constructed a number of buildings in Shillong. "It is claimed that he constructed the first mosque in Shillong, and also a church, the Church of England, near the State Central Library and the Government Press. The latter construction was done under his contractorship".[10]

Kasimuddin's son Mowla Buksh has also contibuted significantly towards the infrastructural development of Shillong, Besides constructing many buildings in Shillong, this renowned contractor took up the construction work of the Shillong. Gauhati road and diverted the Umkhrah river near. Polo ground,

Due to the development of road transport, establishment of government offices and business complexes, besides other groups of people, Muslims from Assam, Bihar, Uttar Pradesh, Punjab and Bengal entered Shillong and settled down. The muslims who came from the district of Sylhet were inducted in the offices in Shillong. This led to a steady growth of Muslim population in Shillong.

Composition

The Muslims of Shillong are concentrated in Laban, Lumpering, Police Bazar, Jail Road, Garikhana, Jhalupara, Barapather and Laitumkhrah. Majority of them are *Sunnis* and only a small section belongs to the *Shia* section.

Barring a few families of early Bengali muslim traders some Muslim males established marital relations with the Khasi women. A few Khasi women were converted to Islam and on conversion they adapted to the Islamic way of life. Mathur's field study has located more than 50 Muslim-Khasi families in Laban.[11] In the majority of such families the tradition of the mother predominate, but they are Muslims so far religion is concerned. Children born of such union suffix the Khasi tiles along with their Islamic names.

A most remarkable trend found in these families is the changing role of the 'Khadduh' (the youngest daughter). In Khasi matriliny she inherits the ancentral property. She has to perform certain specific religious and social obligations. In the Muslim-Khasi families she is not entitled to the lion's share of the property because she does not have to fulfil the above mentioned obligations. Mathur writes, "In a majority of the Muslim-Khasi householsd, the position of the youngest daughter has been changed as she has no longer to perform . . . . the religious rites, and fulfil the social obligations".[12]

Islam could not make such headway in the Khasi society compared to christianity. It is due to the fact that the Muslims never tried to convert the Khasis in an organized manner like the christian missionaries. Only a few women were converted to Islam due to affinal relations, and their children are guided by the regulations of both the traditions. This group of people are basically engaged in sorts of business where the wives stand by their husbands.

The group of Hindustani speaking Muslims include butchers, bakers, quilt makers, barbers, washermen and tailors. There is also a number of Behari muslim beggers, who cali themselves Faqir (Mustim saints), but are engaged in the un-Islamic activity of begging.

There are a number of Assamese Muslim families in Shillong. They basically started their life in Shillong as office goeps. This group of people is hardly attentive to trade and commerce.

During the last two decades, some Muslims entered Shillong and are engaged in petty business. The first category includes the group of Bengali Muslims who belong to the Murshidabad distrist of West Bengal. They are engaged in selling sundries and send a major portion of their earning for their families in Murshidabad. Occupationally, they resemble the 'Bara-Masiyas' —a wandering gipsy like people who move from place to place on certain fairs and festivals. This group of people are temporarily residing in Shillong.

The second category includes the Bangladeshi refugees who first entered Assam and then Meghalaya. The Assam agitation demanding the deportation of foreign nationals during the last two decades made the life of the Bangladeshi refugees insecured. In such situations, migration is the possible solution. A section of such an industrious Bangladeshi Muslim youths have entered Shillong and are engaged in selling eggs and vegetables. Some of them are also engaged as day labourers. Their families are left behind in the *char* (river islet) areas of the Brahmaputra Valley. If this process of silent migration continues unhampered then in near future this group of people will pose a threat to the lower rank (economically) of the Khasi petty business persons which include the hardworking Khasi women.

Number of Muslim Population in Shillong

The census data hardly provide any quantification of the different groups of Muslims residing in Shillong. This gives us the following accounts: In the year 1879, Hunter recorded only 62 Muhammadans in the Khasi hills.[13].

In 1901, in the Shillong town group out of a tolal population of 9621, 646 souls were Muslims. In 1911, the total population was 13,639 and of that 847 persons were Muslims. In 1921, out of

17,203 persons, 991 persons were Muslims. In 1931, of 26,536 persons, 1423 were Muslims. In 1941, of a total of 38,192 persons 3026 were Muslims. In 1951, there was a decrease in numbers due to the partition of India and it was 2418 souls only out of a total number of 58,512 persons. The void so created was gradually filled up and in 1961, the number of Muslim population increased to 5154 while the total population also increased to 1,02,398 numbers.[14] Since 1961 Census, Shillong urban agglomeration has been recorded as Class-I town.[15]

In 1971 Census of India, Meghalaya had a population of 10,11,699 of which 26,347 persons were Muslims. In 1981 Census of India, Muslims constituted 3.10 per cent i.e. 41,434 persons out of a total population of 13,35,819 in the state of Meghalaya.[16]

Muslim Religious Organizations

Shillong is a cosmopolitan town. Churches, Temples, Mosques and Gurudwaras are located in different areas of the town. It is a historical fact that whenever there is a concentration of a religious community there grows a religious organization. Mosques are located in those areas where there are Muslim settlements. There are six mosques in Shillong.

The Police Bazar mosque was constructed before the year 1897. It is known to the people of Shillong, that the devasting earthquake of 1897 took the life of the 'Imam' while he was offering his afternoon prayer. Today, approximately three hundred males offer their special Friday prayer at the 'Masjid'. In the Laban 'Masjid' too approximately two hundred males offer their Friday prayer.

The Laitumkhrah Masjid was established in 1934 on public donation. Its founder President was Late Ali Ahmed, a Chief Engineer of undivided Assam. A huge gathering offer their Friday prayer at the Garikhana Masjid which was donated by Elahi Buksh.

The Iqra Library, which is housed in the Garikhana Masjid compound, has been making significant contribution towards the spread of knowledge of the Islamic religion.

With the intention of providing facilities to devotees, two Masjids were constructed in Bara Bazar and Bora Pathar respectively. These two Masjids emerged after the creation of Meghalaya. Special 'Idd' prayers are conducted in these Masjids and in the 'Idgahs' (field) at Laban and Mawprem. The Muslims have got separate burial grounds. In the old Lumbering graveyard a tomb was built over the grave of a 'Sufi'-sant known as Shah Noor Baba. Muslims and even non-Muslims believe in its spiritual power and visit the tomb to get their wishes fulfilled.

The Shillong Muslim Union

To maintain their separate identity and to consolidate their society according to the Islamic norms, the Shillong Muslim Union was formed long back in 1905. After the formation of Meghalaya, the elaborate constitution of the Union was remodelled in 1975. Now, the jurisdiction of the Union extends to all parts but of the state of Meghalaya only. The aim of the Union is to achieve 'social, cultural, religious, economic and educational betterment of the Muslim of Shillong in particular and other parts of Meghalaya in general'.[17]

According to its objectives it has been offering financial assistance to the poor, handicapped persons, widows and needy orphan children. The Union asists for the better management of the 'Masjids', 'Idgahs' and Kabarstans' (graveyards). It also organizes religious functions and festivals. The Union offers assistance, both in cash and kind to other parts of Meghalaya during crisis arising from natural calamities and also to the victims of social conflicts. By acting as a 'buffer' between the State government and the Muslim public, it draws financial assistance from the government which is percolated down for the welfare of the masses.

The Muslim Trust: *WAKF*

Before the creation of Meghalaya, Shillong was placed under the jurisdiction of the Assam State Wakf Board. After the creation of Meghalaya the independent Meghalaya Wakf Board was constituted, by the Law Department of the Government of Meghalaya. This was constituted under the Wakf Act of 1954. Wakf means the permanent dedication by a person professing Islam of any property for any purpose recognised by the Islamic Law as religious, pious or Charitable.[18] The Board looks after the weifare of the wakf property.

In Shillong, the Wakf property includes:

1. All the 'Masjids', as mentioned above and the 'Idgahs' and graveyards. This category is known as 'Wakf-ul-Lilla'.

2. The Family Wakf or 'Wakf-ul-Aulad': Some of the early Muslim settlers of Shillong purchased considerable areas of land from the British government for business and residential purposes. To keep these family property intact, to stop division and fragmentation and for the benefit of the greater Muslim community, those estates were dedicated to the Wakf Board. Thus, a Wakf property can neither be sold nor divided, not it can be disputed property. A share of the income goes to the descendants of the Wakif (dedicator).

The family Wakf in Shillong are the following:

1. Hazi Elahi Buksh Wakf Estate, surrounding the Garikhana Masjid.

   a) Lila Brothers and Super Bazar areas,

   b) Some areas in Paltan Bazar,

   c) Some areas in Jhalupara and

   d) The Sweeper's Colony in Bara Bazar.

2. Gulam Rahman Wakf Estate, which includes the areas of:

   a) District Employment Office, Keating Road,

   b) An area near the Taxi Stand in Police Bazar (opposite to the Assembly Library),

   c) An area at the junction of the Polo Bazar Main Road and Thana Road, and

   d) A plot near the Dreamland Cinema Hall.

3. Hazi Kasimuddin Molla Wakf Estate: This includes:

   a) The area from the Meghalaya Co-operative Apex Bank in Police Bazar to the Rook Wood Cottage at Kachari Road,

   b) The Police Bazar Mosque.

Another Estate known as Sheikh Umed Wakf Estate at Laban had to be alienated from the Wakf list. The Wakf Board's negligence caused such alienation. The Board remained silent when the Estate was enchroached after the death of the Wakf.

Women's Organization

The Muslim women of Shillong are not lagging behind. With the aim of stabilizing the community and to establish a unity among the Muslim women of Shillong, the Shillong Mahila Majlish was formed in 1958, under the Presidentship of Begum Z.A. Rahman. This is a socio-religious association of the Muslim Women of Shillong. In its 35 years of life, the Majlish has been rendering valuable service. particularly to the Muslim community by providing financial assistance to the widows and divorces and to the poor and needy Muslims. The members have provided shelter to old and destitute Muslim women.

The Majlish used to run an English medium Nursery school at a nominal fee. When the Muslim Union found it difficult to run the Laban Muslim Girls' L.P. School, then it entrusted the responsibility to the Majlish in 1963 and the Majlish could successfully run it till 1983.[19] Later on, the Nursery school had to be closed down due to lack of public cooperation. The administration of the L.P. School was again shifted to the Muslim Union. The Majlish stands by the Social Welfare Board and contributes generously in cash and kind to the flood, draught and riot affected people.

Cultural Activities of the Muslims

Participation of the Muslims in the cultural life of Shillong deserves special mention. Prominent Muslim artists have been participating in various cultural programmes organized by different cultural organizations in the city. People of Shillong acknowledge the contibution of the Music teachers. Mention may be made of Jonab Ershad Ali (before Independence), Jonab Moti Mia (before 1950) and his sons Chuni Mia and Surja Mia and Jonab Phool Mohammad. Jonab Khan is still continuing with his instrumental music.

The artists have been participating in the cultural programmes organized by Kohinoor Club, Manju Smriti Majlish, Giti Notya Samaj etc. Earlier to that (before Independence) some worked for Bengal Institute-concert party, Assam Bengal Theatre and so on Late Mowla Buksh, Late Md. Amanat Ullah popularly known as Tunu Babu and late Md. Ahmed Ullah popularly known as Dhon Babu were the members of the former.

The Kohinoor Club (established in 1932-33) is basically a Muslim cultural organization. Late Aulad Hossain who was a member of the Club could gain considerable appreciation for his stage performance (drama). His son Jonab Afzar Hossain is a founder member of the Manju Smriti Majlish and notably a founder organizer of Ananda Sammelon in Shillong. Assamese Muslim singers include Asad Mahmood (son of Tunu Babu) and Adil and Hosna. Mst. Geetiara Hossain (grand-daughter of

Aulad Hossain) could also acquire considerable recognition as a singer.

Conclusion

In the foregoing pages we have discussed the emergence and growth of the Muslim society in Shillong. Any study in the last 130 years history of Shillong is incomplete without highlighting the contributions of the Muslims in diverse fields as has been depicted above. Political personalities of the composite state of Assam like Syed Saadullah, Fakruddin Ali Ahmed and Moinul Haque Choudhury are remembered for their contribution toward the socio-political life of Shillong.

The Muslims could establish a firm hold in Shillong due to their expertise, religious tolerance and willingness to assimilate with the locals. Due to such tendencies they could bring the isolated, conservative and orthodox Khasi women to their fold through matrimonial alliances. This has produced the Khasi community. Besides establishing affinity with the Khasis, the Muslims have also established cordial relations with other groups of people living in the city. They participate in the non-religious aspect of the religio-cultural festivals and ceremonies of the other groups of people, notably of the Hindus.

The impact of the Khasi matrilineal system on the lives of the Muslim women of Shillong deserve special mention. As in Islam, in the Khasi tradition too, the women are given a high status in society. However, due to socio-historical causes and to protect the women from the social evils there developed the system of 'Purdah' and 'Burkha' for the Muslim women. Practically, it compels the Muslim women to live a life of seculsion and backwardness. The Khasi tradition provides ample opportunities to the Muslim women to progress, which conforms to the Islamic ideology. As a result, the Muslim women of Shillong are marching together with the Khasi women and are getting education and employment. They are progressing in the proper direction keeping in mind the Islamic principles of honesty and modesty.

REFERENCES

1. Robinson, W., *A Destrciptive History of Assam*, (Sanskaran Prakashak, Delhi 1841, Reprint, 1975), p. 408.
2. Hunter, W.W., *A Statistical Account of Assam, Vol. II*, (B.R. Publishing Corporation, Delhi, 1879, Reprint 1982), p. 273, Section (The Statistical Account of Sylhet).
3. *Ibid*, p. 239.
4. *Ibid*, p. 241.
5. M'Cosh, *Topography of Assam* (*Sanskaran Prakashan*, Delhi, 1837, Reprint 1975), p. 161.
6. Pemberton, P.B., *The Eastern Frontier of India*, (Mittal Publications, Delhi, 1835, Reprint 1979), p. 223.
7. Choudhuri, J.N., *The Khasi Canvas*, (Published by Jaya Choudhuri, Quinton Road, Shillong 1, No page number.
8. Shillong Mahila Majlish, *Sliver Jubllee Year*, 1958-1983 No page number.
9. Choudhuri, J.N., *Op. cit*,
10. Mathur, P.R.G., *The Khasi of Meghalaya* (Cosmo Publications New Delhi, 1979).
11. *Ibid*, p. 44.
12. *Ibid*, p. 54.
13. Hunter, W.W., *Op. cit*., p. 215.
14. Mathur, P.R.G., p. 8.

15. Census of India, *General Population, Table*, Series 13. Meghalaya Part II-A, p. 58.

16. Marwein P.T., *Meghalaya Hand Book* (Warphlang, Garikhana Road, Shillong, Second edition, 1987), p. 17.

17. The Shillong Muslim Union, *The Constitution*, 1979, P.I.,

18. The Wakf Act. 1954, Section 3

19. Shillong Mahila Majlish, *op. cit.*

22

The Changing Attitude Towards Working Women : A Panoramic view through Decade in Shillong

Geetanjali Baruah

It is well known that the world today is rapidly changing, and these changes are multidimensional. Socially one of the most fundamental and remarkable change which brought forth since India's Independence is the emergence of woman the exclusive seclusion of their home into the activities of the world at large.

Social change that India has witnessed since Independence have effected it's entire population. Yet in some sections of the society the impact is much more marked than in others. Among the urban educated population, effect of such change is more marked among the women than that of it's counterpart. Particularly after Independence, the socio-economic conditions have expanded opportunities for women's education and employment, which provided them with new avenues to express and assert their equality. The socio economic change lead the urban educated women in India, to achieve a new status and new role that wiped out their age old ideologies.

It is true that every known economic system has been utilizing and perhaps requiring the work of women. They are working not only for their maintenance but also for their satisfaction as human being and as member of the society for the betterment of the country at large.

However, Indian Women working outside their home is not a new phenomenon. As India are always working in the agricultural fields along with men with same tenacity since antique. In urban India also women are working in factories as menial workers and as construction labour since long.

But, taking up of employment outside the four walls of their home by the educated women is comparatively a recent phenomenon. As such the urban educated working women comprise comparatively a recent emerging social group which is drawing attention of laymen as well as of scholars.

While studying social change it is essential to study the changes that are occuring in society due to the spread of education and employment of women. As because, education of women and their position in a society reveals the extent of development of that society. As well as, the economic status of women is regarded and accepted as an indicator of a society's stage of development. However, the status of any given section of population in a society is intimately connected with its economic position, which in turn depends on rights, roles, opportunities for participation in economic activities. Therefore to ascertain women's position is vital, because it will indicate the trend of social change as a whole. At this juncture, it will be relevant to clarify what the term 'status' means. The term status according to social scientists means a position in the society. The dictionary meanings of the term status are condition, position, rank, importance in a society or in any group. Hence, study of women's economic role as well as her position as a worker would definitely help to determine her position or status in the society.

This paper tries to ascertain the attitudinal change towards educated woking women. Because it is important to study this position of urban, educated working women from whom one can assess the pulse of changing Indian womanhood.

In this juncture it should be made clear at the very outset that this study is purely an attitude survey and carried out only among the Assamese and Bengali inhabitants of Shillong. For this purpose 50 working women of different disciplines serving in Shillong are interviewed and 50 relatives of two ascending as well as two descending generations of these women are also interviewed to determine the changing attitude. There might be many scholars who may contend that attitude surveys do not have much to do with reality or practice. However, many social psychologists have assumed that attitudes have something to do with social behaviour. They consider attitudes at precursors of behaviour, as determinants of how a person will actually behave in his/her daily affairs.

Further, attitudes of a person or of a group of persons have a far reaching effect on their covert and overt behaviour-"attitudes are theoretically a component of all behaviours overt and covert" (Remmars, 1954: 3). Therefore to study the social change or the direction towards which the society is moving, it is significant to know the attitudes of a group of persons and the change taking place in their attitudes towards others. Because attitudes of a person determines their thoughts, feelings as well as their behaviour. So to determine the change, it is necessary to investigate the attitudes of various sections of the society towards educated working women. Because it is their attitudes that suggest the possible directions of such change. The change in their thinking would largely shape the social life as well as behaviour of the people who hold these attitudes. Hence it is important to study the changing attitudes of the educated elites of the society, which is of great significance in bringing out social change in the country as a whole.

Though the section of educated working are numerically least in number but is very important in terms of quality. Because this section provides leadership to the nation and set examples for others to follow, formulate social norms goals to be adhered to be achieved by others, and mould the personalities of it's members. So the understanding of the attitudes of people towards this section is of great relevance and significance for analysing the future social trends. According to one scholar "Women workers in India came either from very poor or from very rich strata of society, because the very poor section work to meet the gross economic necessity whereas the very rich work to utilies their intelligence and also for self-ful-filment." (c.f. Kapur: 1974). But this situation has changed. The number of middle class women workers has increased tremendously in the last two decades.

Before Independence and a little later, the middle and upper class women were mostly confined to their homes. This was because of lack of formal education, lack of independent economic status, lack of access to health and nutrition services as well as pre-occupation with child rearing. But however, the most important drawback of women's development was that, as that, at that time it was considered derogatory for a girl, specially for a married women belonging to aforesaid classses to come out from her home to take up employment outside. It was only under dreadful economic necessity or dire economic difficulty that taking up of her salaried job was accepted by the society. However, those who took up such type of job had to face criticism. They were pitied upon and were considered unfortunate, because circumstances had compelled them to take up employment. As such, most of the middle class working women were either widows, divorced or others who had no one to support them economically.

Even when, the middle class working women started taking up jobs, they were supposed to take up the jobs which were considered by the society as 'Respectable' for them. The so called respectable jobs were that of a teacher and later that of a doctor and so forth. Most of these women had to take up such kind of jobs selected by their families. Working in the offices side by side with men, specially in clerical capacity was considered to be most "disrespectable". Women who took up such jobs were not only looked down upon but were discouraged by the society. It was only after the partition of the country in 1947, that middle class women started taking up of jobs in the offices. Thus taking up jobs in the offices in various capacities by the middle and upper class women in India is a post-Independence phenomenon. It is in free India, spinsters as well as married women of these classes have been entering in increasing numbers into various kinds of remunerative jobs and occupations that were largely the preserves of men. (Kapur: 1974).

The government of India labour bureau publication "women in employment (1964)" has also pointed out "the post war period has also witnessed a remarkable rise in the number of women who gain a living through employment in many white collar vocations, in shops, commercial establishments, banking and insurance institutions." However, it is true that the spread of education, particularly in urban areas has opened up more employment opportunities for women in non-manual, clerical, administrative and professional work. The largest expansion of opportunities has been marked in government service too.

However, gradually the attitude of people and of society as a whole has undergone a considerable change. It was once considered below dignity and prestige of a man (whether he is the father or husband) to send their daughter or wife to work outside her home. But with the rising cost of living the middle class family finds it a very difficult to subsist on the father's or husband's income along. Today there is a welcome change from the attitudes mentioned above. This case is applicable to the residents of Shillong also.

The employment of women has come into prominance with the better chances of participation in the economic life. Today, women are the integral part of new economic order and important part of it's manpower resources. As a result, fathers, husbands, relatives as well as members of older generation of Assamese as well as Bengali families residing in the capital city. Shillong also approve or do not mind their educated daughter's, wife's, daughter-in-law's working but rather want and encourage that they should not only help their family by supplementing it's income, or in other words they desired or needed financial help.

These reactions of the relatives of working women undoubtedly reflect the processes of significant change in their attitudes towards women's employment. Today educated working women including women office workers of Shillong in particular and India in general are not only accepted by the society than before but are even respected and admired by a greater number of people than ever before. Thus old prejudice against women's work in offices and shops is gradually changed a lot. Now people do not mind as they did before their daughter's or wife's working in the offices even as clerks or in other capacities. As a result, spinsters as well as married women of middle and upper classes of Assamese and Bengali communities of Shillong are engaged in large numbers into all types of office jobs both in the private and public sectors. Practically almost every office in Shillong today employs women. Women from various social ranks work as clerks, stenographers, personal assistants, secretaries and receptionists, government officials, managers, executives and various other disciplines in large numbers. Women are also being recruited in increasing numbers in responsible services like the Indian foreign service, Indian police service and the Indian administrative service.

Establishment of working women's hostels through out the country is another fact which also reveals the changing attitude. The scheme of providing hostel facilities for working women drawn from rural areas and small towns at cheap rates was started during the Fifth Plan. By December 1986, 405 hostels were sanctioned catering to 26,800 beneficiaries with day care centre in 96 hostels. Financial help is given to registered voluntary organisations by the government on cost sharing basis for their maintenance (Sharma: 1990).

According to a UNI report, at present a total 597 working women's hostels have so far been established in the country having accommodation capacity for 38, 127 boarders. In 201 hostels day care centres are available in the country with a total capacity of keeping 4210 children, the available documents said (Shillong Times: 24th Feb: 1992).

To help and to encourage the educated working women and after recognizing their need for more congenial and safe accommodation specially for those who have come from outside Shillong, there are two working women's hostels in Shillong at present. One is at Stonyland under the management of ladies and children's recreation centre and the other is Fair-haven in Bivar road, Shillong under the supervision of Y.W.C.A. (Young Women's Christian Association). These two hostels are providing accommodation to the working women of all the North-Eastern states as well as other States of India like Bengal, Bihar, Uttar Pradesh, Tamilnadu, Kerala, etc. who has come to Shillong to serve in the offices and other organisations situated at Shillong in various capacities. But these two hostels are not sufficient to meet the increasing demands of accommodation problem of the working women. Though the authorities of these two hostels has increased the number of seats since 1981, but it is not enough. To give the impetus to the working women such type of hostels are very necessary, which can provide them safe accommodation and help them to work safely residing outside their respective homes.

To sum up, the status of educated working women has no doubt changed a lot and is still changing. Because the educated women are now more keen and desirous to acquire and utilize their education and training than earlier. It has improved a lot from the stage when it was considered derogatory to present stage when she has much freedom and opportunities to have education as well as to join in various kinds of occupations and professions. Today they are respected and honoured as a working women for their occupational or professional achievements and position.

However, as a result of this changing attitude, at present an educated woman can take up a job according to her choice in any professions like teaching, medicine, law, administration, management, banking, engineering, architecture, journalism, mass communication etc., etc. This has also been approved by her parents and if married by husbands also, when there is no dearth of economic suppport. The attitude of educated women also changed a lot as they prefers to work in varied disciplines rather than staying at their respective homes under the veil of social prejudice. Today to some extent the right, equality and opportunity brought our daughter, sister and mother in the limelight of social change and these in turn helping in nation building and it is urgently needed to carry out with the world at large. But in true sense, women in India are still in process of struggling for actual equality. Therefore any programme strategy for their welfare and development should necessarily be oriented towards removal of social injustices and disabilities with the ultimate goal of their involvement in the mainstream of national life.

REFERENCES

1. Kapur, Promilla, 1974. *The Changing status of the working women in India*. Vikas Publishing House, Pvt., Ltd. Delhi.

2. Lebra Joycee, Joy Paulson, Jana Everett., 1984 *Women and work in India: Continuity and change*. Promilla and Co. New Delhi.

3. Remmers, H.H. 1954. *Introduction to opinion and attitude measurement*. Harper and Brothers. New York.

4. Sharma, Urmil. Social Welfare Programmes for women and children in India. *Social Change* Vol. 2, pp. 3-12.

5. *Shillong Times*. 24th Feb. 1992 Shillong.

6. *Women in employment*. 1964. Ministry of Labour and Employment Government of India. Labour Bureau, Pamphlet Series-8.

23

The Growth of Science and Technology in Shillong (1981–91)

Sarit Chaudhuri*

Introduction

Since the ancient and medieval periods our country bear a rich scientific tradition. "Science can no longer be looked upon merely as a number of disciplines or independent fields of specialization: in the advanced countries there is a new awareness of the wider role of science and technology. In India and other developing countries out-dated out looks, social conservatism or administrative dominance may effectively prevent science from assuming a wider role in society. Consequently, there is an urgent need to evolve a new image of science and to develop the machinery necessary to support this image" (Rahman: 1974).

After the attainment of national independence, Government of India deliberately tried to spread the scientific and technological institutions throughout the whole country. As a result of it

*Anthropological Survey of India, North East Regional Office, Shillong.

even in small city like Shillong we can find a number of such institutions scattered here and there. Of course this city has some special importance as it was capital of undivided Assam and still after the declaration of Meghalaya as a separate state it is functioning as the same. This paper is just an attempt to enlist various scientific institutions and to throw some light on the activities or achievements of those organisations since 1981 to 1991.

Data collected from various published materials viz., articles, reports, newsletter, journals, etc. as well as by personnel communication. At first a table is given below enlisting most of the institutions with some other relevant information. Then an attempt has been made to throw some light on the activities of most of those enlisted institutions existing at different places in Shillong. In this respect Nandi (1984) rightly remarked, "so far as scientific activities and surveys are concerned, significance of Shillong in particular in the context of whole region is very difficult to assess, except the bare fact that Shillong is the headquarters to all-most all the central scientific activities."

Anthropological Survey of India (ASI))

North Eastern Regional Centre of Anthropological Survey of India established in 1953 in Shillong, has been engaged in anthropological research among the people living in Assam, Arunachal Pradesh, Meghalaya, Manipur, Nagaland and Mizoram.

During the year, the primary focus of research activities of this office centred around the national project on the people of India which is nearing completion. Field investigation was undertaken in Assam, Arunachal Pradesh and Mizoram to collect additional data. All the State Volumes have been finalised. Photographic coverage was completed on 56 communities and the maps prepared. Thematic papers on Demographic profile of Indian people, Ethnogenesis of Muslim population and Hinduism in north-east India were prepared for this project. This

TABLE 1

Information of Scientific Institutions in Shillong

Sl. No.	*Name of the Institution*	*Year of Establishment*	*Type*	*Objective*
1.	Anthropological Survey of India	1953	Central Govt.	Conducting research work on the basis of field data regarding various ethnic groups of North East India
2.	Botanical Survey of India	1956	—do—	Undertaking plant exporation and collection, to survey, study and document the plant resources in the North East Region.
3.	Geological Survey of India	1961	—do—	To carry on extensive geological study in the North East Region.
4.	Survey of India	1971	—do—	Preparation of maps for various purposes and geoletic survey.
5.	Zoological Survey of India	1959	—do—	Collection, identification and survey of fauna of this North East Region.

6.	Indian Council for Agricultural Research	1975	—do—	Promoting and conducting research and training in agriculture, animal science and fisheries for the development of the North East Region as a whole.
7.	Agricultural Finance Corporation Limited	1978	—do—	To resurge the economy of the rural areas of the North East States on the concept of 'total development'.
8.	Central Seismological Observatory	1952	—do—	To analysis of the problem related to evalution of earthquake risk in this region.
9.	Plytechnological Transfer Centre	1979	—do—	Catering to the needs or industrial growth of North Eastern Region and solving problems faced by thriving industries.
10.	Atomic Mineral Division	1976	—do—	To search valuable atomic minerals to generate atomic power.

Contd.

11.	Satellite Communication Project	1979	—do—	For the establishment of Satellite Communication Earth Station for the long distace telecommunication.
12.	National Scheduled Castes and Scheduled Tribes Finance and Development Corporation	1991	Central Govt.	To stimulate economic development of SCs and STs and also function as an apex institution for the agencies engaged in the economic development of SCs and STs.
13.	North Eastern Electric Power Corporation	1976	—do—	For planned development of power generation projects including transmission line for evaluation of power.
14.	North Eastern Hills University	1973	—do—	To initiate different academic wings and research projects.
15.	Tribal Research Institute	1962	Govt. of Meghalaya	To conduct research project for socio-economic development of the tribes of Meghalaya.

Contd.

16.	Indian Council for Social Science Research	1977	Autonomous Body	Providing fellowship for social science research and publishing research articles related to North East India.
17.	North East India Council for Social Science Research	1974	—do—	To promote and co-ordinate social science research in North East and to undertake, organise and facilitate research study course, conference, seminars and lectures in matters relating to social sciences.
18.	Institute of Social Research	1980	—do—	Promoting and publishing higher academic research related to social science and and humanities.
19.	Meghalaya Science Society	1973	—do—	Promoting, developing science in Meghalaya.
20.	North Eastern Council	1972	—do—	To formulate a coordinated plan for development and greater human welfare of the seven states of North East Region.

Contd.

21. North Eastern Institute of Anthropological Research	1987	—do—	The Institute takes up research project/studies in all disciplines of social sciences recognised by the Indian Council of Social Science Research. The Institute believes in interdisciplinary and holistic approach in research.
22. North East India History Association	1979	—do—	Promotion and encouragement of the scientific study of the History of North East India and the adjoining areas historically connected with the region.

apart, other continuing and Seventh Plan Projects were also attended to.

Reports were under preparation with regard to the projects, Tribes in Contemporary India, Agrarian System and Agrarian Laws in Tribal India etc. Field investigation was conducted under the project. All India Anthropometric Survey; Stratification and Social Change, Ethnicity, Politics and Political System in Tribal India and Socio-Political development in the country: Area Study North East India.

The Zonal anthropological museum established in 1979, continued its activities of collection, preservation, maintenance and display of ethnographic specimens depicting bio-cultural profiles of the people of north east India. Several specimens were collected from various states of north-east India. Scientific staffs of this region also published several books and articles in various reputed journals of India (News letter, 1988 and Annual Report; 1989-90).

Botanical Survey of India (BSI)

The Botanical Survey of India was established in 1980 for exploring the plant wealth of our country with Sir George King, the Superintendent of the Royal Botanic Garden. Sibpur, as ex-officio Director. Reorganisation of the Botanical Survey was taken up in 1952. On the recommendations of the Officer on Special duty, the Government of India established a Headquarters Organisation in Calcutta and other four Regional Circles Eastern Circle was established in 1956 at Shillong. It covers the state of Assam, Manipur, Meghalaya, Mizoram, Nagaland. and Tripura. The Circle has the National Orchidarium at Shillong and Experimental Garden at Barapani. The herbarium of the Assam Forest Department having 80,000 specimens was transferred to this Circle in 1956.

The Regional Herbarium has at present 1,15,000 specimens. Detailed studies on the Monocot Flora of Assam, Flora of Jowai,

Nongpoh, Cyperaceae of North East India, Orchids of Khasi and Assam Plains, have been completed and mostly published. New programmes on cultivation or orchids in collaboration with North Eastern Council and studies on the vegetation and flora of Namdapha in Arunachal Pradesh under Man and Biosphere programme are in progress.

BSI is publishing a quarterly journal bulletin of the B.S.I. devoted to plant sciences mainly relating to study of floristics, vegetation, Taxonomy, Ecology, Cytology and Economic Botany. It also published Records of BSI Annual reports and Flora of India (Series 1, 2, 3, and 4) etc. Some of the major programmes between 1981 to 1991 is given below: (1) Flora of Meghalaya, (2) Flora of Tripura, (3) Flora of Manipur, (4) Flora of Mizoram, (5) Flora of Assam, (6) Flora of Nagaland, (7) Lichen Flora of NE India, (8) Orchidaceae of India, (9) Ethnobotanical study of NE India, (10) Insectivorious plants of NE India (11) Orchids of Arunachal and Nagaland, (12) Project on Survey, Study and conservation of Endangered flora, (13) Conservation of rare and threatended plants by Multiplication through tissue culture technique under captive breeding programme, (14) Flora of Kazi Ranga National Park. (15) Flora of Cherrapunjee.

Geological Survey of India (GSI)

To carry on extensive geological study in the NE Region the Assam Circle office of GSI was set up at Shillong on Ist. September, 1961 which was latter redesignated at Assam-Meghalaya Circle. Out of the total geographical area of 254497 sq. km. in North East India, an area of 145605 sq. km. (about 57%) has already been mapped. Now future plan is to cover rest of the area by systemic geological mapping in the coming years in search of mineral deposits.

With in 1981 to 1991 GSI worked extensively in the 7 states of NE India. It is impossible to give detail information. Here only main programmes and some latest findings are given. Main programmes are (i) systematic Geological Mapping, (ii) Mineral Investigation, (iii) Geotechnical investigation and (iv) Geoenvironmental studies.

During the palaeontological investigation a new fossiliferous horizon from Chengapara Formation of Garo Hills; Meghalaya. Fossil evidences also collected from siltstone and calcareous grey sand stone of Upper Diang Formation from Sugnu area, Chandel District, Manipur.

Palaeontological and Remote Sensing input has been provided to the items of systematic geological mapping in Manipur, Meghalaya, Mizoram and Nagaland in order to achieve higher mapping coverage. Particularly in inaccessible and difficult area. One of the most important news is that in Meghalaya near Mawsynram a site was selected and proposed by GSI (NER) for 'National Geological Monument'.

Each year GSI publish Records of GSI (NER) which is the collection of Scientific Papers and also publish annual news mentioning briefly their yearwise achievements briefly.

Survey of India

The North Eastern Circle of the Survey of India, established on March 10th, 1971, has six field units, two photogrametric units and two drawing offices. Prime objective of the Survey is preparation of maps for various purposes and geoletic Surveys.

After independence the major effort of the department was diverted to the surveys for multipurpose development projects planned in the successive Five Year Plans for all round economic development of the country. The NE Region also received its due share. In this region, all projects surveys were undertaken and completed. These include surveys for hydro-electric projects, town development projects, flood control projects, communication projects, oil refinery projects etc.

Surveys for a number of projects which includes the New Capital Site for Assam, Brahmaputra Erosion sites, River trend surveys, Barak and Makru H.E. Projects are being undertaken.

North Eastern Region is rich in natural resources. For optimum utilisation of these resources, various developments, activities are planned by Central/State Government agencies. Survey of India has been interacting with various user agencies in its endeavour to discharge its obligation towards socio-economic developmental demands for surveys.

The Department of Science and Technology had constituted working Group and Task Force to formulate project proposal for the Survey of India. Some of the proposals for this region are briefly mentioned below:

(a) Centre for Advance Survey Technology and Application (CASTA).

(b) Flood Plain Zoning Survey Organisation.

(c) Computer Centres for Survey of India.

Indian Council of Agricultural Research (ICAR)

The ICAR Research Complex in North Eastern Hills Region was established in 1975 with its headquarters in Shillong, Meghalaya to cater to the needs of the region. The major objective of the Institute are (i) to develop improved and sustainable farming systems for different agro-climatic and socio-economic conditions of the region, (ii) to maintain analyse and project resource date base for perspective planning; (iii) improvement of crops live stock, fishes management of resources and development of local competence through training.

In the last decade ICAR carried out extensive research work to improve different varieties of crops viz, rice, maize, pulses, oil-seeds, vegetable crops, fruit crops and spices and plantation crop in relation to the existing ecological and geomorphological situation.

The multidesciplinary research project on cropping system was continued in 1989 at Barapani (Meghalaya) and Bazar (Arunachal Pradesh) to identify the appropriate cropping pattern to improve total productivity and net return without hampering the soil health on the long term basis. Data on productivity of different cropping systems at both the locations revealed that the inter-cropping systems (rice + ground nut, maize + ground nut bean) were more productive and profitable than the sole cropping. However, among the sole crops groundnut was found to be more profitable than either maize, rice or soyabean.

Under Animal Husbandry Programme various research projects are already done on breeding, feeding, production, nutrition and diseases of rabbit, goat, pig, cattle, fish and poultry and ducks.

Besides these other research projects on soil and water resources, Farm Tools, and Implements, Mushroom, Transfer of Technology and Farming System are successfully completed. A lot of research articles is published in various reputed journal by their scientist. They also participated in various seminar/symposium/workshop/meeting all over India to expose their extensive research achievement.

Central Seisomological Observatory (CSO)

The whole of North East India is well known as one of the Seismically most active regions of the world. A number of earthquakes shook the area in the past, of which the earthquakes of June 12, 1897 and August 15, 1950 last and indelible brand in the mind of the local people (Nandi; 1984). CSO is established in Shillong in the year 1952 to record and analysis of the problem related to evaluation of earthquake risk in this region.

Under Seismological Studies, programme mainly relate to natural hazards reduction. Under this programme several earthquake monitoring studies/projects have been taken up and considerable works by ERE Centre on data/information collection, processing and dissemination have been undertaken. NE Region under which several automatice remote stations in the NE Region have been telelinked with the Central base station at Tezpur having computer and Microwave reception facilities.

Atomic Mineral Division (AME)

North Eastern Circle of AMD was opened in Shillong in 1976 with an objective to find out raw atomic minerals for the generation of nuclear power. One of the most striking achievement which is recently done and came in almost all major news papers, is the identification of uranium mines from Domistat and Nonghkhirimey area situated about 120 km. away from Shillong. AMD expecting that this uranium may be richest one in comparison to earlier identified uranium mines in India. Already scientists of AMD collected 13,000 mineral samples from that region. After primary testing they send those to their head office for further wider analysis. Naturally Atomic Energy Commission wanted to take possession of 85 sq. km. land in that area from the Meghalaya Government. But 2000 tribals living in 10 villages in that particular area already gave objection not to transfer their land for atomic mineral mines.

National SC & ST Finance and Development Corporation (NSFDC)

NSFDC has been set up by Govt. of India under section 25 of the Companies Act, 1956 with the objective of stimulating economic development and growth of the members of Scheduled Castes and Scheduled Tribes. North East Zonal Office is open in this year at Shillong.

Besides economic development it also attempt to identify and fill the critical gaps in the programmes of State-level SC and ST Development Corporations and other agencies. It is also to function as an apex institution for the agencies engaged in the economic development of SCs and STs.

At present as a new organisation NSFDC attempt to collect secondary information regarding SC and ST of N.E. India to carry out their following functions:

(i) Identify potential schemes and economic activities of high relevance for development of SCs and STs.

(ii) Finance viable economic development schemes through Central/State level Institutions and other agencies promoting programmes for development of SCs and STs. NSFDC also provides grants for importing training to SCs and STs to improve their skills and knowledge.

North Eastern Electric Power Corporation Limited

The North Eastern Region is blessed with the highest Hydro-power potential in the country on account of mighty Brahmaputra and its tributaries which is estimated to be about 37400 Mw. Development of power in the North Eastern Region of India with its stategic border and predominantly tribal states has lagged very much behind the rest of India. The socio/economic development of the North Eastern Region which has already assumed National importance is linked with the development of power. There can be no doubt that the most important factor which has stood against industrial development in the North Eastern Region has been lack of availability of power.

To harness this enormous power potential, the North Eastern Council part forth the idea of having an electric utility Corporation for planned development of power generation projects including transmission lines for evacuating power. Thus North Eastern Electric Power Corporation Ltd., (NEEPCO) came into being in April 1976. It is today all set up to plan, promote, investigate, survey, design construct, generate, transmit operate, and maintain power stations, transmission lines and sub-stations in the entire North Eastern Region. It will thus enable in harnessing the power from the rivers of North Eastern Region and for the country, various projects related to generation and transmission during sixth and Seventh plan periods by NEEPCO is given below:

TABLE 2

Projects at a Glance

Name of the project	Cost in Rupees Crores	Installed Capacity
A. Generation Project		
Kopili H.E. Project	149.02	150 MW
Garo Hills Thermal Project	43.20	60 MW
Doyang H.E. Project	128.61	105 MW
Ranganadi H.E. Project	267.23	405 MW
Kameny H.E. Project	555.50	600 MW
B. Transmission Project		
Kopili Transmission Scheme	7.42	220 KV
Additional Transmission Scheme	20.28	132 KV
Doyong Transmission Scheme	40.87	220 KV
Transmission Scheme for Power Supply to Arunachal Pradesh	11.16	220 KV
Kopili Extension Transmission Scheme	17.05	220 KV
Kameng Transmission Scheme	24.25	400 KV
Ranganadi Transmission Scheme	389.12	400 KV

Tribal Research Institute (TRI)

The Government of Meghalaya established Tribal Research Institute in the year 1962 to conduct research projects for socio-economic development of the tribes of Meghalaya as well as collecting evidences of material culture of the tribes of NE India for state Museum. Other objective is to study and prepare booklets on various subjects and topics concerning the tribal people of the state right from their dim past to the present time, so that a clear picture can be obtained regarding their changing way of life, beliefs, health, moral etc. Institute believes that this will help to the genuine welfare of the people without cutting a drift from their moorings. The tangible result obtained thereby will provide a basic and informed advice to the administrative machinery to plan their welfare in a manner befitting the present modern development. Owing to the various handicaps which the Tribal Research Institute is facing since its inception and the difficulties which are beyond its control, the above objectives as earmarked in the Original Scheme could not be achieved.

In recent year 1988-90 one project 'Socio-Economic development among the tribal people' was conducted among the Khasi-Jayantia. Any report is yet to publish. Now this Institute became one man department and reached at non-functional stage. Last in 1978, TRI published 'Assortment from Tribal Research Institute Sri R. Kostan Ray Science then no publication is available.

North Eastern Council (NEC)

The North Eastern Council was constituted under the North Eastern Council Act, 1971 with the principal objective of promoting and accelerated and balanced socio-economic development of the North Eastern Region. Though NEC has been formed as an Advisory Body in the North Eastern Council Act, it is now essentially an advisory, planning, funding and developmental body for the entire North-Eastern Region. It focuses on matters of common interest extend inter-alia, to critical spheres of planning for power generation, flood control, inter-state transport and communications. Broadly, the NEC Plan has two components, namely, one implemented by the Constituent Units directly and the other by the Central Agencies and Regional Corporations sponsored by the NEC. The main thrust has been on schemes of regional importance whose benefits can be shared by all units.

The performance of the NEC during the Seventh Plan has been outstanding both in terms of utilisation of Plan funds and also the work on the ground. The entire outlay of Rs. 780 crores has been utilised and 154 schemes have been completed.

During the 7th Plan period 1124 kms. or roads and 1660 meters of major bridges had been included in NEC's Plan. The completion of the second bridge over the river Brahmaputra is a land mark in the history of the development of transport and communication in the North-Eastern Region. Third bridge over the Brahmaputra at Jogighopa has also been started.

The NEC has financed surveys and studies for undertaking Railway Projects out of which 15 projects are very much important.

NEC is working extensively for the development of power through NEEPCO. Moreover, the Council has also funded 6.5 MW Baramura Gas Thermal Unit in Tripura which has been successfully commissioned in March 1990.

Starting from Fifth Five Year Plan, the NEC has been laying considerable emphasis on the Development of agriculture and Allied Sectors together with Irrigation, Flood Control and Soil and Water Management Programmes in an Integrated manner. The thrust areas of development during the 7th Plan with NEC support were those of establishment of Regional Centre for

Bio-fertilizers, setting up of Input Testing Laboratory, Training-cum-Production of Mushrooms, Regional Cotton Seed Multiplication Centre, Regional Breeders Seed Farm, Pilot Project on Dryland Agriculture, Water Harvesting and Weed Control Schemes, etc.

In the Animal Husbandary Sector, a total of 25 Projects were implemented at the cost of Rs 14.46 crores during 7th Plan and in the Horticulture Sector. a total 23 projects have been supported involving an outlay of Rs. 9.88 crores.

In order to reduce the sufferings of people in the Brahmaputra valley as well as in Barak Valley of Assam implementation of the master Plans prepared by the Brahmaputra Board for both the basins are of paramount importance. NEC decided to implement the flood moderation component of the Pagladiya in the Brahmaputra basin and Tipaimerkh project in Barak basin.

Several other projects are also taken for the development of Sericulture, Weaving, Tissue Culture, etc., within this period of 1981 to 1991. The Annual Plan outlay for the year 1990-91 for North Eastern Council has been fixed at Rs. 202.00 crores out of which 108.78 crores have been earmarked for Transport and Communication while another Rs. 74.7 crores have been allocated for Water and Power Development in North East India and Rs. 9.14 crores and Rs. 4.94 crores have been earmarked for implementation of various schemes and projects under Manpower Development and Agriculture and Allied Activities respectively.

Over the last few years, the NEC has been engaged in identifying the basic problems and assessing the potentialities of the region and in the setting in motion the much needed pace for integrated development. The North Eastern Region has certain basic constraints which seem to impede the growth of economy in the region. In the Eighth Plan a number of important Schemes and Projects will be taken up on selected priorities so that the region's basic socio-economic maladies can be remedied for greater welfare of the people inhabiting the region.

North-East India Council for Social Science Research (NEICSSR)

It is one of the most important and active voluntary organisation in this region established in the year 1974. According to Pakem (1984) prior to that Shillong had no institutional social science research facilities except in the Anthropological Survey of India and the Research Department of Arunachal Pradesh. One of the important objects of the NEICSSR is to promote and co-ordinates social science research in the states of North East India and to undertake, organise and facilitate research study courses, conferences, seminars and lectures in matters relating to social sciences in all its aspects and ramifications. Latest activities and achievements done by NEICSSR within last decade is given below briefly:

Seminar

1. Continuity and Change in the Hills of North-East India with a special reference to Garo Hills as a tribute to Dr. D.N. Majumdar on 14-15 December, 1990.
2. Shillong 1981-1991 on 22-23rd August, 1991,

Book Release

1. Tea Garden Labourers of North-East India 1990 (ed) Fr. Sebastian Karotemprell and Dr. B. Datta Ray.
2. Shifting Cultivation in North-East India 1990 (ed) Dr. D.N. Majumdar.
3. Social and Political Institutions of Hill People of North East India 1991 (ed) J.K. Sarkar and Dr. B. Datta Ray.

NEICSSR, a registered member of United National Environment Programme, observed World Environment Day on 5th June 1991 by holding a Panel discussion on Strategy towards North-East India Development and Strain on Environment.

Institute of Social Research

In the year 1980, Institute of Social Research, a voluntary organisation was established by Dr. M. Kar in order to encourage academic research. From 1981 this institute publishing a journal, Social Research. It is a quarterly Journal publishes articles in all branches of social science and humanities pertaining to any region of India specially the North East. It also publishes research findings, theory and critical analysis in Social Science and Humanities. Under the editorship of Dr. Bimal J. Dev this institute published more than 30 issues of 'Social Research' with about 150 articles highlighting socio-economic life of the tribes, Agrarian Situation, problem of tribal development, tribal identity, Unemployment problem, demography, educational problem, Tea Industry, Urbanisation, Regional Planning mainly in relation to all north eastern states.

North Eastern Institute of Anthropological Research (NEIAR)

This institute established in the year 1987 with its Headquarters in Silchar (Assam) and a Regional Office at Shillong (Meghalaya). Objective of the institute is to guide as well as conduct various research projects/studies in all disciplines of social sciences recognised by the Indian Council of Social Science Research. The institute believes in inter-disciplinary and holistic approach in research and also published a bi-annual journal named 'SOCIAL SCIENCES' which publishes original research papers. review articles, brief notes, book reviews and other information pertaining to research facilities of collaborative organisations. NEIAR organised a two-day seminar on status of women in Barak valley in collaboration with ICSSR-NERC, Shillong on 26th and 27th November, 1988. Another two important seminar on Dynamics of Social Movements in Southern Assam with collaboration with ICSSAR-NERC, Shillong on 27th and 28th January 1990 and 'Youth and Psychotropic Drug Abuse in North East India with reference to Meghalaya on 23rd and 4th May of 1991 sponsored by the Director, Social Welfare, Government of Meghalaya.

Indian Council for Social Science Researeh (ICSSR)

The North Eastern Regional Centre of ICSSR was set up in Shillong on 4th March, 1977 in collaboration with North Eastern Hill University with following objectives—(a) act as the agent of the ICSSR within the region, (b) act as the representative of the social scientists of the region and bring their ideas and problems to the ICSSR, (c) provide a platform for the social scientists of the region to come together for promotion of social science research and (d) serve as the link between the social scientists of the region and the national and international community of social scientists. Science its inception this centre contributed a lot to create a conducive academic atmosphere in this whole region. Within 1981 to 1991 the centre arranged several important seminars, symposia, conference, Research Methodology Course, Social Scientists' Meet, Special Lectures at different states of North East Region and also given study grants to different scholars. From 1981 to 1986 about 47 seminars were held in different parts of North East India related to Social Cultural, Political, Economic, Administrative and Planning aspects of North East India from macro as well as micro level analysis (Report ICSSR: 1977-87). In the year 1986-87 besides various important seminars viz. Impact of Land Reforms in North East India, Development and Environment in North East India, Psychology and Development in North East India, Problem of Hill Area Development, etc. some important panel discussion on "Problems of Social Science Research on North East India" took place in Assam, Manipur, Mizoram, Nagaland and Arunachal Pradesh (Annual Report: 1987-88). In order to improve the research capacity of scholars and research workers in North East region this NERC every year selected a central academic theme. One such theme was 'Status of Women in North Eastern Societies' on which a number of seminars were sponsored. Other two regional seminars were organised by the Centre on the 'Constraints of Development in North East India' (Annual Report: 1988-89).

Summing up

From the whole discussion it appears that starting from 1952 to 1991 several scientific institutions gradually established in Shillong and these are working tremendously for the overall development of the seven sister states of North East region. Of course we can place these Institution categorically into three level viz.: (i) National, (ii) Regional and (iii) Local. But irrespective of categorical level, all these institutions contributed substantially for the decadal growth of science and technology in and around Shillong in particular and North East India as a whole through the implementation of hundreds of valuable projects, conducting seminar symposium/workshop and by publishing various books and scientific research articles. But this onward march of science and Technology some times create a huge problem for a particular community or particular area. As for example due to the discovery of extremely valuable high quality Uranium in the Domiostat-Nangthirimei area 10 Khasi villages with a population of about 2000 individuals are in danger. They are really afraid of loosing cultivable land which is their prime source of livelihood. Even they will not be able to work as a labourer in Uranium mine as it requires skilled and specially trained labourers. Of course the displacement of various ethnic groups due to installation of dam, thermal project, missile testing range etc., are not new phenomena in our country. It is true that the interest of nation some times a particular community or communities of a particular area has to sacrifice a lot but their proper rehabilitation also deserve scientific outlook.

REFERENCES

1. Inaugural Issue, 1981 State Museum, Meghalaya, Shillong,
2. Chadha, Colonel SM 1984. The Mapping Status Projects and Plans for the North Eastern Region. In *Survey for Development* North Eastern Council Survey and Survey of India. pp. 3.1-3.8.

3. Annual Report 1989-90. ICAR Research Complex for N.E.H. Region, Barapani, Meghalaya, India.

4. An Introduction 1991. National Schedule Caste and Scheduled Tribes Finance and Development Corporation, Shillong.

5. Assortment 1978. Tribal Research Institute Meghalaya, Shillong, Department of Education, Shillong.

6. News 1989. Geological Survey of India North Eastern Region-Vol-8, Shillong.

7. News 1990. Geological Survey of India North Eastern Region, Vol-9, Shillong.

8. Botanical Survey of India 1984. Director, Botanical Survey of India, Calcutta.

9. Annual Report 1986-87. Botanical Survey of India, Calcutta.

10. Newsletter 1981. Botanical Survey of India, December Vol-7, No. 3, Calcutta.

11. Report 1980. Botanical Survey of India, Eastern Circle, Shillong.

12. Annual Report 1984. Botanical Survey of India (In Hindi) Calcutta.

13. K.P. Singh for Scientist-'SE', B.S I. Eastern Circle, Shillong (Personal Communication).

14. Basic Statistics of North Eastern Region 1987. North Eastern Council Secretariate, Shillong.

15. Report—North Eastern Electric Power Corporation Limited (A Govt. of India Enterprise) Shillong.

16. —— 1990. Role of North Eastern Council in Socio-Economic Development of North Eastern Region and NEC Plan for 1990-91. *Journal of North Eastern Council* Vol-XI No. 2 and 3, April-September, pp. 24-39.

17. Rahman, A. 1974. *Science, Technology and Economic Development*, Delhi, National. pp. 1-2.

18. Nandi Kamal 1984. Scientific Activities in and Around Shillong, *In Shillong* 1971-1981 (ed.) B. Pakem, Calcutta, Research India Publication for NEICSSR. p. 135.

19. Pakem, B 1984. A Survey of Social Science Research Works Conducted in Shillong. *In Shillong 1971-1981* (ed) B. Pakem, Calcutta. Research India Publication, for NEICSSR. p. 158.

20. Newsletter 1981. North East India Council for Social Science, Research Vol. XXX.

21. Annual Report 1989-90. Anthropological Survey of India, Calcutta.

22. Newsletter 1988. Vol-VII, No. 1, January-April, Anthropological Survey of India, Calcutta.

23. Decadal Report 1977-87. ICSSR (NERC) Meghalaya.

24. Annual Report 1987-88. ICSSR (NERC) Meghalaya.

25. Annual Report 1988-89. ICSSR (NERC) Meghalaya.

ACKNOWLEDGEMENT

Author is highly indebted to Dr. S.B. Chakrabarti and Zahid Hussain of Anthropological Survey of India (NERC) Shillong for their continuous guidance in writing this paper.

24

Status of Education in Shillong During 1981 to 1991

Parijat Chakrabarty
and
Ms. Sarbani Bhattacharya

1. Background

Looking at the history of Shillong in the educational field, formal education started around later half of the 19th Century. Informal education existed in the form of Khasi traditional dances, social structure, culture, etc. before introduction of any formal education. According to H. Syiemlieh, "Primary school was opened at Nongthymmai a locality of Shillong in 1857". Perhaps this was the first formal school opened in Shillong. In 1876, U Babu Jeebon Roy established a high school in Shillong.

Thereafter dramatic changes with regard to the expansion of educational institutions occurred and Shillong happened to be one of the most important learning centre in the whole of North-East. Educationally, Shillong has established herself as an ideal and attractive learning centre in the North Eastern region.

Climatic condition, geographical location, higher standard of schools, provision of well maintained and disciplined residential schools, natural environment, hospitality, general maintenance of cleanliness and discipline, past history, communication facility, and many other factors combined together might be the root cause.

The educational environment prevailed before 80's and that in 1981 to 1991 are quite different. During 1981 to 1991, the people of Shillong able to experience effective changes with the comming of television, VCR's, computers—due to rapid urbanisation of the capital city, expansion of the city, development of roads and buildings, the existence of the University, promotion of tourism industry and other factors. On the other hand unrest among the students, students movement, instability in the political sphere, price rise, drugs and the like brought in major changes in every aspect of life of the people residing particularly in Shillong which in turn affected the State, Meghalaya.

Taking into account of the affective and effective changes in majority of cases the nature of change happened to be spontaneous. Any kind of change that takes place in the society influences the whole environment in particular either directly or indirectly. Any kind of change is essential for growth and development of human beings, place, region or society. Whether the change is worthwhile or not is to be judged by the people. Therefore, people must be knowledgeable and aware. Knowledge and awareness can be developed only through appropriate form of education and training. Education as we all know brings in change in behaviour, which gives an individual the power of understanding, decision making, judging and becoming aware of the present and future impact of the affective and effective changes. Since, the capital city, Shillong is well known as a learning centre for quite long time it would be interesting to know whether education really help human being to judge, understand, and make aware with the modification of behaviour.

Confining ourselves to educational sector only, the paper attempts to focus on the status of education in Shillong from 1981 to 1991 and then analyse the affective and effective changes occurred.

2. Status of Education in Shillong

(i) *Population structure and Literacy Status*—

According to the 1991 census (provisional), the population of Shillong is 222273. Table 1 shows the growth of population in Shillong at different periods.

TABLE 1

Population Growth in Shillong

(in thousands)

Year	1881	1891	1901	1911	1921	1931	1941	1951
Total	11.3							
Population	11.3	9.3	9.6	13.6	17.2	26.5	38.1	58.5
in Shillong								
	1961		1971		1981		1991	
	102.3		122.7		174.7		222.2	

Source: (i) Census of Assam, 1901.

(ii) Statistical Handbook of Meghalaya, 1984.

(iii) Census of Meghalaya, 1971.

(iv) Office of the Census, Government of India, Shillong.

The population given in table indicates the population of Shillong Urban Agglomeration, which comprises of Shillong

Municipality, Shillong Cantonment, Mawlai, Nongthymmai, Pynthorumkrah and Madanrting. Distribution of population in these areas as per 1991 Census (provisional) follows—

Locality	*Population*	
	1981	*1991*
Shillong Municipality	109244	130691
Shillong Cantonment	6620	11075
Mawlai	20405	30442
Nongthymmai	21558	26816
Pynthorumkrah	6165	14322
Madanrting	10711	8927

In 1981, literacy percentage of Shillong Urban Agglomeration was 65.65. Literacy percentages of Shillong Municipality in 1981 and 1991 (Provisional) found to be 69.18 and 77.26 respectively, During early part of 1991, Shillong Literacy Drive was started. Mass participation of individuals and educational institutions are taking part in making the drive successful.

There are 66 numbers of Primary schools in the Shillong Municipality. During 1981 to 1991 a good number of Pre-Primary and Primary schools were established.

(ii) *General and Technical Education—*

In a study, Chakrabarty (1989) reported that out of 94 High Schools (in 1988), 17 High Schools were established during 1981 to 1988. The study observed that 5 numbers of High Schools were established in the year 1985 and this was the record growth of High Schools in a single year within a period of 112 years (i.e., from 1876 to 1988). The study also observed that there is a high degree of correlation (0.987) between the growth of number of high schools and that of population.

Another study conducted by the author (1990) suggests that by 1989 Computer Education course was introduced in 20 high schools in Shillong. St. Edmund's School was the first one to introduce computer education course in 1986. The study found that there is a significant difference between the attitude of boys and girls towards computer education.

The Society for the welfare of the Disabled only of its kind in Shillong established the School for Children in Need of Special Education in 1986 and the Centre for the Disabled Child in 1989. The aim of the society is to train up disabled children to become as independent as possible. These institutions are providing necessary education and training to the disabled children to look after their own personal needs, to earn a living when they grow up. The number of disabled childrens' enrolment is increasing every year. Main function of these institutions are to provide remedial teaching, diagnosis, Parent Counselling, Vocational Training, Social Integration, and to develop the sense of equality and awareness of the people.

In the share of technical education, courses on new subjects like computer applications and electronics were introduced in Shillong Polytechnic during 1987. A number of technical institutes like typing school, computer education institutes, electronic training institutes (Television, Radio, etc.) were set up during the ten years period to meet the technical manpower demand.

In 1985 and in 1987, Women's College and Raid Laban College respectively came into existence.

North Eastern Hill University in 1986 introduced quite a good number of vocational courses at the Pre-University and Under-Graduate levels. New departments like Bio-Chemistry, Regional Sophisticated Instrumentation Centre, Centre for

Creative Arts, Centre for Eco-Development, Centre for Science and Mathematics Education, were established in thc 1981-1991 decade.

In order to encourage young boys and girls towards games and sports in a more organised way two stadiums were inaugrated in this decade. Jawaharlal Nehru Stadium at the Polo Ground, Shillong was inaugrated in 1989 for promotion of games and sports in the State. Donbosco Stadium was build up by the Don Bosco organisation, where inter school games and sports takes place.

3. Effective and Effective Changes

Human beings like changes. Change brings in transformation, growth, diversification, development, differentiation and competition. Human by nature is dynamic and not static. In any field of activity people wants change. Changes in the educational environment during the decade were quite remarkable and significant.

Continuous growth of education in Shillong is helping in bringing out effective changes.

Every year students in quite large number from the North Eastern States come here in Shillong to seek education. Shillong as a centre of learning not only helps in imparting knowledge to thousands of students every year but also plays a very important role in integrating the students of different regions whose language, culture, lifestyle, etc. are different from one another. It would be appropriatte to name Shillong as a Cosmopolitan Integrating Centre or Socio-Educational Integrating Centre.

A section of students from Meghalaya are sent every year to different parts of India for seeking professional education. Professions like Engineering, Medical, Management and other courses demand adequate knowledge of Science, Mathematics or both. Performance of the local students in Science and

Mathematics was quite critical before 80's. But in 1981-1991 performance of the local students improved significantly. Phobia for Mathematics and Science is diminishing at a faster rate. People's urge to compete and to adapt to new things showed a marked increase during the last ten years in order to keep pace with the developed regions. Any new product introduced in the international markets or in the markets of big cities in India is observable in Shillong within a very short period of time. This has a great impact on the behaviour of the people of Shillong. Adapting to new situation, new product, or new things by the people of Shillong especially by the youngsters warrant more income and for which to acquire knowledge and skill are essential. These lead everyone for higher and higher education.

For example, modern technological aids like computers, television, VCR, were adopted by the people during 80's in no time. With the coming of these scientific aids in the city enthusiasm for teaching-learning process also increased effectively besides, entertainment. Educational institutions are adapting modern educational aids in order to promote the quality of education. In depth research activity is essential to know the extent and quality of effective changes in educational field.

Due to increase in infra-structural facilities in Shillong students from all the five districts of Meghalaya come here to receive school, technical or higher education and also to get jobs. Since, 1981 flow of students from urban and rural areas increasing day by day. This became possible mainly due to the effort of the State Government in constructing and improving roads, providing transportation facilities and opening up of offices in various parts of Meghalaya which require qualified manpower for functioning. Growing awareness of the people and or providing scope to the people tends to an effective change.

Since, Shillong is the capital city and an important learning centre, rapid expansion of population is taking place from 1981 onwards. Which suggests that Shillong is growing and developing almost in every field.

Marathon, Walkathon, Book Fair, Conferences, Seminars, Exhibition are some of the effective things which are common affair since 1981 in Shillong helped in broadening the outlook of the people.

In the year 1988 Conference of SAARC countries on "Development of Women" was held in Shillong which had a great impact on the people of Shillong.

Alongwith the effective changes certain affective changes could be noticed during this period.

Students' movement, unrest and indiscipline affected the educational environment to a great extent. A group of women studying at the Pre-University and Undergraduate levels were asked about their feelings towards Shillong and the existing educational climate prevailing in Shillong. Out of 200 women about 90 per cent responded that the situation in Shillong has changed a lot. Today's Shillong is not the same as it was earlier. Marked changes in the educational environment took place in the past four or five years in terms of quality of education, motivation of teachers and students and the urge for learning which is affecting the prevailing climate. The responses of the students indicate that educational institutions and the educational environment is affected badly due to various factors.

Another affective change that is noticeable for quite sometime is increase in number of vehicles on the road. In a paper, Chakrabarty (1990a) on Road Safety Education emphasised the need for road safety education for the school children and suggested a curricuium for it in order to reduce the number of road accidents and hazzards. In Shillong too, time has come to provide road safety education to all, specially to the school children. Traffic jam, congestion on the roads, accidents are quite common during school hours these days.

Consumption of drugs by the students at various levels brings in affective changes among the student community and is badly affecting the educational environment.

Increase in population, houses, unemployment, inflation are some of the factors which has some affective bearing on educational environment either directly or indirectly.

4. Conclusion

There are a number of effective and affective changes taking place since 1981. Considering the good side and bad side together we observe that growth of Shillong in any field is not stagnant. Changes are occurring and people are also becomming more and more aware and conscious. Effecient and effective changes are adapted and implemented by the people readily. Managing the education sector in changing circumstances is a huge task. Principals, teachers, students and the people must work together for effective and effecient management of educational status and the educational institutions. Taking certain factors like competition, diversification, differentiation and protactive, reactive, evolutionary and revolutionary changes into consideration management of educational institutions require manpower with conceptual and technical skills. Changes will occur and bound to occur in the society, accordingly, style, strategy, tactics, approach and practices in managing educational institutions must change time to time. People, structure, task and technology are four important factors in management. Efficient and effective management of the educational institutions can only be perceived when the above mentioned four factors are integrated together so that innovation or change of any kind can be adapted and put into use for the welfare of the students community as well as the society.

REFERENCES

1. Chakrabarty, Parijat. 'Management of High Schools of Shillong'. Unpublished Project Report (Self Financed), 1989.
2. Chakrabarty. Parijat. 'Computer Education in the High Schools of Shillong—A Study', M.A. Dissertation Education, North Eastern Hill University, Shillong 1990.

3. Chakrabarty, Parijat. 'Educational Technology and Human Resource Development in SAARC Countries'. Paper presented at the International Conference on Educational Technology: The Futures organised by AIAET held at New Delhi from 31st October to 3rd November, 1990.

4. Chakrabarty, Parijat. 'Road Safety Education at School Level: A Bare Necessity'. Journal of Indian Education, NCERT, Vol. XV, No. 5. pp. 48-54, 1990.

5. Syiemlieh, H. 'The role of School in the Intellectual Development in Khasi and Jaintia Hills'. Centenary Celebration. Shillong Government High School (1880-1980), 1980.

25

Mass Media and a Changing Shillong

M.P. Hazarika

Shillong 1981-1991 is undoubtedly an important topic for discussion. We always feel that Shillong grows but at a pace that never helps in obliterating its rural face, its ethnic image. When we discuss 'Shillong 1981-1991', we have to do it in some historical perspective. We have to take into account the exodus of population that followed the formation of Meghalaya as a State. The Capital city saw its first fragmentation in the seventies as the cosmopolitan character has received some jolt with the migration of vast number of composite population alongwith the shifting the capital of a major state. The eighties therefore were a period of consolidation on a different footing. John Baxendale, an eminent British Social Scientist, referring to British National culture said, 'Intelectuals turned against industrial Society criticizing the social effects of economic growth and looking instead to a gentlemanly culture, and to an idealised version of pre-industrial life. Henceforth, ideals of national growth and technological change were held back by contrary ideals of 'stability', 'transquility' closenes to the past, and 'Non-materialism'. These altitudes were reflected in a persistently rural image of the nation, a romantic culture of the countryside. . .". In a parallel situation in Meghalaya, the entire development theme seems to have been dominated by traditional, rural themes of continuity, 'stability' and 'The eothmic quality of life'. Shillong being the nerve centres of the State of Meghalaya could hardly exert its aggressiveness to jump the limits of rural world and overcome its rural image. It has no stirrings within its own soul; it can hardly exert its influence to link between the culture of the enthmic groups and those of other minorities and the process of economic change. The mass media has changed technologically at an incredible speed. But barring a limited manifestations of urbanity in the rural society, Shillong in the eighties was yet to shad its rural image. Social changes have their obvious influence on the needs of the communications and the various media of mass communication respond to the challenges of a society in a process of Socio-Cultural transformation whatever its pace and tempo. Shillong has however witnessed a few changes over the last one decade or so in the Socio economic spheres. The ecology in and arround has undergone a pathetic transformation, the environment has received deadly as saults from various directions. The sylvan beauty of the city has lost its charm, its lustre and serenity. These changes have their impact on the media of mass communication and Shillong could not escape being affected by these changes and then the definite and revolutionary changes in mass communication technology seem to affect the patterns of behaviour of the people inhabiting this city. Although cable systems are yet to make a dent, the video cassettes and video parlours have mushroomed in the city and video cassette sellers have virtually invaded the households in a big way and domestic life has been subject to tremendous pressures and to use the term as coined by an American media specialist with proliferation of video parlours, video carsettes, 'any time can be prime time.' In any case, the number of video cassette can no longer be counted in the tips of fingers.

The expansion of Doordarshan network in the NorthEast has indeed influenced the projection of development image of the region and Shillong is always brought into focus because of the constant coverage of events in the city and in the process it comes into limelight. The eighties were the period that witnessed an sffulgence of T.V. advertisement doing about the consumer goods sponsored by the advertisers. This has given a new dimension to the market of consumer goods and urban population has been under tremendous influence and spell and the music that is associated with. And was it possible for Shillong in the eighties to remain unaffected by these influences?

Regarding dessemination of information, the media have been fragmented. There is Doordarshan news, features, the A.I.R. broadcasts and again the vides news casettes are all around. There is information all besides the printed media. Apart from the availability of national dailies in the city, there are more than thirty local news papers for the local audience and readers. While the national dailies could hardly bring into focus the problems of the people that inhabit the city, the local language papers could bring into bold relief various local issues that concern the citizens. The local ethnic newspapers provide a forum for discussing so many local issues and what is more important is that these news papers, being aware of their ethnic richness and identity and their cultural heritage, should extend an outlet to the great national mainstream. We saw flow of such ethnic problems into the mainstream papers and the unfortunate part is that in the late eighties quite a number of National Dailies have shifted their representatives to Guwahati.

The population has increased in the city (Municipality area) from 1,09,091 in 1981 to 1,13,138 in 1991 and the literacy rate in the city might be much higher than 48% of the Meghalaya's total population of 17,60,626. The literate people of the Greater Shillong area and the elite sections in the city itself constitute a vulnerable part of the Meghalaya's population from the media point of view. One has to understand one very basic fact: the public's reaction to the programmes broadcast or telecast as the constant flow of feedback seems to suggest. We very often come across in the solumns of the newspapers in the form of criticism about the programmes put out by these powerful electronic media. The local papers in Shillong are also unsparing. Infact, Shillong citizens in the decade that has gone by spoke in a united voice for immediate starting of the local T.V. Centre of the Doordarshan. Perhaps Doordarshan will open the door now to such popular reaction the moment a local production centre is opened up. Video culture has gripped the city in a very significant manner as the Video Home Service operating in important occasions like marriage, birthday etc, is an usual scene in the city. The first video feature film in Khasi language by the eminent Khasi film-maker, Rapsang, is a very important step in the video filming in Shillong. Perhaps the successful Khasi movie 'Manik Raitong' by Ardhendu Bhattacharya has not only inspired a groups of Khasi Youths interested in film-making to bring out the richness of Khasi legends, its literary beauty but has with the production of 'Manik Raitong' proved that there is a cultural viability of bringing the ethos of a tribal society into significant focus, that, the richness of a tribal cultural heritage should not remain isolated in the confines of the tribal world. Shillong has made significant strides in this direction during the eighties. The film Society movement as paintakingly run by group of enthusiasts in the city has done some very substantial works that has helped in getting to the movie lovers an oppurtunity to see some very select film classics. But the new media technologies have their obvious effects and Shillong cannot remain aloof from these. As Albert Collin, an American mass media specialist, very appropriately refers to, "The new technology is failed for its potential benefits to people's lives, removing burdens and contributing to human Progress. The contrasting perspective is symbolised by the image of the juggerhaut—the machine that is unstoppable crippling, or constraining human freedom". Compared to the power of T.V. and radio, what Shillong witnessed in the eighties is the reporting of events reasonably honestly on a number of occasions. The Press Corps in Shillong had demonstrated not only their power but a sense of responsibility in bold interpretation of facts and daring probe into situations thereby bringing into light sensational facts. The small press is one of the Great Social and cultural forces and without their being tied to the rich capitalist Groups they can raise their voice for the underdogs and against the political evils. The small press in Shillong is gradually coming up whose emergence we have seen in the eighties.

As I have already indicated that Shillong has suffered quite a bit particularly in the preservation of its ecological balance. Shillong lost much of its pristine beauty and as referred to as the "Scotland of the East", the environment pollution in variety of ways, mass feeling of trees have marred the beauty of Shillong' greenery, the tourist's major attraction. We have not seen a marked upswing in the tourist traffic as Shillong has not been able to offer much to them and the tranquility and peace get disturbed more often then not by internal troubles. By the end of the eighties, we have not seen anything remarkable that could stimulate the flow of tourists. The media as a whole have done a good job by widely publicising the many International, National and Regional Conferences held in Shillong on important subjects; Seminars and symposiums held on many important themes and crucial issues and the deliberations made in therefore had a direct bearing on the process of development of the region.

Shillong has a glorious past. The eighties had seen many important happenings in this capital city. Shillong has its own entity, it has a folksy character. Let its vibrancy sustain amidst its rural serenity, let the folksy character of its culture endure, let the ethmic groups living in this place make their own contribution. Shillong has to make a very substantial stride in its march to the twentyfirst century.

26

Crime Profile in Shillong (1981-1991)

Mrinmayi Banerjee

Introduction

Crime is a universal phenomenon and an age old problem of every society that is being faced by all since the advent of the world. Perhaps crime existed since beginning of civilization and both the sexes are the victims of crime. The nature and extent of crime is regarded as barometer of social health.

It has been the general consensus among social scientisits and particulary criminologists that crime is the result of complex social and cultural factors, which become operative only by going through the transformation of psychological and psychiatric factors. Relationship between crime and population and also linkage between crime and urbanisation have been noted by many researchers. They reported that "most developing countries find it difficult to cope with increasing crime rates resulting from rapid socio-economic changes including spread of education, industrialization and urbanisation" (Clinard and Abbort, 1973; Singh and Khan, 1983).

Different forms of crimes are occurring since ancient and medieval times and have carried themselves forward to the contemporary times. Offences are grouped into two broad categories, viz., cognizable and non-cognizable offences. 'Cognizable offence' means, an offence for which and 'cognizable case' means a case in which a police officer may, in accordance with the first schedule or under any other law for the time being in force, arrest without warrant. The offences committed against persons are murder, arson, kidnapping, dacoity and rape, and offences against property are burglary, theft and cheating etc., and many others such as practicising untouchability and giving or accepting dowry. 'Non-cognizable offences' means an offence for which and 'non-cognizable case' means a case in which a police officer has no authority to arrest without warrant. These offences are less serious in nature like possessing illicit arms, consumption or trading of narcotics, smuggling of goods etc., (Singh, 1981).

But before going into original problem we should know what crime actually means. According to law 'crime' is any form of conduct which is forbidden by under pain of punishment. Different authors defined crime in many ways. According to Donal (1958). "A crime may be defined as an act which the law prohibits and punishes, which is almost always immoral according to prevailing ethnical standard, which is usually harmful to society as originated at a given time and place; and whose repression is in the long run, necessary or supposed to be necessary for presentation of the existing social order." Again "crime may be defined as anti-social behaviour which the group rejects and to which it attaches penalties" (Elliot and Merril, 1941) (See Datta Ray majumdar and Doley, 1986).

Psychologists and Sociologists conducted lot of research works on crime and criminality. The majority of the investigators agree upon environmental causes like poor homes, over-crowding, rejecting and indifferent parents, illigitimacy, illiteracy, parental and familial conflicts, lack of parental control and bad associations etc., are main contributing factors for delinquency

(Ganguly and Maitra, 1966). Francis (1970) reported that the violent criminals are more extrovert as compared to those with criminal offences against theft, treasing or cheating. Singh (1980) on the other hand found that murderers are significantly more anxious, more neurotic and more psychotic than other types of offenders. According to Kundu and Mukherjee (1960), the child of middle position became the worst victim of unhealthy condition following by other position in the siblinghip".

Sociologists on the other hand reported that rate of urban growth is an important factor in stimulating crime (Singh and Khan, 1983). Carleton (1967) has enquired at length into the consequences of urbanisation. He attributes causes of a variety of riots, agitations and terrorist activities to industrial urban growth. Elliot (1952) in her study reported a definite relationship between crime and urbanisation and according to her the incidence of crime was visibly higher in cities than town and villages. She further observed that urban crimes were mainly centered over the properties like theft, cheating of property, fraud and embezzlement of money and also the social problems like abortion, drug abuse and political corruption. On the contrary the rural crimes tend to be direct and often arises due to inexperience, lack of judgement or interpersonal conflict situations.

Most of the work reported above are mainly centered in Western and Southern parts of India. No systematic work has yet been done on crime and criminality in North-Eastern India except Datta Ray, Majumdar and Doley (1986) who made an intensive work on crime and criminality in North-Eastern Region especially in Assam and Meghalaya. They have made an attempt to study socio-cultural back-ground of prisoners and their rehabilitation. There study was concerned only with prisoners, who were imprisoned in different prisons of Assam and Meghalaya and they collected datas from May, 1982 to December, 1982.

Present Study

In the present investigation an attempt was made to study the rate of incidence of crime during the last ten years in Shillong from 1981-1991 upto July. The study was largely focussed on (1) types of offences took place during the period of 1981-1991, (2) the community mainly responsible for committing such offences, (3) also the age group of the criminals.

To gather a broad based idea of different types of crimes taking place both in micro and macro level in Shillong during the period of 1981 to 1991 upto July, the Author intended to collect data from all the police stations and jails of Shillong. But due to paucity of time the datas were collected only from the registers of different jails of Shillong and under trial prisoners therein.

Data so collected from the jail register of district jail of Shillong were tabulated in the following heads to get a clear idea about the rate of crime and criminality in Shillong during last ten years, i.e., from 1981-1990.

Discussion

Criminological analysis is often handicapped for want of consensual crime-index. Lumping all offences together is hardly a satisfactory procedure or measure. Datas so collected from register of district jail of Shillong was tabulated on frequency method. Frequency less than five in any community was not taken into account. From frequency, number of convicts were converted into percentage. In the analysis main focus will be on three distinct aspects, yet intimately related as follows:

(1) Which community is prone to commit more offence.

(2) Age group of criminals.

(3) Different types of offences committed under Indian Penal Code/Criminal Act in Shillong during the period 1981-1991 upto July.

(1) Community-wise Number of Convents in Shillong (1981-1991 upto July)

Table—1 gives a statistical idea about which community is more prone to commit crime in Shillong. Khasis are the main inhabitant of Shillong followed by Bengalis, Nepalease, Assamese, Muslims, Beharis, Punjabis, Marwaris, Jayantia, Mizos, Geros, Nagas, Manipuris, etc. Hence among the convicts also they figure a large percentage over other communies. In an average nearly 38% of the criminals in Shillong belong to Khasi community. From 1981-1985 it is observed that percentage of crimes within Khasi community is almost remaining the same to the extent of 43.7% on an average but in the second half of the decade i.e., from 1986-1990 the percentage registered a declining trend of 32.7% on an average. Hence, it is seen that percentages of Khasi criminal varied with a downward trend to a clear range of 11% from 1981-1990.

Nepalese are coming second in reckoning in respect of criminal activity in Shillong. On an average they are responsible for 27% of the crime committed during ten years 1981-1990. During the first half of eighties, i.e., 1981-85 nearly 21% of the crimes were committed by Nepalese in Shillong but in the later half, i.e., 1986-90, 33.85% on an average in Nepalese community are involved in criminal activity. An increase to the extent of 12.7% in nearly a perceptable variation in percentage and matter of concern to the law and order problem of the city.

Bengalis are coming third in respect of criminal activity taking place in Shillong. Bengalis are on an average responsible for 9% of the total crime committed during last ten years (1981-1990). During the first half of eighties the percentage of crime committers were approximately 11.5% but during the later half of eighties the percentage came down to 6%, i.e., almost half in comparison to the previous half of the decade, which however is a healthy sign for the society and also to the peace keeping forces of the city in particular.

Muslims in Shillong coming next to Bengalese in order as crime committer. They constitute on an average 8% of the crimes committed during the year 1981-1990. Percentage of crime in both halves of the decade were 9% and 7.74% respec. tively. A percentage of variation which is not as high as was noticed among the communities discussed earlier.

TABLE 1

Community-wise Number of Convicts (Figure in the Parenthesis Indicate Percentage)

Year / *Community*	*1981*	*1982*	*1983*	*1984*	*1985*	*1986*	*1987*	*1988*	*1989*	*1990*	*1991* (*Up-to July*)
1. Khasi	342 (43.51)	406 (44.42)	396 (44.54)	419 (44.76)	425 (39.76)	315 (30.88)	397 (32.62)	394 (34.44)	394 (30.78)	423 (34.19)	213 (39.44)
2. Nepali	168 (21.37)	179 (19.58)	150 (16.87)	181 (19.34)	290 (27.13)	348 (34.12)	509 (41.82)	306 (26.74)	450 (35.16)	380 (31.43)	95 (17.59)
3. Bengali	121 (15.39)	125 (13.68)	67 (7.54)	128 (13.68)	85 (7.95)	67 (6.57)	68 (5.59)	66 (5.77)	73 (5.70)	88 (7.28)	26 (4.81)
4. Muslim	50 (6.36)	81 (8.86)	107 (12.04)	82 (8.76)	98 (9.17)	77 (7.55)	89 (7.31)	112 (9.79)	107 (8.36)	69 (5.71)	70 (12.96)
5. Behari	14 (1.78)	23 (2.52)	38 (4.27)	30 (3.21)	18 (1.68)	24 (3.33)	22 (1.81)	46 (4.02)	37 (2.89)	11 (0.91)	16 (2.96)

6. Jaintia	12 (1.53)	28 (3.06)	54 (6.07)	18 (1.92)	47 (4.40)	93 (9.12)	43 (3.53)	55 (4.81)	65 (5.08)	90 (7.44)	24 (4.44)
7. Assamese	12 (1.53)	17 (1.86)	28 (3.15)	34 (3.63)	32 (2.99)	33 (3.24)	31 (2.55)	69 (6.03)	63 (4.92)	77 (6.37)	34 (6.30)
8. Punjabi	14 (1.78)	6 (0.66)	7 (0.97)	7 (0.75)	—	11 (1.08)	8 (0.66)	18 (1.57)	31 (2.42)	9 (0.74)	14 (2.59)
9. Garo	13 (1.65)	13 (1.42)	18 (2.02)	22 (2.35)	29 (2.71)	14 (1.37)	24 (1.97)	54 (4.72)	32 (2.50)	37 (3.06)	42 (7.78)
10. Manipuri	12 (1.53)	20 (2.19)	7 (0.79)	7 (0.75)	11 (1.03)	12 (1.18)	8 (0.66)	11 (0.96)	7 (0.55)	8 (0.66)	—
11. Mizo	22 (2.80)	16 (1.75)	17 (1.91)	8 (0.85)	34 (3.18)	11 (1.08)	—	7 (0.61)	12 (0.94)	8 (0.66)	6 (1.11)
12. Naga	6 (0.76)	—	—	—	—	5 (0.49)	18 (1.48)	—	9 (0.70)	—	—
13. Hajong								6 (0.52)			
14. Bangla-deshi										9 (0.74)	

Among the other communities in Shillong the Jayantias on an average responsible for 4.7% of the crimes committed during the year in study. Whereas, Assamese are coming next to them recording an average percentage of 3.6% during the same period.

Beharies on an average are responsible for 2.6% of the crimes committed during the period 1981-1990. Next significant position in the crime table is occupied by Garos who are responsible for 2.4% of the crimes on an average committed during that period. Punjabis, Manipuria, Mizos and Nagas are on an average registered 1% each for Punjabis and Manipuris, 1.3% for Mizos and 0.3% for Nagas in respect of crimes committed during that period which are not that significant in respect of the communities discussed earlier.

(2) Age-group of Criminals

From the Table·2, it is observed that the largest number of convicts were found in the age group of criminals belonging to 15 to 24 years registering 44.18% of the total convicts. If we go for the individual analysis among the communities residing in Shillong, it is observed that highest percentage of criminals in all the communities are in the age group of 15 to 24 years. Criminals belonging to the age group 25-34 years are coming next recording 36.09% of the crimes committed during the period 1981, 1990. The percentage shows a steep declination to 12.73% with the more aged criminals belonging to the age group 35-44 years. The criminal activity with the more aged person within the age group of 45-54 years registered only 5.46% of the crimes committed during the year in the study. A negligible percentage of 1.0% of the crime are found to be restricted within the age group of 55-64 years, whereas 0.53% of crimes are committed by people in the age group of 65-74 years who can be termed as strayed criminals.

In general crime is seen to be restricted within the youngesters and with the ages as good sense starts growing in them they

TABLE 2

Age-Group of Convicts

Year / *Age-Group*	*1981*	*1982*	*1983*	*1984*	*1985*	*1986*	*1987*	*1988*	*1989*	*1990*	*1991 (Upto July)*	*Percent-age*
15-24	253	262	372	408	450	431	544	459	613	505	186	44.18
25-34	267	319	321	307	384	364	394	406	433	397	212	36.09
35-44	103	114	90	149	121	97	153	145	120	175	52	12.73
45-54	46	60	32	54	54	51	56	70	65	55	22	5.46
55-64	7	16	9	0	12	5	17	5	11	18	8	1.00
65-74	5	6	6	5	6	0	6	8	0	11	0	0.53

refrain from indulging in criminal activity which however gives the society a respect and good health. But the reason in decline in percentage of criminals with the ages can be attributed to the factors that during 15-34 years most of the individuls faced lost of problems due to unemployment, lack of proper training and education, socio-economic in security, social and cultural pressure. All these factors compel the persons to resort to some anti-social activities and as a result they become the victim of criminal offences knowing or unknowingly.

(3) Different Types of Offences Committed Under Indian Penal Code/Criminal Act in Shillong during the Period 1981-1991 upto July

It is found that same person was convicted with more than one charges under IPC, creating confusion in categorising them with a specific singular charge. Keeping the main charge in mind, this infact is a major limitation on the part of the author in analysing the table-3. However, the Table-3 was prepared on the furmula one man one charge (under-IPC) basis. The Table-3 shows that during the period under study i.e., from 1981-91 (upto July) the *Dangerous Drug Addicts* in Shillong are heading the list. The total number of convicts during this 10 years rose to 1731. This shows that drug addicts, are causing a vital law and order problem in Shillong because the age group of drug users range from 20 to 32 years, i.e., the young generations are falling victim to this social evil. Coming to year-wise analysis it is seen that in the early eighties, i.e., in 1981 the total number of convicts under this section was only 53, in 1982 the number was 40. The figure almost remained same upto 1984. But since 1985 the number of convicts started rising, it reached to 207 in that year, remained same in the next year too. But in 1987 the figure was nearly doubted, it rose to 412 a record highest in the eighties but in 1988 the number fell to 104, a healthy sign for the society. In 1989 the figure was 361 and in 1990 it reached to 229 and upto July 1991 the figure was only 36. The addiction not only kills the user but it cripples the society also, because frustration which is the root cause of spreading this social evil spoils the very basement of the society, i.e., the youth who the future rests upon.

Theft is the crime that comes next in order of convicts during the decade 1981-1990. During this period the total number of convicts rose to 1668. The table-3 shows that maximum number of convicts under theft charges was 204 in the year 1982 and the minimum number of convicts 116 were recorded in the year 1987. Hence, it can be inferred that the variation is not wide as it is found in case of drug addicts.

Coming next in order of numerical number is charges for *Criminal Trespass/Lurking house trespass.* The total number of convicts recorded during this 10 years rose to 1182 with minimum number of 95 in the year 1986 and maximum 127 in the preceeding year. Another feature is that the variation is not that high through-out the decade recording an average of 112.

Murder/Attempt to murder is coming next in order recording 960 in totality throughout the decade. The number 53 reads lowest in the year 1984 and highest of 120 in the year 1990—a number which is more than thrice in comparison. Another thing that can be inferred from the table-3 is that during the first half of eighties, i.e., from 1981-1985 the average was much below 100, but during the later half it was well above.

Arrest without warrant stands next to murder totalling 893 in number for the decade 1981-1991 (July). The maximum number of convicts recorded was 141 in the year 1984 and the minimum 37 was noted for the eighties throughout.

In *Rioting* charges number of convicts rose to 657 coming next in reckoning as per the table-3. It was 95 in the year 1984 a record high, rising from a very low number of 9 in the year 1982. The average figure was very much on lower side in the yearly eighties but in the later half it started rising appreciably. The cause of which may lie with the communal disharmony in Shillong during those days.

TABLE 3

Different Types of Offences Committed Under Indian Penal Code/Criminal Act in Shillong During The Period 1981-1991 (Upto July)

Pattern of Crime	*1981*	*1982*	*1983*	*1984*	*1985*	*1986*	*1987*	*1988*	*1989*	*1990*	*1991 (Upto July)*	*Total*
Dangerous Drug Act	53	40	52	40	207	207	412	104	361	229	26	1731
Theft/in building	134	204	181	195	173	135	116	136	153	156	85	1668
Criminal Trespass	114	108	119	104	127	95	103	119	103	125	65	1182
Murder/Attempt to murder	90	82	72	53	70	96	104	119	114	120	49	969
Arrest without warrant	37	128	94	141	66	89	77	72	65	85	39	893
Rioting	24	9	34	95	94	77	58	71	75	81	39	657
Robbery/Dacoity	25	44	68	45	53	54	54	54	55	60	21	533
Abetment of Offence	30	37	14	16	24	21	19	44	67	83	43	398

Causing grievious hurt	24	39	23	35	39	29	40	40	46	52	16	383
Wrongful restraining of person	30	23	12	10	12	27	25	34	19	51	44	303
Cheating	16	11	20	14	14	11	14	14	16	13	7	150
Kidnapping	17	17	6	12	17	10	22	12	12	15	4	144
Rash Driving	8	3	5	7	17	11	18	17	28	13	5	132
Rape	6	12	2	9	12	14	12	13	12	22	5	119
Criminal Intimidation	4	14	13	3	3	6	19	8	10	37	26	143
Criminal breach of trust	2	1	3	12	6	2	3	11	8	16	2	66
Forgery	—	4	4	4	5	1	2	5	7	4	4	40
Criminal conspiracy	8	3	2	—	5	—	1	43	9	—	—	71

Robbery/Dacoity/or Attempt to Commit Robbery come next to rioting in order of numerical number. In the decade throughout the total number of convicts stand to 533 recording highest figure 68 in the year 1983 and the lowest number 25 in the year 1981. Another analysis of the table-3 reveals that during the eighties the variation in number was very close in that particular crime.

Abetment of offence ranks next to robbery/dacoity, and total number of convicts for the period under survey stood to 398 in Shillong. It was lowest in the year 1983 the figure stood to 14 and in the year 1990 the figure was 83, highest in the eighties. During first half, i.e., 1981-1985 the number of convicts were lower than the second half of eighties. i.e., 1986-1990.

Coming next in order of ranking as per the table-3 is convicts accused of '*Causing Grievions Hurt Voluntarily*'. Total number of convicts under these head stood to 383 in totality recording 23 in the year 1983 and highest 52 in the year 1990.

Wrongful Restraining of Persons comes next in order or reckoning totalled 303 in the eighties. It recorded lowest figure 10 in the year 1984 and highest 51 in the year 1990. A figure which is 5 times as high as that of in the year 1984. A comparison between two halves shows that second half of eighties, i.e., from 1986-1990 recorded spurt in crime than the first half, i.e., for the year 1981-1985.

Cheating and Kidnapping, using as bait for money totalled 150 and 144 respectively throughout the decade, i.e., 1981-1990. In cheating the lowest number of convicts recorded was 11 in the year 1982 and 1986, and the highest number recorded 20 was in the year 1983. Kidnapping too had almost same level of variation. The lowest number recorded was 6 in the year 1983 and the highest 22 in the year 1987. Yearwise variation is not wide which creates less problem for the administration as the number of crime committed almost remained same in the decade.

Convicts for *Rash Driving* totalled 132 in the years from 1981 to 1991 (July). In the first half of eighties, i.e., from 1981 to 1985 total number of convicts were only 40 whereas in the second half, i.e., 1986-1990 number of convicts were 92.

Rapists totalled 119 during last eighties, i.e., from 1981-1991 (July). Like other crimes number of convicts was much less in the first half of eighties and recorded only 41 rage cases, whereas, in the second half, i.e., from 1986-1990 recorded rape cases were 78, a figure almost double.

Convicts ofCriminal Intimidation totalled 143 in 10 years from 1981 to 1991 (July). The crime was at a low ebb upto 1986 but after that there was a spurt and in 1990 the figure stood to 37. The upward trend is seen to exist for the year 1991 too, as the figure available upto July the recorded convicts in this 7 months rose to 26, which is not at all a healthy sign.

Convicts classified as *'Criminal Breach of Trust'* totalled 66 throughout the eighties. Mischief by fire or explosion is a serious type of crime and convicts totalled 155 in 10 years. The number of convicts were almost same in every year and in both halves the variation in number of convicts were almost same. The lowest number of convicts was recorded 9 in 1981 and 1988 and the highest number recorded was 33 in the year 1990.

Forgery/Forgery with Notes is also a serious type of crime and during the period 1981-1990 total number of convicts stood to 40. The number of convicts almost remained same in all these 10 years.

Criminal Conspiracy totalled 71 for the period under study i.e , from 1981 to 1991 (July). The number of convicts were maintaining a humble figure in almost all the years but surprisingly in the year 1988 the figure reached upto 43, reason for which may lie with the administrative authority of Shillong. The administration was so much aware that in the next year i.e., 1989 it again felt in line with other years and in the year 1990 none was found to be convicted under this charge, a healthy sign both for society and the administration of Shillong.

Conclusion

Data supplied in the present study are so authentic that they can be relied upon even by the Govt. for any sort of crime orieted information in Shillong. The tables are giving information regarding criminal offences taking place in Shillong during the past decade. It is obvious that the youngsters were crime prone in Shillong like other places in India and the trend was very much on rise in the later part of the decade. Khasis being the main inhabitant in Shillong they have lion's share in criminal activities in the locality. Author's alarming feature is conspicuous from the analysis in that the drug addiction in this city is one of the major crimes. Present investigation is also informative for the personnel who are responsible for keeping law and order of the locality in proper shape.

Acknowledgements

I must express my gratitude to the Inspector General of Prison of Shillong, who very kindly allowed me to collect data from the register of District Jail.

I am equally thankful and appreciate for the help extended to me by other members of the District Jail of Shillong.

It would have remained truncated if I don't admit my indebtedness to Dr. S.B. Chakraborty, Superintending Anthropologist, Anthropological Survey of India, Shillong for his valuable suggestion, and encouragement and enthusing me in taking up this project.

REFERENCES

1. Carleton, W. 1967. "Cultural Roots of American law enforcement". *Current History.*

2. Clinard, M.B. and Abbort, D.J. 1973. *Crime in the developing countries.* London, John Wiley.

3. Datta Ray, B., Majumdar, D. N. and Doley, D. 1986 *Crime perspective in North-East India*, New Delhi. Omsons Publications.

4. Donal, E.J. MacNamara 1958. *'Criminology' The Encyclopedia Americana* (ed.) Dudley, Vol. 8, 200-203.

5. Elliot, M.A. 1952. *Crime in Modern Society.* New York: Harper and Brothers.

6. Francis, R.D. 1970. Recidivism, type of crime and extraversion. *Australian and Newzealand Journal of Criminology*, 3, 92-94.

7. Ganguly, D. and Maitra, A.K. 1966. Some environmental correlates of Juvenile Delinquency. *Indian Journal in Social work*. 27, 205-210.

8. Kundu, S. and Mukherjee, K. 1960 Study of birth order and family positions of the criminals. *Proceedings of the 47th Indian Science Congress, Part-III, Section-XII.*

9. Singh, A. 1980. A Study of personality of Murderers and the Psycho-social factors related with Murder. *Indian Journal of Criminology*, 8, 15-20.

10. Singh, D.R. 1981. Current trends and forms of crime against women. *Indian Journal of Social work. XLII (1)*, 33-40.

11. Singh, D.R. and Khan, M.Z. 1983. Crime urbanisation linkage in India: An exploration. *Indian Journal of Social work.* XLIV (3), 243-252.

27

Tension in Shillong in 1979 and 1990 : An Overview

U. S. Bhattacharya

Tension is a psychological term, it connotes a state of restlessness or unease, especially when some goal or satisfaction is blocked. The world is co-releated with the term stress which means any strain or psychological stresses, such as frustration, deprivation, and conflict, evoke psychological defenses. The confrontation between the tribals and the non-tribals in Meghalaya, like other hill regions of the north-east, is not a phenomenon of receut origin. The long history of their interaction has been one of the tension and conflict either overt or covert. But unlike in Mizoram or Nagaland they never allowed their collision to take a violent turn. But events of 1979 and late eithties in Shillong and in other places of Meghalaya have shattered this belief.

Unrest of 1979 & 1990: A Resume

Meghalaya—the abode of clouds—which came into existence in February 1972, without any bloodshed has witnessed a spate of violence, looting, and arson, especially in and around its capital town Shillong for a few months since October 1979. The state can no longer boast of being an island of peace in the turbulent north-eastern region. It will not be out of place to mention here that the then Union Home Minister M. M. Syed observed in Shillong in the early part of August 1990 that Meghalaya is an oasis of peace in the north eastern region. But the statement was nuffified by the subsequent violent incidences started from the end of August 1990.

In 1979, the trouble started following alleged defacing of a Kali idol on the afternoon of October 22, 1979, in Lait-umkhrah area, and lingered on for about three months, 34 lives were lost, 147 injured, over 100 shops looted, 84 shops and houses and a taxi set ablaze despite night curfew and heavy deployment of police and para-military forces.[2] Six thousand Bengalee families left Meghalaya, number of families uprooted and shifted to safer area as 5000 and total loss of property was rupees twenty crores.[3]

In 1987, 5000 Nepali families mostly from Jaintia Hills coal mines and some families from the East and West Khasi Hills left the state; whereas 2000 families were uprooted and shifted to safer areas, and total loss of property was about rupees nine crores.[4] Although casuality figures were not available, but a conservative estimate by some voluntary organizations put the figure at 6 killed and 11 injured.[5]

In 1988-89, as well as in early part of 1990 some Marwaries, Punjabis and Muslim communities lost several lakh of rupees worth properties and some sustained injuries but due to absence of authentic data, analysis was not undertaken in this project; on similar grounds disturbances in Garo Hills in 1988, was not included in this study.

Let us now take up the black year of 1990. It may be noted here that the political atmosphere in Meghalaya in general and

Shillong in particular started changing since the resignation of Congress Ministry headed by Sri Purno Sangma in March 1990. Instances of selected killings and extortion of big amounts by extremist groups in Assam is another contributory factor for unrest in Meghalaya. In March 1990, a new coalition ministry consisting a number of regional parties and groups headed by Sri B.B. Lyngdoh came to power. It was interesting to note that Sri Lyngdoh was the Chief Minister of Meghalaya in the turbulent year of 1979 also. Lyngdoh in 1979 was a strongman and put down the riot with an iron hand; but Lyngdoh in 1960, was physically and politically a weak person, due advance age and compulsions in the state politics. He was presiding over a cabinet consisting of strange bedfellows with different idiologies and interests. It was a contributory factor in the continuance of disturbances for a prolong period especially in Lower Mawprem and Burra Bazar areas of Shillong.

In 1990-91, the trouble started in the last part of August 1990, when a non-issue became an issue in the form of a demand by newly formed Federation of Khasi Jaintia and people who gave a bund call in Shillong, against alleged 'illegal trading' by non-tribals in Burabazar and also as a protest against issue of trading licenses to non-tribals by the Khasi Hills District Council. The matter came to a head when one non-tribal young businessman of Burabazar Sri Gopinath Banik (22) was killed in his shop and certain alleged comments by the Civil Surgeon of Shillong, during postmortem examination sparked off tension and incidents of stone throwing and damage of some vehicles on 29 August 1990 took in a bizarre turn of events, which practically affected all non-tribal communities including Bengalees, Biharis, Marwaries, Nepalis and muslims. In comparison with events of 1979, loss of life and property was less. Since August 1990 upto February 1991, 12 non-tribals and 2 tribal lives were lost, number of families uprooted and shifted to safer areas was 25 (upto 22.10.90) and total loss of property amounting to 0.25 crores (as on 22.10.90).[6] Outcome, Durga Puja in Shillong practically devoid of enthusiasm and community Kali Puja or Diwali observed. In mid-October Mawprem Durbar served quit order on six non-tribals and in November 1990 and in January-February 1991 because of a series of petrol bomb incidents several non-tribal shops were gutted and several lives were lost either due to severe burn or liberal use of knives, some time even in front of the state police personnels.[7] In 1990-91, disturbances mostly confined to two localities namely, Burrabazar and Lower Mawprem, with occasional incidents of assult and vehicles set on fire in Mulki area two non-tribal houses were set on fire in Upper Mulki area. In various memorandums submitted to Union and State authorities non-tribals of Meghalaya in general and residents of Shillong in particular alleged that they were facing discrimination, intimidation, and physical annihilation in the recent past for the partisan pro-tribal state government of Meghalaya, although the non-tribals constitute 20% of Meghalaya's population and a great factor in the economic growth of the State. They cited the example of draconian Meghalaya Land Transfer Act. 1971. They further alleged that under this unconstitutional Act, non-tribals' basic human right of residing in any part of the country and to have landed property etc. have been violeted. Further, under this 'Black Act', the non-tribal permanent residents of Meghalaya are debarred from purchasing landed property in almost cent percent area of the state. The memorialists alleged that the State government's policy of apar-thied-cum-genocide towards non-tribals was revealed in the murder of one Debashis Deb, 25 years, in Lower Mawprem in the evening of October 10, 1990 and subsequent apathy of police and medical authorities, either reaching the place of occurrence and postmortem with questionable haste are pointer in this direction.[8] On the other hand, tribals alleged that they were exploited by the non-tribals. Meanwhile, it became so shockingly bad that Sri Subodh Kant Sahay, Union Minister of States for Home, 'curtly told Sri B. B. Lyngdoh that he should set his house in order'.[9]

Historicity of Confrontation

The confrontation between the tribals and the non-tribals in Meghalaya, like other hill areas of North-East, is not of recent origin. The history of their interaction has been one of tension and conflict. But unlike in Mizo and Naga hills they never took a violent turn. There has been some accommodation. But the fusion of the two ways of life is still an open issue.

The traditional people of the Khasi Jaintia and Garo Hills, as in the rest of the country, had till the middle of the last century lived in isolated and closed societies; although the people in the border areas of Bengal and Assam had frequent intercourse with plains people specially or trade and commerce. The traditional society in the interior had feared and resented any intrusion in its life style. Some change came after the advent of the British in the second half of the 19th century. The British imperial policy of conquest, legal administration land tenure, spread of education, added with the policy of Christian missions, went to expose these traditional societies to the quicker tempo of modernization, to a dew legal administration and to a new economic process. But the colonial masters also added to the fear and distrust of the tribals by following a policy of 'divide and rule' and a policy of segretating the tribals from the Indian main stream. After the departure of the British, the tribal culture and way of life had undergone a great change. A number of tribals had embraced christianity in preference to their indigenous faith. They had Roman script, took western costumes, music and dance. The process of social change from traditional life to modernity during the 100 years long interaction with the British was so rapid that the tribals lost their value and belief system completely. They faced a crisis of identity.

Aftermath of Independence

Immediately after independence, the tribal leaders of the North-Eastern region raised the demand for autonomy to preserve their tribal heritage and identity. According to some observers sense of group belongingness cemented them into a socio-psychological unity or 'we groups' with strong emotion of ethnocentrism and parochialism while viewing 'other groups' and their ways with hostility. Although special protection and concessions were offered after independence; but fear psychosis persists in the psyche of the tribals.

The Coming of Meghalaya and After

Meghalaya was carved out of Assam on February 21, 1972. But due to clash of personalities and scramble for power and office the All Party Hills Leaders' Conference (APHLC), which was instrumental in the creation of Meghalaya, broke up into groups. The rich dividents that the 'most militant party HSPDP', induced even the most liberal sections in other parties to adopt an openly hostile posture against the non-tribals. The poison of parochial political culture started spreading through the body politics of Meghalaya. The emerging political culture was oriented more to sub-nationalism than to a broader national indentity. The same spirit is reflec'ed in the resentments either against the construction of Canto nent at Umroi or construction of railways in the state.

Revenue Deficit State

The non-tribal minority of Meghalaya and their tax-paying friends in rest of the country, contribute about 84 paise out of every rupee that is spent on the welfare of the tribals.[10] (Meghalaya Budget for 1989-90 is in the round figure Rs. 670 crores and its revenue is a bare Rs. 43 crores; the balance being made up through central assistances). Wonders why they should be deprived of their basic constitutional rights to conduct business or adopt any occupation in the state. Hence the non-tribals argue that being minorities in the state, they expect safety of life, protection of property and some psychological security.

The non-tribals are not convinced by the theory of exploitation of tribals by the 'dkhars' or outsiders. In the matter of land rights, jobs, scholarships, allotment of seats in professional institutions, the non-tribals were completely kept out as a matter of state government policy. Even admission in College is now restricted by government's orders to 80 : 20 ratio. So, if the tribals have apprehensions, the non-tribals too have a stronger case. Those who are trying to exploit these area of tension seem to overlook the compulsions of multi-racial societies, which are a reality of the present day life, and there can be no going back to isolated ethnic sanctuaries.

Fear Psychosis

Even after six months since the trouble between tribals and non-tribals shok the lovely town of Shillong, residents continue to suffer from a fear psychosis and return home soon after dusk. The roads are mostly deserated in the evening. Tourists are advised to stay indoors. A Khasi journalist felt that the state government had not done much to defuse the tension and promote fellow feelings. Others argued that Shillong residents were too peaceloving to be embroiled in trouble and if they stayed back at home in the evenings it was more an act of caution than anything else. A section of the non-tribal businessmen expressed fear that if the present movement lingers there would be more trouble which might result in a flight of capital.[11]

The dispute over Bura Bazar has not been finally resolved. The shops were closed down after violence spread and attained a communal confrontation. Subsequently, the Bura Bazar Merchants' Association moved Gauhati High Court and obtained a stay order permitting them to resume business operations temporarily pending the final verdict.

Some Concluding Observations

We think that the fear of losing culture and identity of three major tribes of Meghalaya is unfounded in reason, due to adequate constitutional and other safeguards. The history of mankind is replete with instances of ethnic groups getting wiped out merely because instead of competing to live honourably as equals with those around them, they asked for some kind of protection or crutches to survive. When a society is reduced to the state of having to make such a demand, it publicly proclaims that it can survive only on crutches. It is a defeatist demand. The Red Indians in the U.S.A. had clamoured for protection and special privileges. They got them, but they neither have their languages nor their culture today. They remain as ethnic groups that are only fit for anthropological study, and are referred to as 'Indians' rather than 'Americans' even though they are the original inhabitants of the land. They are unable to move with the times. The same is true of the tribals of Australia.

This writer feels that culture as a way of life is manifest best of all in the way people work, function and behave as part of their society. Hence any preoccupation with culture cannot be moored solely in the past. It must include in its ambit the present way of life too, characterised by a strong desire to work in all spheres of life with a competitive spirit. A preference for short-cuts to a good life by eliminating a section of competitiors through violence and indulgance in lawlessness by youths is really a suicidal outlook. It is only a society that is unsure of its own performance that can make such preposterous demands, or feel that it should close all windows on the world for fear of being 'swept way' even by mild breezes. Here lies the real challenge before the tribal youths of Meghalaya.

REFERENCES

1. Encyclopaedia Britannica, Vol. IX, 5974 ed., p. 612 and 890.

2. India's North-East In Flames by V.I.K. Sarin, New Delhi, 1980, p. 76.

3. & 4. Statement prepared by the Non-Tribal Communities and indicated in various Memorandum.

5. Sources like to be anonymous.
6. Ibid, 3 & 4.
7. Press Reports (Shillong Times, 29 August, 26 Sept., 14 Oct. and 18 November 1990).
8. Ibid 5.
9. Sunday (Calcutta), Vol. 17, Issue 41, 21-27 Oct., p. 82-83.
10. Ibid 2, p. 79.
11. The Statesman, Calcutta, 14.3.91.
12. Rudolph and Rudloph. The Modernity of Tradition, New Delhi, 1967.
13. Rao, V.V., A Century of Tribal Politics in North East India, New Delhi, 1975.
14. Bhattachariya, U., Local Government in Khasi Hills, New Delhi, 1980.
15. Myron Weiner, State Politics in India, U.S.A., 1968.
16. V.I. Lenis, Imperialism, Moscow, 1969.
17. Robin Blackburn, Ideology in Social Science, London, 1976.
18. Myrdal Gunnar, Asian Drama: An Inquiry into the Poverty of Nations, New York, 1968.

28

Social Instability in Shillong, (1980–1991)

Rakhal Kumar Purkayastha

Shillong (25° 34' N: 91° 53 'E) is situated at an elevation of 1,496 metres above mean sea level. Before 1864, Shillong was an unknown nomenclature except for a small village under the then United Khasi State of Shillong.[1] During the year 1864, the headquarters of the Chief Commissioner of Assam was shifted from Cherrapunjee to Shillong.[2] Accordingly, on March 20, 1874, by a Government Notification No. 49, Shillong was declared the capital of Assam Province with effect from that data.[3] Shillong became a station in 1878 apparently in accordance with the Bengal Municipal Act of 1876. In 1905 to 1911, Shillong received a minor set back due to reconstitution of the Province of Assam into the Eastern Bengal under Lieutenant Governor based in Dacca but still half of the Secretariat continued to function from here and in April 1912, with the reversal of partition of Bengal, Shillong once again gained her lost glory as the capital of Assam.[4] Shillong continued to be the capital of United Assam after independence till Meghalaya was born as the 21st State of the India Union. On January 20, 1972[5] and the capital of Assam was shifted to Dispur and Shillong, the land of blue mountains and red stream became the capital of the newly born hill state of Meghalaya.

The coming of the Britishers and the growth of administrative establishments—civil, military and para military in and around Shillong brought along a large influx of people from the plains to aid the administration in its routine matters. As such the contact of the people of this region from the plains were not unknown and there was a long tradition of trade relations with the plains and many "merchant kings used to take up their residence in the villages near the frontier of Sylhet to take advantage of the trade . . . In view of the importance of trade with the people of neighbouring countries, the chief sought concessions for opening of markets in the former's jurisdiction sometimes acknowledging political supremacy of foreign sovereign."[6] The people of the hill were keen trader and a considerable proportion of the people earned their living by travelling from one market to another.[7] During this period a few Bengali traders from Dacca visited the hills though they did not take up any permanent residence. With the advent of British administration many traders settled in Shillong with Office workers. During this period after 1864 and also after independence Shillong continued to grow not only as an administrative centre but also became one of the prominent centres of learning, judicial organisation, trading activities, church organisation, banking system etc. in the entire north eastern region. After independence Shillong was not only capital of Assam which included now Assam, Meghalaya, Mizoram, Nagaland but also the headquarters of North East Frontier Area (now Arunachal Pradesh) besides the Eastern Air Command, the Assam Rifles, the Assam Regiment, 101 Communication Zone, North Eastern Council and host of other Central Government organisation. Thus this lead to large influx of people from outside the region in order to explore the job potentialities and trade.

Shillong gradually developed into a cosmopolitan set up and in its more than 100 years of recorded history there was no incidents of communal violence as witnessed in its neighbouring states till October 1979, when ethnic conflict originated in Laitumkhrah quickly gripped the entire city and reached its climax in December when bus passengers were lynched by an angry mob, during the clashes which lasted till the end of the year. According to official records, 37 persons were killed, many were injured, people had to flee from their houses and take shelter in refugee camps and properties worth crores were damaged. The people were shocked and surprised at this outbreak of communal carnage and even the Statesman in its editorial of November 1979, commented "There can be no other explanation for the present drift into narrow parochialism in every educated and enlightened Meghalayans which has been relatively free from communal disturbances."[9]

The decade of 1980 to 1990 has been the most turbulent period in the history of the city with persistent social tensions often breaking into social conflict threatening the stability of the society and often resulting in severe or widespread violence requiring intervention of the administration. This regular and persistent social instability has necessitated us to make a modest attempt to comprehend and present this phenomena existing in our cosmopolitan milieu eroding the image of Meghalaya as a multicultural and secular state so that social scientists can appreciate the magnitude and complexity of this crisis and offer suggestion towards its solution.

In 1980, the lingering impact of 1979 continued to haunt the people and administration, additional police reinforcement had to be maintained and Army alerted to prevent and avoid further flare up. The Chief Minister, B.B. Lyngdoh in his Republic Day address reminded the people of the solemn promise that the leaders of all parties in the state made to the national leadership at the time of creation of the state that they would give fair treatment to all protecting the rights and interests of the minorities.[10] In the month of February the officials expressed concern over the involvement of students in anti government demonstration[11] and arrested two students leaders belonging to North Eastern Regional Students Union[12] and in March the district authorities declared Sec. 144 CrPC apprehending breach of peace during the celebration of Holi.[13] In May 1980, Shillong city witnessed a 12 hours bandh to demand expulsion of unauthorised immigrants.[14] This added to the underlying tension in the city as the mass campaign organized by Meghalaya Students Union (virtually a new name of KSU) looked like a carbon copy of Assam movement.[15] The agitation resumed by MSU also had its impact in Tura and Jowai, the district administration retaliated by imposing Section 144 CrPC.[16] In July secessionist leaflets appeared in Shillong[17] and an abortive attempt was made to raid an armoury of Coy HQ of Meghalaya Police situated at Bishnupur,[18] and consequently Army was called in[19], subsequently the raiders were arrested and Army withdrawn. Further the administration had to impose restrictions on celebration of Durga Puja but it passed off peacefully[20] and 1980 did not witness social conflict on any large scale as witnessed the previous year.

The year 1981 did not witness any serious tension except clashes in Iewduh in August originating from teer bookies[21] and killing of Dr. S.C. Banwar, Acting Vice-Chancellor of NEHU by unknown assailant on October 30.[22] In the year 1982 in the month of October the District Administration imposed Sec. 144 CrPC apprehending breach of peace[23] on October 20, a student was assaulted in NEHU Mayurbhanj Campus, the origin of the incident could be ascertained to the tension prevailing in the Campus on the issue of election to Post Graduate Students Union. The local students were of the view that all key post of the Union should be given to them whereas the Nagaland and Mizoram students sought an equal opportunity to contest for all posts since the University catered to the need of these States.[24] The Meghalaya Post Graduate Students Union threatened to close the University Campus if elections were not held.[25] In the year 1983, major social tension centred around death of a young local boy Babu Muthiang, a student of Class X of Laban Khasi

School due to beating by a drunken police personnel performing duty inside a Cinema Hall in the month of April.[26] The students called for class boycott on May 3, and there were incidents of stone pelting at Don Bosco, Laitumkhrah.[27] The administration diffused the situation by suspending the Police Havildar involved in the incident and consequently stir was called off.[28] In the same year there was also an attempt to whip off communal passion capitalising on two stray incidents reported at Lower New Colony and Rynjah (Umpling).[29] On October 19th and 20th, the students gave a call for bandh in protest against the construction of railway line in the state,[30] In November, there was tension prevailing in the southern fringes of Shillong due to intra tribal clashes.[31]

In the year 1984, there was no major incidents except cases of stray assaults in the month of September as a result of which one person was killed.[32] The police immediately launched a man-hunt and six persons were taken into the custody on the basis of confessional statement made by two of them.[33] In the year 1985, there was mild tension arising out of the incident of abuse of a girl student from Shillong College in the month of July and this incident lead to a sequel of retalisation and counter retaliation.[34] In September, there was revival of anti-alien stir starting with mass poster campaigning on September 19, coupled with two hours black-out, seven persons were injured in the incident of stone pelting, it climaxed with 12 hours Meghalaya bandh on September 20[35]. In November, there were cases of assaults in which two persons lost their life. In the year 1986, there was no report of any major incidents.

In the year 1987, it was almost a repetion of 1919, mobs went on rampage burning and stoning houses and property. Janata curfews, bandhs and rasta roko became almost a daily occurrence from the month of May onwards. The prelude to the trouble came in form of an angry crowd that went berseck in NEHU parmanent Campus at Mawlai in the month of May in which nine persons were injured.[36] The main tension centred around certain alleged incident of assault at Nongmynsong where a police driver was attacked by some drunkards.[37] As a sequel to it 12 hours bandh was called on 25th May in which there were incidents of stone pelting at MTC buses and police vehicles. The situation was further percipitiated by the formation of GNLF Unit in the city.[38] The students called for expulsion of foreign nationals from the State, and on June 17, there was a pitch battle between public and police as a result of which two persons were killed in police firing, 8 vehicles damaged, 3 shops plundered at Umsohsun and neighbouring areas of Mawkhar and Jaiaw.[39] The agitation continued almost throughout the year with liberal use of force by both the agitationists and the district administration. Several persons were assaulted and arsoning was witnessed not only in the city but also in the villages. The State Government had to time and again declare curfew and seek help of Army and para military forces to contain the violence and the backlash of Meghalaya incidents were reported even from the Himalayan kingdom of Nepal.[40] According to information contained in a letter written by five non-tribals MLAs to the Chief Minister, Capt. W, Sangma nearly 20,000 people left the state empty handed, 10,000 were sheltered in camps and about 20,000 more were living in mortal fear of eviction and property worth Rs. 5 crores were destroyed as a result of this agitation.[41]

The year of 1988, began with a call of public curfew given by KSU to prevent public from attending Mr. Rajiv Gandhi's meeting scheduled on 28 January and to press on their demands which included extension of Inner-Line Permit, Cent per cent reservation of Assembly seats and solution to foreigners issue.[42] This was followed by KSU call of seven hours strike of school, colleges and cinema halls on June 17, to pay respect of Paul Makri and unknown youth named U Tirot Nongkhlaw who fell victim to police firing on the same date last year.[43] The District Administration imposed Sec. 144 CrPC to prevent the students from taking out procession but ultimately allowed to students
from taking out procession but ultimately allowed to students to

take out procession from Mawkhar to Mawprem Catholic Cemetry via Jaiaw[44] and the programme passed off peacefully with no untoward incidents.[45] In another incident of the year which took place in November there was severe clashes between police and youth at Malki but situation was immediately brought under control due to intervention of the Senior District Official.[46] In the year 1989, the KSU called for 'Public Curfew' on April 20, as a mark of protest against the Government's failure to respond to public sentiments expressed against construction of railway link within the State.[47] On April 24, the KSU threatened the State Government to either scrap railway project or face agitation coupled with nine point charter pending since 1987, which among others included the demand for extension of Inner Line Permit.[48] In May, there was a police action against KSU volunteers and two persons were arrested,[49] this lead to incidents of stone pelting at Police Bazar, G.S. Road, Malki, Lumparing.[50] On May 26, the youths decided to defy Sec. 144 CrPC and a group of mob set fire to the Dy. Chief Minister Mr. D.D. Lapang's house at Jaiaw and clashes were reported from different parts of the city.[51] The State Government decided to buy peace by stopping railway head project, releasing NSA detenus and withdrawing Sec. 144 CrPC and KSU in its turn decided not to hold any immediate agitation. In 1990, the agitation was spearheaded by united front of Khasis, Garos and Jaintias under the banner of FKJGP demanding expulsion of non-tribal traders not holding licenses from Iewduh. Following closely the issue of trading licenses a non-tribal trader was stabbed in Iewduh on August 27. On August 29, an angry mob gathered near Civil Hospital and in the incidents that followed there was liberal use of knives and stones in which many vehicles and houses were damaged though the business establishment remained closed as a mark of protest against the murder of non-tribal trader.[52] A youth was killed in an incident of stone throwing in Wahingdoh and consequently curfew was declared and Army called in to assist civil authorities to maintain law and order. In another incident of violence a youth was killed in Mawprem,[53] besides reports of assaults were there from different parts of the city including academic institutions. The local durbar served quit notice on six non-tribal traders of Mawprem in October for their alleged involvement in the incidents of August 29.[54] In October, the Police used tear gas shell at Mawkhar to disperse procession organised by school students to protest against holding of selection test. Thus the tension which initiated through the earnest efforts of FKJGP in the first part of August by asking the traders to quit Iewduh continued to simmer till the close of the year.

Fear and uncertainty once again gripped the inhabitants in 1991 when college were closed down indefinitely on July 1st, by the FKJGP educational wing over the admission issue,[55] however, the strike was called off on July 3, following an assurance given by the State education department officials that students will be assisted in matters of admission and amount of fees scholarship will be increased to match the hike in the college fees. The license issue which rocked the city the previous year was once again brought into limelight by FKJGP in the second week of July coupled with demands for removal of evil practises like sale of illicit liquor, gambling etc. at Iewduh.[56] A procession taken out by FKJGP in this connection was prevented from proceeding to Iewduh and consequently went on rampage.[57] There were also cases of stray incidents of assualts on July 20, and one person was killed.[58] The situation was brought under control with arrest of 15 persons[59] and non-tribal traders of Iewduh got a temporary respite by filing a writ at Gauhati High Court Order License issue.

All our above facts point out to the fact that a wide gulf has been created which has generated widespread tension between the tribal and non-tribal population of the State. Though no single factor can be pointed out as the cause of this animosity, the tribals believe that for decades the non-tribals have taken advantage of their financial insecurity and illiteracy and simply went around the laws to procure land and business by keeping the name of the tribals as the frontmen while the actual profit of the business went to the non-tribals and they may not be off the mark. The non-tribals on the other hand, believe that they are being unnecessarily harassed in the name of rules and regulations created to preserve the cultural identity, given second class citizen treatment in a State that runs on the money paid by the tax payers and in which they have contribute their mite in its development. But keeping in view the agitations that were launched during the decade it can be traced economy lies at its base. The youth today are utterly frustrated at the lack of job opportunities and other avenues which could afford them meaningful livelihood. The government job remains the only source of major employment and the youth even find it difficult to gain admission in higher educational institutes due to increase in the number of candidates passing their school finals. This frustration among the youth has also been taken advantage of by the political leadership and tribal economic elites to divert the attention from the major issues and keep themselves in the seat of power. This issue of unemployment is likely to increase as noted from the population trend. The population of the city which was estimated to be 1,22,752[60] in 1971, has increased to 2,48,639[61] in 1991 thus indicating 100% increase in the past twenty years and basing it on this increase we can assume that this may touch a figure of 3,53,862 by 2301 A.D. added to it will be problem of migration from the rural areas due to lack of employment facilities. Thus it is time for us to realise that agitations and violence will not contribute to any long term gains but instead a climate of confidence has to be generated and a solution found by people from all sections, all localities, experts, elders, youth leaders etc. Men in his march to progress has overcome many greater odds and definitely problem of our city is not insur-mountable but required sincere efforts of all its inhabitants.

REFERENCES

1. Pakem, B. (Ed.), *Shillong 1971-1981*, NEICSSR, Shillong, 1984. p. 1.

2. Bareh, Hamlet. *Meghalaya*, North Eastern India News and Features Service, Shillong, 1974.

3. Pakem, B. *Op. Cit.*

4. Chowdhury, J.N. *The Khasi Canvas*, Chapala Book Stall, Shillong, 1978, pp. 326-331.

5. Datta Roy, B. (Ed.) *Electoral Politics in Meghalaya*, NEICSSR, Shillong, 1978.

6. Lish, A.B. Calcutta Christian Observer, Vol. III, 1838, pp. 133-34 as quoted in Dutta, P.M. Impact of West on Khasis and Jaintias A Survey of Political Economic and Social Change, Cosmo Publication, New Delhi, 1982.

7. Allen, B.C., Gait, E.A. *et. al. Gazetteers of Bengal and North East India.* Mittal Publication, New Delhi, 1984, p. 492.

8. Hunter, W.W. *A Statistical Account of Assam, Vol. II, 1879*, B.R. Publishing Corporation, New Delhi, 1982, p. 241.

9. As quoted by Rymbai, R.T. in *Social and Political Tension in North East, in Social Tension in North East India*, Bhattacharjee, J.B. (Ed.), NEICSSR, Shillong, 1982

10. Shillong Times, June 26, 1980, p. 1.

11. ————————, Feb. 2, 1980, p. 1.

12. ————————, Feb. 9, 1980, p. 1.

13. ————————, March 1, 1980, p. 1.

14. ————————, May 3, 1980, p. 1.

15. ————————, May 31, 1980, p. 1.

16. Shillong Times, June 28, 1980, p. 1.

17. ————————, July 19, 1980, p. 1.

18. ————————, Aug. 2, 1980, p. 1.

19. ————————, Aug. 9, 1980, p. 1.

20. ————————, Oct. 8, 1980, p. 1.

21. ————————, Aug. 29, 1981. p. 1.

22. ————————, Oct. 31, 1981, p. 1.

23. ————————, Oct. 16, 1982, p. 3.

24. ————————, Oct. 23, 1982, p. 1.

25. ————————, Nov. 6. 1982, p. 1.

26. ————————, May 1, 1983, p. 1.

27. ————————, May 7, 1983, p. 1 and 6.

28. ————————, May 14, 1983, p. 1.

29. ————————, Sept. 17, 1983, p. 1.

30. ————————, Oct. 8, 1983, p. 1.

31. ————————, Nov. 19, 1983, p. 1.

32. ————————, Sept. 8, 1984, p. 1.

33. ————————, Sept. 15, 1984, p. 1.

34. ————————, July 20, 1984, p. 1.

35. ————————, Sept. 21, 1984, p. 1.

36. ————————, May 6, 1987, p. 1.

37. ————————, May 24, 1987, p. 1.

38. ————————, May 23, 1987.

39. ————————, June 18, 1987.

40. ————————, Nov. 2, 1987, p. 1.

41. ————————, Nov. 9, 1987, pp. 2 and 3.

42. ————————, Jan. 28, 1988, p. 1.

43. ———————, June 11, 1988, p. 1.

44. ————————, June 17, 1988, p. 1.

45. ————————, June 18, 1988, p. 1.

46. ————————, Nov. 12, 1988, p. 1.

47. ————————, April 14, 1989, p. 1.

48. ————————, April 25, 1989, p. 1.

49. Shillong Times, May 24 and 25, 1989, p. 1.

50. ————————. May 25, 1989, p. 1.

51. —————————, May 27, 1989, p. 1.

52. Meghalaya Guardian, 30 Aug. 1990.

53. Shillong Times, Oct. 13, 1990, p. 1.

54. ———————, Oct. 14, 1990, p. 1.

55. ————————, July 2, 1991, p. 1.

56. ————————, July 17, 1991, p. 1.

57. —————————, July 20, 1991, p. 1.

58. —————————, July 21, 1991, p. 1.

59. —————————, July 24, 1991, p. 1.

60. Census of India, 1971.

61. Census of India (Prov.), 1991.

TABLE 1

Records of population in Shillong UA* in 1971
(Community wise break up)

Assamese	9033
Bengali	6031
Hindi	8085
Gorkhali	17302
Khasi	49152
Others	33149
Total	122752

*Shillong UA includes Nongthymmai Town, Mawlai Town, Shillong Cantt. and Shillong (M).

Sources: Census of India, 1971 Meghalaya series 13 Meghalaya part II C-Social and cultural tables, Director of Census Operations, Meghalaya.

**Census 1971 Series 13-Meghalaya, District Census Handbook, UK and J Hills Director of Census Operations. Meghalaya.

Part XA villages and Town Director Part XB Primary Census Abstract.

TABLE 2

Projected population with base year 1971 Shillong UA*

Year	*Actual*	*Projected*	*Percentage Decadal Variation*
1971	1,11752	----	
1981	1,74,703	——	42.32
1991	——	2,48,639	60.23
2001	——	3,53,862	85.72
2011	——	5,03,617	121.99

TABLE 3

Record of Major Agitations in Shillong City during 1980-1991

Year and Months	*Place of occurences*	*Organisation spear-heading agitations*	*Issues*	*Leaders*	*Govt's response*
1987 May to November	Different localities	Khasi Students Union	Foreign nationals	Bull N. Lyngdoh.	Sec. 144 CrPC curfew Army called preventive detention
1989 April and May	Different localities	Khasi Students Union	Scraping of Byrnihat Railway project	Bull N.-Lyngdoh	Sec. 144 CrPC curfew Army allerted preventive detention
1990 August to October	Mainly Iewduh	Federation of Khasi, Jaintia and Garo people	Trading-license	S.S. Cajee	Sec. 144, Curfew Army called Preventive detention

TABLE 4

Records of Bandhs in Shillong City during 1980-1991

Year	*Date/ week*	*Month*	*Type of Bandh declared*	*Any reported violence/during after bandh*
1980	3rd	May	12 hrs. city bandh	Nil
1981	—	—	—	—
1982	—	—	—	—
1983	3rd week	Sept.	12 hrs. Laitumkhrah	—
1984	—	—	—	—
1985	20th	Sept.	Meghalaya bandh	—
1986	—	—	—	—
1987	25th	May	12 hrs. bandh	Incident of stone throwing at Mawlai,
	10th	Nov.	14 hrs. Public curfew	Jaiaw and Riatsamthiah

Contd.

Contd.

	17th	Nov.	Road Blockade	——
	3rd week	Nov.	Bandh in different localities	——
1988	28th	Jan.	Public Curfew	——
1989	20th	April	3 hrs. Public Curfew	——
199	5th	June	12 hrs. city bandh	——
1990	1st week	Sept.	12 hrs. bandh	——
1991	20th	Aug.	12 hrs. Laitumkhrah bandh	——

Source: Compiled from Newspaper Clippings.

TABLE 5

Records of persons killed in Shillong City during 1980-1991

Year	*Date/Week*	*Month*	*Locality of incident*	*Nos. of persons killed*	*Reason of killing*
1980	——	——	——	——	——
1981	——	——	——	——	——
1982	——	——	——	——	——
1983	Last	April	Cinema Hall	1	Beaten by Police personnel on duty
1984	1st week	Sept.	Not reported	1	Stray assaults
1985	1st week	Nov.	-do-	2	-do-
1986	——	——	——	——	——
1987	17th	June 7	Umsoh sun	3	Police firing
	2nd week	Oct.	Upper Shillong	2	Communal violence

Contd.

Contd.

1988	—	—	—	—	—
1989	—	—	—	—	—
1990	—	Aug.	Iewduh	1	Not reported
		Oct.	Wahingdoh	1	-do-
			Mawprem	1	-do-
1991	20th	July	Wards-Lake	1	Group assault

Source: Compiled from Newspaper clippings.

29

Electoral Politics of Shillong

A CASE STUDY OF LAITUMKHRAH BY—ELECTION 1990

S. K. Mukherjee

Meghalaya has a Legislative Assembly. For the electoral purpose the state has been divided into sixty constituencies. The 17th constituency of Meghalaya is the Laitumkhrah Constituency for the last Assembly election. Historically speaking Shillong is an administrative centre planted in the Khasi Hills by the alien British rulers in 1863. To-day, Shillong is the capital of Meghalaya situated in the midest of blue hills of the Khasi Hills district. About 103 km south of Gauhati and surrounded by the beautiful forest pines. Prior to the formation of the state of Meghalaya, constituted two districts of the composite state of Assam, Garo Hills district and United Khasi and Jaintia Hill district. The present state of Meghalaya was curved out of the composite state of Assam as an autonomous state passed on 24th December 1969 by the two houses of the Parliament and consequently on January 21, 1972 it emerged as a full fleged state.

Shillong being the capital of Assam and later Meghalaya play an important role for the politics of Meghalaya. Shillong is known as non-tribal town in a tribal setting. Situated in the centre of Shillong, Laitumkhrah is well known for its multi-ethnic character. This constituency is mainly populated by the following ethnic groups: (i) Khasi, (ii) Bengali, (iii) Assamese, (iv) Bihari, (v) Mizo, (vi) Nepali, (vii) Punjabi and (viii) Garo.

The Khasi society is characterised by matriliny. Among the Khasi though all of them share the language and social structure, there are five groups segregated into well defined cultural areas and each developing a different shade of economy and dialect. On the basis of religion Laitumkhrah has a large number of Christian population, particularly the Roman Catholic.

In the Laitumkhrah constituency the areas like New Colony and Bhagyakul are dominated by Bengalis who are mostly govt. servants and traders. Among the Assamese most of them are engaged in Govt jobs. With the shifting of Assam Capital from Shillong Assemese population has reduced to a greater extent.

Biharis are also engaged in various types of jobs, such as hair cutting, shoe reparing, laundering, pan-bidi cigerette selling, grocers shop etc. Besides many of them sell milk and milk products.

The Nepalis are mostly engaged as porters, pony cart drivers domestic servants (mostly female). Mizos and Panjabis are residing in Nongrim Hills and Goraline areas. Apart from the Khasi the other non-tribals also play an important role in the election process of Meghalaya.

In 1990 Laitumkhrah by-election was important from the various point of view in the Meghalaya Politics. With the election of Mr. P.G. Marbaniang to the Lok Shabha as Congress-I candidate in November 1989 the 17th Laithumkhrah Assembly Constituency fell vacant. Initially four candidates, filed their nomination to contest for the election later on the Janata Dal candidate Mr. H. Anionties Roy Kharpuli withdraw his nomination on 17th February. The other three candidates are

Mr. Robert Kharsiing (HPU), G.M. War (Cong. I) and G.R. Marbaniang (Independent). Mr. Robert Kharsing has taken the 'Rising Sun' as his election symbol and scale has been alloted to Mr. G.R. Marbaniang. An open hand is Mr. War's symbol.

In selecting a candidate the total demographic picture of the state and for that matter the composition of the electorate has to be considered from various angles e.g. ethnic, religions, linguistic, sex, age and working force. Moreover, the selection committee also consider his length of association with the party, whether he changed parties, his income and source of income, social activities etc. In Meghalaya the knowledge of English is essen-t al. Apart from that candidates with high degree of intelligence, political shrewdness and with persuasive powers ate normally considered to be meritorious for the party. Sitting M.L A's and traditional tribal leaders opinion is also play an important role in selecting a candidate in Meghalaya. All the parties now wanted represation from youth and women too.

The sitting M.L.A Mr. P.G. Marbaniang, a Catholic and was popular among the tribal and non-tribal voters of the constituency. As a headman, MDC member and M.L.A, he served this constituency for quite a long time and had a strong hold in this constituency. The Cong.-I Candidate Mr. G.M. War is very close to Mr. Marbaniang who feels that Mr. War is an well experienced man and associated with Catholic Chruch and he has long involvement in sports organizations and well aware of the problem of Laitumkhrah. Mr. War has served in various capacities in and outside the government and has held the post of Public Relation Officer in North Eastern Hill University till two days before filing his nomination papers. His greatest advantage is that he has the sitting M.P. and outgoing M.L A. of the constituency Mr. P.G. Marbaniang as his chariot driver.

Robert Kharsing (HPU) the regional opposition parties concensus candidate is a dynamic young man who had served Laitumkhrah from 1983 to 1985 as its headman. He was also the President of Khasi Student Union for some years. Mr. Kharshing helds a Master's Degree in Anthropology has the credit of serving as Research Associate at the St. Xavier's Institute of Education (Bombay). His recent association with leaders like Rajmohan Gandhi, George Fernandes and others had broadened his political outlook. A member of the Moral Rearmament (MRA) movement which believes in absolute Honesty, truth and humanity. Above all he is the eldest son of Late Martin Narayan Majaw who died recently was very actively associated with Meghalaya politics Mr. Kharshing's Catholic connection also have weighed heavily in a constituency where Catholics out number other Christian denominations.

George Richard Marbaniang (50) was an Independent candidate. He rebelled against the Congress (I) after he was not given the party ticket. He turned against the party he said on 'grounds of principle'. He is not a Catholic but belong to Presbyterian Church. He was a formar headman of Laitumkhrah was associated with Congress (I) and served also a General Secretary of Shillong City Congress (I) Committee.

In Laithumkhrah Constituency one gets into an election spirit immediately after the flag starts fluttering in different house tops. Even the vehicles plying round the constituency flew party flag. Like 1989 Parliament election religian has been an important issue in this constituency.

The campaigning for the Laitumkhrah Assembly seats in the heart of Shillong city has gained mementum with street corner meetings by filmstar and Congress-I, M.P. Mr. Sunil Dutta on 16th Feb., 1990 in Don Bosco square. In his speech he said that the Deputy Prime Minister, Mr. Devilal make irresponsible remarks against the christians which is really very shamful. Keeping in mind the constituency's overwhelming christian population, Mr. Sunil Dutt made special mention of the contribution made by christians particularly of Mother Teresa and said Christianity brought better education facilities and health facilities for the people. Mr. P.G. Marbaniang, the elected M.P.,

Mr. J.D. Porhmen, Mr. G.M. War, the party candidate were among others who addressed the meeting. Among other things they also remined the audience that the National Front Government fought the election on three recent principal issues, price rise, corruption and Punjab. But the National Frond Govt. failed to do anything about all these poll promises. Mr. P.G. Marbaniang referred Mr. G.M. War as an well experienced in administration and one qualified to render series to this constituency. As regard local issue Mr. G.M. War sees the local problems of the constituency as shortage of water, repairing of roads, and drains as well as cleaning up of Laitumkhrah market which according to him is congested and full of illegal liquor shops and anti-social elements.

As a HPU candidate Kharsiing got support from HSPDP, the PDIC and other Independents. He committed truth, fair play and justice for all. The following issues are raised by him.

(a) Value based politics,

(b) The strengthening of traditional democratic institutions,

(c) The protection of environment,

(d) Communal harmony,

(e) Character, honesty and faiplay in all dealings,

(f) Certain urgent problems of the constituency such as the acute shortage of drinking water and absence of a Community Hall.

Apart from that he also raised the question of 'Foreigners problem' in Meghalaya, Introdiction of Inner Line Permit to check outsiders. In a meeting at New Colony, a Bengali dominated area which was attended by Mr. G.G. Swell, Nicolas Roy, Mr. Kharshing and other influential persons of the area, they say that they are sorry for the unpleasant things which happened in the past in the name of 'Foreigners Movement' by a section of Local youth. They assured the voters that this type of thing will not occur again. Here they do not raise the question of

'Foreigners issue, Inner Line Permit and the question of introducing Railway line in Meghalaya. They also assured that they will try to solve their other problems too. Such campaigns were held in the evening in order to contact as many voters as possible.

In a matrilineal set up the role of women is important. Out of 14,686 voters, there are 7,413 female voters and 7,273 male outers in this constituency. Therefore the role of women and their organization also important. In Meghalaya the *Twwadam* (Tribal women's Welfairs Association) play an important role in electoral politics. Mrs. T. Shadap is the president of this organization. She after consulting with the other members. Generally decide to support the candidate whom they believe will look after their problem and also helpful in maintaining their traditional system. This time they have decided to support Mr. Kharsiing and requested its members and volunters to support in favour of the HPU candidate. Moreover, Mr. Kharsiing's mother is also associated with Lritumkhrah *Long Kmie* (Respectable Lady's organisation) a local unit of Twwadam. His mother Mrs. Edith Kharshiing Majaw, is a co-worker of Mother Terasa. So it was easier for Mr. Kharshiing to get support from this organisation as Mrs. T. Shadap and Mrs. Kharsiing was able to mobilize support of women voters. Their volunteers were also able to collect a good amount from the areas like Nongrim Road, Lum shora, Nongrim Hills, Laithumkhrah Police point, New Colony, Nongkanriah of this assembly constituency.

The last two-three days of campaigning for the Laitumkhrah Legislative Assembly Constituency saw hectic political activity with all three candidates addressing a series of meetings. In a show of strength the Congress (I) took out a rally in a procession of vehicles that included bus and cars. In the evening the Chief Minister Mr. P. A. Sangma and M.P. Mr. P.G. Marbaniang held the meeting at the Laitumkhrah Police point. The meeting was attended by a large number of ministers. The Chief Minister said, 'It is upto you to choose, Mr. Sangma told the gathering between a man who has connections with government and can get things done for you or a man in the opposition who will only show in the street without accomplishing anything for you'. Mr. S.L. Marbaniang, Minister of State for Information and Public Relations, in his speech denounced the opposition leaders for spreading slur that Congress (I) is a non-tribal party, while the opposition was itself allied with the National Front of which BJP was a part, are well known for its antiminority stance.

The opposition party's consensus candidate Mr. Robert Kharsiing informed the gathering that he has 25 acres of land, moveable assets amounting Rs. 2,000 and a bank balance of Rs. 9,025. He told the gathering that his personal asset was a strategy of rooting out corruption.

All the three parties, the Congress (I) HPU and the Independent are emerged in wooing out the non-tribal votes, who form a sixeable chunk of non-tribal votes of the total Laitumkhrah electorate. The non-tribal vote banks which has so for with the Congress promises to disintegrate as the two other candidates are also making at all out effort to win them over to their side. Leaflets were circulated in Bengali, English to woo the minorities.

The results of the Laitumkhrah by-election shows that one of the greatest factors contributing to the victory of the joint opposition candidate, Mr. Robert Kharshiing was the split in the Congress camp. Due to the emergence of a rebel candidate in the fray, the more intellectually advanced electorate Laitumkhrah were 'put off' or alienated from the Congress camp. United regional parties joint campaign for Mr. Kharshiing ensured his victory. The large support from the non-tribal section of the electorate that the regional parties could muster was also a major factor for Mr. Kharshiing's victory. Never before the non-tribals voted such a large number for a regional party candidate. The non-tribal pockets have been traditional vote banks for Congress I. The victorious candidate Mr. Robert Kharshing attributed his victory to the hard work of his party supporters and the support from all sections of people. He added that the split in Congress I and change of government at the Centre also influenced the electorate and were responsible for his victory.

The Congress I in Meghalaya was death with a severe blow with the loss of prestigious Laitumkhrah seat to the concensus opposition candidates. Mr. Robert Kharshiing who won by a margin of 857 votes. A senior leader of HPU Mr. S.D. Khongwir said that now with the new equation in the State Assembly and results coming in from other. The coalition government in the state was bound to fall. Shortly after the result of Laitumkhrah by-election, the political scene of Meghalaya was also changed. On 25 March 1990 with the resignation of six Ministers, Parno Sangma Ministry was reduced to a minority. On 20th morning Sangma ministry tendered its resignation and on that very day in the evening B.B. Lyngdoh, leader of the newly formed Meghalaya United Parliamentary Party was sworn in.

REFERENCES

1. Dutta, P.S., 1986. Electoral Politics in North East India, Omsons Publications, New Delhi.
2. Nakane Chie, 1967. Garo and Khasi: A comparative study in Matrilinel system, The Hange. Mouten and Co. Paris.

30

Urban Development in Shillong
An Overview

S.K. Agnihotri

Located in the East Khasi Hills District of Meghalaya at an altitudes varying between 600 m to 1400 m above sea level, Shillong is a State capital, a District Headquarter as well as a centre of regional importance. The main approach to the city is by the National Highway No. 40 which links it to Guwahati in the north and by the National Highway No. 44 to Jowai in the east.

The growth of Shillong has largely been a result of British Administration, and as a consequence, a sleepy village of 1363 inhabitants in 1872 has grown to a city of nearly two and a half lakh inhabitants. The independence of the country and creation of the State of Meghalaya in 1972 further helped in enhancing the process of growth of Shillong. Till 1971, Shillong acted as the capital of the States of Assam and Meghalaya and prior to that of the States of Assam, Meghalaya and Arunachal Pradesh. Important institutions like North Eastern Council, North Eastern Hill University, Eastern Air Command are located in Shillong.

(2)
HISTORICAL GROWTH OF THE CITY

In December 1863, the British Government bought large tracts of land from the Syiem of Mylliem and the Headquarters of the Khasi a Jaintia Hills District was shifted from Cherrapunjee to Shillong. The British located a sanatorium and a cantonment in the town of Shillong. In 1874 with the separation of Assam from Bengal, Shillong became the headquarters of the new province of Assam. The administrative headquarters was planned around 1875. Besides, areas like Laban, Laitumkhrah and Mawkhar were rapidly growing and the town then had a population of about 4000 persons. The early growth of Shillong was due to the expansion of offices and commercial activities to serve the administrative population. After independence, the process was accelerated with the influx of people from the neighbours States as well as from other parts of the country.

In 1951, Shillong consisted of the municipality and the cantonment. The municipality did not provide enough scope for residential colonies and the town began to grow outside the municipal limits. By 1961, Nongthymmai and Mawlai acquired urban characteristics and became integral parts of the Shillong urban agglomeration.

(3)
GENERAL FEATURES

Geography

Shillong (25° 34'N latitude and 91° 53'E longitude) is located in the valley formed by the Khasi Hills. The general topography is characterised by undulating terrain with deep gorges and narrow valleys.

Geomorphology

Shillong and its suburbs fall on the central up-land zone of the Shillong plateau which is mainly a dissected plateau with an intervening valley zone. The upper-most part is a mildly undulating plateau of limited width stretching roughly along the east-west direction and having an average altitude of 1800 to 1900 m above mean sea level. The highest point in the area, that is, Shillong peak (1964 m) falls in this part. Its northern side, a rain shadow forested zone, descends at 2°0 slope to the lower surface of Greater Shillong which is an undulating terrain of average elevation of 1400 m above mean sea level on which practically all the localities of Greater Shillong fall. The topography comprises rolling hills and valleys. Wah Umkhrah and Wah Umshyrpi are the two main streams which drain the area. The common varities of social are redloam and laterite.

Climate

The climate of Shillong is characterised by moderate warm-wet-summer and cool-dry-winter. Shillong has a mountaneous climate which is sub-tropical and characterised by high rainfall mostly during summer. The overall landscape gives it a picturesque appearance for which Shillong is often referred to as the 'Scotland of the East.

The mean daily maximum and minimum temperature during the summer season are 24°C and 18°C respectively, while in winter the maximum and minimum temperature are 14°C and 2°C respectively. However, the daily range of temperature in winter is greater than that in summer. The high variation in temperature makes the winter season more severe. January and February are the coldest months of the year.

The mean annual rainfall of Shillong is 242 cms. Of the total rain, about two third falls in the monsoon months of June to September brought about mainly by the south west monsoon winds. Pre-monsoon gets only one fifth of the total rain, mainly by thunder storms. The retreating monsoon season is less rainy, while winter is almost dry.

Except in March, the relative humidity is always more than 50 per cent. During the rainy season, when the winds are mainly from the south-west, the relative humidity is over 75 per cent.

Natural Vegetation and Forests

The natural vegetation of Shillong is dominated by rolling grass lands and pine forests. In the depressions, some pockets of broad leaved evergreen forests are found. The trees are heavily laden with festoons of moss and contain orchids as well.

There are four protected forests around Shillong. The Riat Laban forest (1157 hectares), Upper Shillong forest (3113 hectares), Laitkor forest (1932 hectares) and Short Round forest (648 hectares).

Demographic Features

During the past few decades, Shillong has experienced a steady urban expansion as would appear from *Table I*. Selected demographic characteristics as per 1981 census in Shillong Urban Area are given in *Table II*.

The town has been expanding beyond the municipal limits due to the growth of numerous regional institutions. As a result, the Master Plan covers an area of 10,373,60 hectares.

The shifting of the capital of Assam in 1971 did effect the population of the town to some extent but the establishment of new offices of the Central Government like North Eastern Hill University, North Eastern Council, Indian Council of Agriculture Research etc, has neutralised this impact.

TABLE I

Growth of Population (1901-1991)

Year	*Population*	*Percentage increase*	*Remarks*
1901	9,621		
1911	13,639	41.76	
1921	17,203	26.13	Shillong
1931	23,536	36.81	Municipality
1941	38,192	62.27	
1951	58,512	53.20	
1961	1,02,398	75.00	Town Group
1971	1,22,752	19.87	Standard
1981	1,74,703	42.32	Urban Area
1991	2,22,273	27.23*	

Source: Census of Meghalaya 1981.
*Provisional Census 1991.

TABLE II

Selected Demographic Characteristics (As per 1981 Census) in Shillong Urban Area

Town	*No. of Houses*	*Population*	*No. of Literates*	*No. of Workers*
Shillong (M)*	21,289	109,244	75,582	36,320
Shillong (Cantt**)	1,321	6,620	3,799	2,036

Mawlai	3,593	20,405	11,638	6,476
Nongthymmai	4,349	21,558	14,502	6,946
Pynthorumkhrah	2,244	10,711	5,837	3,211
Madanryting	1,182	6,165	3,339	1,672
Total	33,978	174,703	1,14,697	56,661

Source: Census of Meghalaya, 1981.
*M—Municipality.
**Cantt—Cantonment.

(4)

URBAN ADMINISTRATION

Shillong has a unique urban administrative structure. The municipal board is only one of the components, the others being the District Council, the *Syiemship* and the *Dorbar Shnongs* (Village dorbars),

District Council

The District Council has been constituted under the provisions of the Sixth Schedule of the Constitution of India. It acts as the executive and legislative authority in respect of specific matters provided in the Sixth Schedule of the Constitution. Some powers of the District Council are:

(a) the allotment, occupation, use or the setting apart, of land, other than land which is a reserved forest, for the purpose of agriculture and residential or any other purpose likely to promote the interest of the inhabitants of the village or town; (b) management of forest not being a reserved forest; (c) establishment of town committees; (d) powers to access and collect land revenue and impose taxes: (e) matters relating to village or town administration, public health and sanitation etc.

Syiem

The District Council appoints a Syiem. The Syiem is elected by an electoral durbar consisting of Myntris representing various clans. The Syiem governs the State with the help of the durbar, an executive council constituted by the Myntris.

Both the District Council and the Syiem take up schemes within their respective jurisdiction relating to creation and management of civic infrastructure. The Syiem of Mylliem is managing the biggest wholesale and retail trade centre in the State and the District Council has been constructing footpaths, drains etc. in areas outside the area of the Shillong Municipal Board. The Durbar Shnong is the grass root traditional institution which is involved in the civic affairs of the locality. It is elected directly by the male members of the tribes. Each locality has its 'Shnong' headed by 'Rangbah Shnong', and assisted by the executive members elected by the people. The Durbar articulate the need of the people and also primarily look after the welfare of the locality.

Municipal Board

The Shillong Municipal Board was constituted in 1910 under the Bengal Municipal Act, 1884. After independence, the functions and powers of the Board were regulated by the Assam Municipal Act, 1956 which was subsequently adopted by Meghalaya as the Meghalaya Municipal Act, 1973. The Board is at present without an elected body and is managed by a nominated body. Besides the Chairman and the Chief Executive Officer, there are ten members representing various municipal wards. There are 27 municipal wards namely; 1. Laitumkhrah, 2. Laitumkhrah, 3. Laitumkhrah, 4. Laitumkhrah, 5. Malki, 6. Malki, 7. European Ward, 8. European Ward, 9. Police Bazar, 10. Jail Road, 11. Jail Road, 12. Mawkhar, 13. Mawkhar, 14. Jaiaw, 15. Jaiaw, 16. Jaiaw, 17. South East Mawkhar, 18. South East Mawkhar, 19. Mawprem, 20. Mawprem, 21. Mawprem, 22. Kench's Trace,

23. Kench's Trace, 24. Laban, 25. Laban, 26. Lumparing and 27. Lumparing.

There has been no elected Board since 1973 and the last election to the Board was held in 1966. At the time of election, the approximate population of the municipal area was 80,000 whereas its present population is 1,30,691.

The total area within the municipal limit is 10.36 sq. km. which has remained unchanged. However, the operational area of the Board has increased considerably as most of the vacant lands within the municipal area have been built up.

The main functions of the Board are to provide civic amenities like roads, footpaths, drains, street lighting, conservancy services, management of water supply etc. It does not provide education and health facilities and other services as offered by other local bodies. However the existing services are not being provided to the desired level because of inadequate funds and trained manpower.

The Shillong Municipal Board has a total strength of six hundred and sixty persons. There appears to be surplus of hands at the ministerial level. However, there are very few technical hands to manage civic facilities.

The sources of revenue of the Board are limited to holding tax, water tax, lighting tax, sanitation tax, fees, rent and toll tax. During 1981-82, the total receipt was Rs. 37.02 lakhs, which rose to Rs. 114.94 lakhs in 1990-91; an increase of over 210 per cent. The revenue receipt of the Board from different sources during 1981-92 was Rs. 43.55 lakhs which rose to Rs 226.33 lakhs during 1990-91. Table III shows the revenue receipts of Shillong Municipal Board from different sources during the period 1981-1991.

The State Government sanctions grants-in-aid to the Board to carry out development programmes. The assistance extended by

TABLE III

Revenue Receipt of Shillong Municipal Board from Different Sources during 1981-1991

Year	*Receipt from own sources i.e. Rent, Taxes, Fees etc. (Rs. in lakh)*	*Percentage of the total Revenue*	*Fund Received from State Govt. Grant-in-aid (Rs. in lakh)*	*Govt. Loan (Rs. in lakh)*	*Percentage to the Total Revenue*	*Loan from Financial Institutions (Rs. in lakh)*	*Percentage to the Total Revenue*	*Total (Rs. in lakh)*
1981-82	37.06	85.10	3.49	—	8.01	3.00	6.89	43.55
1982-83	32.72	61.14	4.80	—	8.97	16.00	29.89	53.52
1983-84	45.02	44.67	43.77	12.00	55.33	—	—	100.79
1984-85	45.99	68.54	21.11	—	31.46	—	—	67.10
1985-86	108.92	44.89	67.60	65.00	55.11	—	—	240.62
1986-87	43.46	43.18	57.19	—	56.82	—	—	100.65
1987-88	86.00	48.52	91.25	—	51.48	—	—	177.25
1988-89	51.38	39.87	77.50	—	60.13	—	—	128.88
1989-90	106.14	52.29	96.85	—	47.71	—	—	202.99
1990-91	114.94	50.79	111.38	—	49.21	—	—	226.32
Total	670.73	49.99	574.94	77.00	48.59	19.00	1.42	1341.67

the State Government during 1981-82 was Rs. 3.49 lakhs which rose to Rs. 111.38 lakhs during 1990-91. Table IV shows the item wise break up of assistance extended by the State Government during 1981-1991.

Performance of the Board has to be examined in terms of the level of services provided namely water supply, street lighting, sanitation and solid waste disposal and also in terms of improvement in its revenue generation. An analysis of the data indicates that the Board has not been able to supply 100 litres of water per capita per day, and there is a net shortage of water. Street lighting is relatively good and the municipal area is by and large well lit.

As regards revenue generation, Table III indicates that over the years, the Board has depended largely on government funding. During 1981-82, its own receipts contributed nearly 85% of the total revenue which declined to 51% during 1990-91. Government grant which was only 8% in 1981-82 shot up to 49.21% during 1990-91.

As per Table IV the investment in the upkeep of civic services has been varying. There has been an increase in the public works sector and a decrease in the water works. Poor availability and quantity of water may be attributed to low level of investment. If the level of water supply services is to be improved, higher investment is required and the investment pattern needs to be changed. Inspite of the fact that expenditure under conservancy has been maintained at an adequate level, the service is far from satisfactory.

There has been considerable increase in the establishment cost; from an expenditure of Rs. 1.49 lakhs during 1981-82 to Rs. 56.88 lakhs during 1991-92. The vast increase is partly attributed higher emoluments of the municipal employees due to revision of pay and allowances but mainly due to the increase in the number of employees.

TABLE IV

Itemwise Break-up of Assistance Extended by the State Government to the Shillong Municipal Board During 1981-1991

(Rs. in lakh)

Year	*Public Works*	*Water Works*	*Conser-vancy and Health*	*Establish-ment*	*Others (Interest on Loan Electri-city Charges)*	*Total*
1981-82	—	—	2.00	1.40	—	3.49
1982-83	—	—	0.50	4.30	—	4.80
1983-84	8.27	19.00	14.00	2.50	—	43.77
1984-85	10.00	5.16	—	5.95	—	21.11
1985-86	28.01	23.59	—	16.00	—	67.60
1986-87	6.40	—	9.09	41.70	—	57.90
1987-88	—	—	9.00	45.79	24.10	91.25
1988-89	13.27	2.10	6.13	48.92	7.58	77.50
1989-90	18.99	4.47	—	39.53	33.59	96 58
1990-91	14.26	5.50	10.23	56.88	24.51	111.38
Total	99.20	59.82	50.95	263.06	89.78	575.38

The Board over the years has been given additional responsibility of implementing development schemes such as (1) environmental improvement of slum areas (2) urban basic services for the poor (3) nehru rozgar yojana and (4) integrated scheme on liberation of scavengers and improvement of sanitation etc.

(1) Environmental Improvement of Slum Areas

The emergence of slums in Shillong may be attributed to the fact that Shillong was originally planned for a population of about 20,000 persons but over the years the economic character of the town has undergone a change from a hill resort to an administrative-cum-commercial centre. The rapid influx of migrants both from the rural areas of the State as well as from other States has resulted in straining the service facilities to the limit creating slum-like conditions.

Under the provisions of the Meghalaya Slum Areas (Improvement and Clearance) Act, 1973 total 31 slum pockets within the urban areas of Greater Shillong have been identified (Table V). The poulation of slum dwellers in these pockets is estimated to be 58,420 persons.

TABLE V

Details of Slum Pockets and Population in Different Urban Areas of Shillong

Name of the Urban Area	*No. of Slum Pockets Identified*	*Estimated Slum Dwellers*
Shillong Municipality	21*	42,000
Pynthorumkhrah	2	3,750
Cantonment	2	3,045
Nongthymmai	3	4,310

Mawlai	3	4,080
Madanryting	1	1,235
Total	32	58,420

*Name of the 21 identified slum pockets within the Shillong.

Municipal Board are Naspatighari; Qualapatti, Laitumkhrah (Harijan Colony) Polo Bazar, Part of Jail Road, Sweeper Lane, Part of Laitumkhrah, Demseiniong, Malki, Madan Laban, Riat Laban, Lumparing, Lower Mawprem, Upper Mawprem, Wahingdoh, Barapathar, Wahthapbru, Laban, Part of Lama Villa, Part of Riat-samthiah and part of Umsohsun

To improve the physical environment of the slum areas 'Environmental Improvement of Urban Slums' scheme was introduced in 1974-75 under the 'Minimum Needs Programme' which was subsequently included under the 20-point programme in 1982-83. The main objective of the scheme is to improve the physical environment and to improve the quality of living conditions by providing basic civic amenities and facilities such as approach road, footpaths, public water tap/hand pump, cumminity sanitation facilities, street lighting, drainsboth for stromwater and effluents. This scheme was introduced in Shillong during the fifth five year plan period and schemes in four slum areas viz, Naspatighari, Qualapatty, Harijan Colony (Laitumkhrah) and Polo Bazar were completed by 1981. In Malki, Lumparing, Madan Laban and Riat Laban schemes were under progress However, the coverage till 1981 was meagre due to organisational problems as well as lack of funds. During the decade 1981-91, a conserted effort was made to tackle the problem extensively and 9 slum pockets i.e. Malki, Lumparing, Madan Laban, Riat Laban, Lower Mawprem, Wahingdoh, Laban, Upper Mawprem, Jhalupara were fully covered whereas

5 slum pockets (Laitumkhrah, Demseingion, Wahthapbru, Pynthorumkhrah-I and Pynthorumkhrah-II) were partially covered. An amount of Rs. 92.09 lakhs was spent in providing the services and 34,472 persons were benefited.

The Board was expected to maintain the assets created but due to paucity of funds, these could not be maintained properly.

Although there is considerable improvement of the physical environment after creating the basic amenities in the slum areas, the over all impact of development could not be achieved as the scheme only took care of improvement of community infrastructure whereas the housing conditions and social inputs were missing. Hence, recently two new schemes have been introduced viz. "Urban Basic Services for the poor" and "Nehru Rozgar Yojana" in the slum areas for over all development of these areas.

2. Urban Basic Services for the Poor

The urban basic services scheme now known as the urban basic services for the poor (UBSP) was sanctioned by the Government of India in the year 1987-88. This scheme was earlier assisted by UNICEF and Government of India. The scheme is a social input scheme meant for the urban poor with special emphasis on women and children. The main components of the revised scheme enable urban poor to have access to basic services like non-formal education health care, nutrition supplementation, immunivation, assistance to handicapped, assistance to juveniles delinquents, assistance for rehabilitation of alcoholics/drug addicts, assistance for sports, cultural activities and activities geared to promoting communal harmony, national integration and civic consciousness. The scheme provides social services to the urban poor in a convergent manner along with physical amenities to be provided through the scheme on Environmental Improvement of Urban Slums. The main aim of this scheme is to improve the quality of life of the poor, especially the women and children members of Scheduled Castes, Scheduled tribes and minorities. People's participation in planning, implementation and evaluation of the project activities and convergence, constitute the basic principles of this scheme.

So far 42 low cost sanitary units, 100 smokeless chullahs, 200 low cost water filters, 10 baby beds have been provided under this scheme. In addition, water connection to a creche at Lumparing has been provided. Basic infrastructure like community halls have been provided at Madanryting, Jaiaw Pdeing, Jaiaw Laitdom, Madan Laban, Riot Laban and Oakland and a creche building at Laban. These buildidgs will be utilised as centres for immunization as well as for motivation and for holding awareness campaign.

During the year 1990-91, Rs. 10.02 lakhs was sanctioned for implementing immunization, nutritional programmes and adult literacy programmes. The scheme is being implemented in Barabazar (Sweeperline), Barapathar, Demseiniong (Laitumkhrah), Lumparing, Lower Mawprem, Laban, Malki, Wahingdoh etc. So far 9 immunization centre and nutrition centres have been started and the beneficiaries covered so far in these centres are 2022 and 1600 respectively. Six adult literacy centres have been set up covering 600 beneficiaries.

3. Nehru Rozgar Yojna

The scheme introduced by the Government of India in October, 1989. The main objective is to provide and generate employment for the urban unemployed and under-employed poor by promoting self employment ventures and by increasing opportunities for wage employment through creation of socially economically useful assets through the urban local bodies. While the target group is urban poor, women beneficiaries and beneficiaries belonging to Scheduled castes and Scheduled tribes constitute special target groups. The Nehru Rozgar Yojna has 3 (three) components namely:— (a) urban micro enterprise; (b) urban wage employment through public assets creation; and (c) employment through housing and shelter upgradation. These schemes have two components namely, (i) loan and subsidy and (ii) training and infrastructure support. The subsidy component is 25% with a ceiling of Rs. 4000/- for beneficiaries belonging to the scheduled castes and scheduled tribes. Seventy five per cent of the unit cost is met through loans at the same rate as sanctioned for integrated Rural Development Programmes. The 2nd part of the scheme relates to training and infrastructure support. It has three components namely (i) training of urban poor beneficiaries; (ii) support to training institutions; and (iii) infrastural support for setting up of urban micro-enterprises. The duration of the training is 3 months. The fund required for the same is met entirely by the Central Government. In the year 1989-90, the Government of India had released an amount of Rs. 20.74 lakhs as its share for this scheme. The State's share was Rs. 9.78 lakhs. In the year 1990-91 Rs. 6.30 lakhs was released as State's share and Rs. 4.77 lakhs as administrative and operational expenses.

Out of 26 schemes proposed under wage employment scheme, 9 scheme have been completed and others were in progress.

Under the scheme of urban micro enterprises, the total number of applications under process in the different banks was 113 out of 257 beneficiaries proposed for the year. As regards housing and shelter upgradation, the Board have sent a scheme to the Housing and Urban Development Corporation for sanction which will cover 295 beneficiaries.

4. Integrated Scheme on the Liberation of Scavengers and Improvement in Sanitation

The scheme was introduced by the Government of India towards the end of the seventh five year plan period with the objective of eliminating manual scavenging of dry latrins and their conversion into low cost sanitation units. The scavengers so liberated would be rehabilitated under this scheme.

Prior to the introduction of this scheme, construction of low cost sanitation units was also taken under the scheme of urban basic services and environmental protection and development.

5. Water Supply

The first water distribution system in Shillong was commissioned in 1910 when raw water was tapped from the surface sources viz., Wah Jalynoh, Wah risa and Madan Laban. With the growth of population over the years and increasing demand, new sources have been explored such as Umkhen, Umjasai, Crinoline, Sericulture spring etc. At the same time, ground water sources have also been explored, such as at Polo, Lady Hydari Park and near St. Edmunds School etc., to replenish the supply. However inspite of all effort, the gap between demand and supply has widened due to steady increase in population. In order to overcome this problem a Water Suppply Scheme for Greater Shillong has been prepared. The first phase of the project has been implemented.

The responsibility of supply of potable water within the Municipal Limits rests with the Board whereas in Mawlai, Nongthymmai, Madanrynting, Pynthorumkhrah towns and other rural settlements, it is being managed by the Public Health Engineering Department.

The quantum of water supplied till 1981 within the municipal area was around 0.6 million gallons per day which works out to be 27.46 litres per capita per day. However over the years, the supply has been considerably enhanced after the commissioning of the first phase of the Greater Shillong Water Supply Scheme and at present 1.60 million gallons per day of water in being supplied. Out of the total quantum, 0.6 million gallons per day is supplied out of the water tapped by Municipal Board from its own sources i.e. Wahjalynroh, Wah risa, Mada Laban, Pattakhana, Umjasai, Wahdienglieng and Crinoline and the water tapped from Umkhen by Public Health Engineering Department whereas remaining one million gallons per day is released to the municipal reservoir from Mawphlang by Public Health Engineering Department. The per capita supply of water is 63.00 litres per capita per day which is much below the ideal standard of 200 litres per capita per day. The level of supply is also much below the recommended minimum level of 100 litres per capita per day.

The scarcity of water aggravates during the lean period as the sources dry up. Figures pertaining to the quantum of water supplied outside Municipal area are not available but in general, the situation is much worse. People depend mostly on unprotected natural sources.

The raw water tapped from the source is stored in the reservoirs located at Bara Bazar, Lower Mawprem, Lachumiere, Upland and Nongrim hills etc. and then released to the subsidiary reservoirs located at different places. Household connections are then allowed from the subsidiary reservoirs or storage tanks through individual pipe lines. As a result of this unscientific distribution, not only the initial cost of connection for the consumers is very high, but also maintenance is a problem as at times the distance from the storage tank to the household is more than one kilometer. Concurrently, frequent damages to roads and footpaths are common due to crossing and leakage of water. On account of the damages to pipe lines, the wastage of water is more than 10% of the total supply.

The raw water tapped by the Municipal Board is supplied untreated except post-chlorination stage. On the other hand, Public Health Engineering Department release 1.0 million gallons of water per day to the municipal reservoirs after treatment.

Taking into account a minimum of 100 litres per capita per day of water, the present requirement of water within the municipal area alone is 11.30 million litres per day against the supply of 7.12 million litres per day. The minimum water requirement for Greater Shillong area during 1991 is estimated to be 25.90 million litres per day which will increase to 34.70 million litres per day by 2001.

6. Sewerage and Sewage Disposal System

With the increase of population, the untreated sewage and other wastes have been creating a threat to the purity of the natural streams criss-crossing Shillong city. In the year 1976, Public Health Engineering Department had prepared a scheme for disposal of sewerage in Shillong municipal area for statement of water pollution of the streams and for preventing the imbalance in basic ecological ingredients. The estimated cost of execution of the scheme for Shillong municipal area at that time was about Rs. 427.00 lakhs. The scheme was technically approved by the Government of India. Due to paucity of funds, the scheme could not be implemented.

In 1988, the Meghalaya State Pollution Control Board carried out an investigation on the water quality of Barapani reservoir. The result of the said tests were alarming. It was observed that the untreated sewage of Shillong and the eroded soil of the catchment areas were polluting the Barapani reservoir. As a first step to check the onslaught of this pollution, Meghalaya State Pollution Control Board have prepared a scheme for sewarage system and its subsequent for Greater Shillong. The estimated execution cost of the project is about Rs. 5.00 crores. To facilitate stage-wise execution of the project, the scheme has been segregated in four phases.

7. Power Supply

The Shillong Hydro Electricity Company Limited established in 1922 was taken over by the Meghalaya State Electricity Board in 1977. Since take over, considerable improvement has been made to meet the growing power demand.

The peak demand in the city is more than 20MVA. The source of supply to Shillong is from the 132 KV grid sub-station at

Mawlai. Eevn though power supplied is adequate, poor conditions are experienced in many areas. This is due to mainly to technical reasons.

The power supply system requires renovation and augmentation not only to meet the present demand of the consumers but also the future requirements of the ever increasing population. Meghalaya being surplus in power, the Meghalaya State Electricity Board should take the initiatative to have a properly designed distribution system for Shillong to give better service to its consumers. The Electricity Board has recently taken up construction of a few grid sub-stations at different localities within the town to cater to the needs of Shillong and surrounding areas.

Proper street lighting is necessary for the safety of drivers and pedestrians. At present, street lighting schemes are being implemented by the Meghalaya State Electricity Board with funds released by the Urban Affairs Department and the Municipal Board. Table VI shows the nature and power of lamps and number of lams within the Shillong municipality.

Due to the severe resource constraint, Shillong Municipality is not in a position to pay energy charges and as a result, Government gives assistance to the Municipal Board from time to time to clear the bills of Meghalaya State Electricity Board. Government have sanctioned installation of sodium and mercury vapour lamps even in areas outside the Shillong municipal limits and have also sanctioned fund for their maintenance. In the absence of any local bady outside the limits of municipal board, extension of such facilities in non-municipal areas has been minimal.

8. Implementation of Schemes

The schemes mentioned earlier proposed to be implemented cover the entire master plan area which is nearly 10 times the jurisdiction of Municipal Board. The water supply and sewerage schemes have to be maintained by a non-government agency as the burden of maintenance and upkeep cannot be on the Government departments. The Municipal Board has to implement schemes like Environmental Improvement of Urban Slums, Nehru Rozgar Yojana, Urban Basic Services for Poor, Integrated scheme for elimination of scavenging and liberation of scavengers. This may be possible only if a civic body is set up having jurisdiction over the master plan area. Since in the State, the District Council' the Syiem, the Rangbah Shnong are involved in the civic affairs, there is duplication and overlapping of functions. proposed civic body (Municipal Corporation) must have representative from the above institutions to make it more effective. The Government of Meghalaya have already taken a decision to establish a Municipal Organisation for the entire master plan area.

9. Management of Urban Administration

There are many agencies and local institutions who are responsible for providing civic amenities or are involved in this process directly or indirectly. In addition, there are Government Departments and agencies like the Public Works, the Public Health Engineering, the Urban Affairs, the Meghalaya Urban Development Authority, and the Meghalaya Urban Development Agency which implement various schemes and Programmes of the State Government.

Meghalaya Urban Development Authority is mainly responsible for enforcement and implementation of Master Plans. Meghalaya Urban Development Agency has been set up to implement all the poverty alleviation schemes through the local Municipal Boards. Public Works Department executes all the schemes pertaining to roads and Buildings. Public Health Engineering Department's task is to implement water supply and sewerage schemes. The Urban Affairs Department has been implementing environmental improvement of urban slums schemes and providing civic infrastructure. Meghalaya State Electricity Board has been implementing street lighting schemes with funds released by Urban Affairs Department and Municipal Board. Shillong

Municipal Board also constructs footpaths, drains and maintains them within their jurisdiction.

It is apparent from above, that within the same city, atleast as seven agencies of the Government are operating and implementing various development programmes. Most of them are not aware of the programmes of other agencies. The result is uncoordinated development of infrastructure facilities. There is, therefore, a need to co-ordinate the activities of the various agencies in the field and also assign functions clearly to each of them. The question is who can co-ordinate. The Meghalaya Urban Development Authority is an umbrella body and expected to take on these functions as all schemes have to be implemented within the framework of Master Plans and Zonal Plans. If that be so, the above agencies have to be represented in the Authority. At present there is no representative of these Agencies except the Municipal Board and the Cantonment. It may be necessary to make amendments in the Meghalaya Town and Country Planning Act, 1973 so that the Government agencies including Syiemship and the District Council are represented and contribute to the development process of the city.

10. Recent Developments

There have been several major developments as regards urban administration of Shillong and improvement of urban services during last few years. The first relates to the final publication of the Master Plan for Greater Shillong area. The plan broadly indicates the land use pattern showing specific areas for residential, commercial, industrial and administrative uses. It also recommends transportation net-work suitable to the terrain of the city. Zoning regulation prescribed in the Master Plan is a tool to regulate the growth of the city and to ensure that development takes place in accordance with the recommendation of the Master Plan.

The second important development relates to the proposed setting up of a new township near Shillong to accommodate the estimated population of 1,50,000 by 2011 A.D. The new township will be in close proximity to Shillong and will be self-contained unit. It will have all the required urban infrastructure and necessary civic facilities will be provided.

It is also proposed to set up a urban corporation which will have jurisdiction over the entire master plan of Shillong and will be responsible for providing and maintaining the civic facilities. The proposed civic body will have representation from all the local bodies and also the tribal institutions involved in the civic affairs of the city.

Urban poverty has been one of the biggest problem which needs immediate attention. The centrally sponsored scheme of Nehru Rozgar Yojana to improve the economic condition of people below the poverty line, has been launched and Shillong Municipal Board has been made the implementing agency. In addition to the above programme urban basic services scheme has been introduced with a view to improving the health and hygience conditions of urban poor, particularly women and children. It has also been decided to eliminate the practice of manual scavenging.

Shillong has been facing acute traffic congestion. This has led to increased travel time and also degradation of urban environment. A comprehensive traffic and transportation study has been carried out by National Traffic and Transportation Centre, New Delhi. The study recommends both the short term and the long term measures to ease traffic congestion in the city.

Disposal of solid waste in the city is far from satisfactory and is one of the causes for the dirt and filth, a common sight in the city. A comprehensive study on the improvement of solid waste disposal system has been conducted by the National Environmental Engineering Research Institute, Nagpur. The study proposes to set up new dumping sites, conversion of garbage into bio-gas and improvement in the collection and transport of solid wastes from diffcrent localities to the dumping sites. Its implementation is in progress.

estimated population of 1,30,000 by 2011 A.D. The new township will be in close proximity to the new [illegible] and will be a self-contained unit. It will have all the [illegible] and necessary civic facilities will be provided.

It is also proposed to set up a urban corporation which will have jurisdiction over the entire master plan of [illegible] and will be responsible for providing and maintaining the civic facilities. The proposed civic body will have representation from all the local bodies and also the [illegible] institutions involved in the civic affairs of the city.

[illegible] has been one of the biggest [illegible] which [illegible] are attention. [illegible] Nehru Rozgar Yojana to improve the [illegible] of people below the poverty line has been launched. [illegible] has been taken up [illegible]. In addition to the above program [illegible] has been introduced with a view to improving the [illegible] and living conditions of urban poor particularly women and children. It has also been decided to eliminate the practice of manual scavenging.

[illegible] has been facing acute traffic congestion. This has led to increased travel time and also detrimental to [illegible] environment.

[illegible]

carried out by National Traffic and Transportation Centre, New Delhi. The study recommended both the short term and long term measures to ease traffic congestion in the city.

Disposal of solid waste in the city is far from satisfactory and heaps of the garbage together with [illegible] a common sight in the city. A comprehensive study on the improvement of solid waste disposal system has been conducted by the National Environmental Engineering Research Institute, Nagpur. The study proposes to set up new dumping sites, conversion of garbage into bio-gas and improvement in the collection and transport of solid wastes from different localities to the dumping sites. Its implementation is in progress.